IMAGES
of America

ANDERSON COUNTY

I0806327

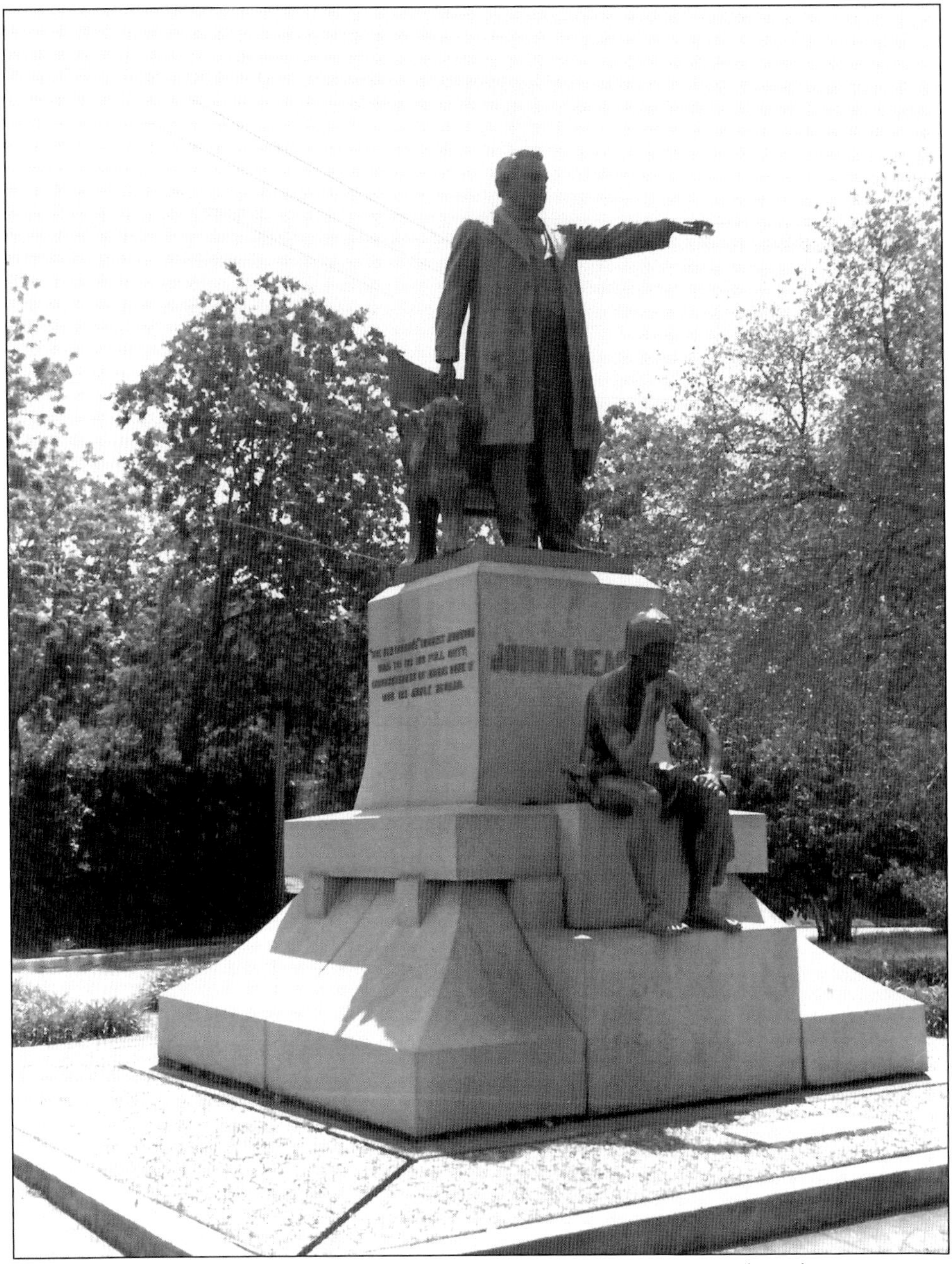

On February 10, 1908, a resolution was passed by the Palestine City Council to place a monument to John H. Reagan at the intersection of Avenue A, Houston, and Main Streets. The base of the monument was placed at that location until being moved to the new Reagan Park. On July 6, 1911, the new monument, complete with a statue of Reagan, was unveiled at the park. (Courtesy of METC.)

On the Cover: Green's Bluff, formerly Cook's Bluff on Cook's Plantation, was located on a high ridge overlooking the Trinity River in western Anderson County, south of Cayuga. In the late 1800s, the bluff was sold to a group of freed slaves who renamed it Green's Bluff and named the community Yard. The ferry was at the southern end of the bluff. (Courtesy of Louise Spaith.)

IMAGES
of America

ANDERSON COUNTY

Beverly Odom, Louise Goff, and the
Anderson County Historical Commission

ARCADIA
PUBLISHING

ISBN 978-0-7385-8462-1

Published by Arcadia Publishing
Charleston SC, Chicago IL, Portsmouth NH, San Francisco CA

Printed in the United States of America

Library of Congress Control Number: 2010925133

For all general information contact Arcadia Publishing at:
Telephone 843-853-2070
Fax 843-853-0044
E-mail sales@arcadiapublishing.com
For customer service and orders:
Toll-Free 1-888-313-2665

Visit us on the Internet at www.arcadiapublishing.com

This book is dedicated to the all the historians of Anderson County, both past and present, who have devoted their time and energy to preserving the history of our county in both words and photographs.

Contents

ACKNOWLEDGMENTS

As the primary producers of this book, Beverly Odom and Louise Goff would like to express their appreciation to the following for the sharing of their pictures and time: Danny and Paula Trigg, Sue Price, Jimmy and Kathy Odom, Nancy Maddox, Edwin Dabbs, Johnnie Belle McDonald Faucett, Anita McReynolds, Lamar Roberson, Elsie McGee, Jimmy and Kathy Odom, Wallace Odom, Louise Redwine Spaith, Marita Denson Stovall, Veda DeShazo, Reginald Browne Jr., Floyd Barthel, Versalean Logan, Dick and Sharon Atwood, Karla Lang (Palestine Public Library, special collection librarian), Museum for East Texas Culture (Dan Dyer, director; Elizabeth Mason, office manager, Carl Avera Collection; and Lizzie Langenkamp, archivist). Unfortunately we were unable to publish all of the pictures that were shared.

Thank you to the current Anderson County board members: Rudy Ramirez, chair; Bonnie Woolverton, vice chair; Kay Gresham Szabo, secretary; Mary Billups, treasurer; Jimmy Odom, marker chair; Beverly Bailey Odom, cemetery chair; Dorothy Odom Bruce, webmaster; Bill Bruce, computer technician; Dan and Paula Trigg, Elkhart representatives; James Henry, Neches representative; Mildred Smith, African American representative; and Charlene Hutchinson, historian.

Special thanks go to the reporters, both past and present, of the *Palestine Herald Press* for their contribution through numerous articles. In addition, thanks go to the Mary Kate Hunter Collection at the Palestine Public Library, James Neyland's works, and the Carl Avera Collection at the Museum for East Texas Culture.

Thanks also go to the commissioners court and Judge Linda Ray for their support.

Courtesy Keys:

Museum For East Texas Culture	METC
Carl Avera Collection, Museum for East Texas Culture	CA
Palestine Public Library	PPL

Unless otherwise noted, all images appear courtesy of the Anderson County Historical Commission.

Anderson County Historical Commission
101 E. Oak Street
Palestine, Texas 75801
903-723-3065
Fax: 903-723-3771
achccommission@yahoo.com
www.achc.info

INTRODUCTION

When the first white settlers pushed through the wilderness, they knew that life on the frontier would bring tremendous hardships and danger. Anderson County is the microcosm of the indomitable spirit that formed the United States into the great nation it is today. Not only is it a wonderful place in which to grow up, it is a wonderful place in which to grow old.

Anderson County is located in central East Texas. The Neches River forms its eastern boundary, and the Trinity forms its western boundary. The county seat of Palestine, the largest town in the county, is located in the geographical center of the county. Anderson County has a total area of 1,077 square miles of hilly terrain, which ranges from 198 to 624 feet above sea level.

The area was once the home of the Comanche, Waco, Tawakonis, Kickapoo, and Kichai Indians. On the east, along the Neches River, were also friendly Cherokee Indians who were hunters and farmers. As the white settlers came, they began to settle in the rich fertile Trinity valley about 2 miles southwest of the present city of Palestine.

Concerned about the dangers to the pioneers along the frontier, Gen. Sam Houston ordered new posts to be built in strategic locations along the frontier. As a result, in 1835 and 1836 Fort Houston was built to protect the new settlers. Life flourished in and around the new fort. The population grew as more people came to settle the area.

Originally a part of Houston County, the settlers around the rapidly growing Fort Houston petitioned for a new county. On March 24, 1846, the legislature of the State of Texas passed an act creating Anderson County. It was named for Kenneth Lewis Anderson, the last vice president of the Republic of Texas. Although both Fort Houston and Mound Prairie vied to be the county seat, state law required that the county seat be located near the geographical center of the county. As a result, a new town was established. The town was named Palestine after Palestine in Crawford County, Illinois, original home of some of the early settlers. After the decline of the population at Fort Houston, John Henninger Reagan, one of the leading citizens of Palestine, bought the land on which the fort had stood.

The steamboats that plied the Trinity River in the mid-19th century played a vital role in the economy of Anderson County in the era when cotton was king. Magnolia, located 10 miles southwest of Palestine, was the principle port from which cotton was shipped to Galveston and other destinations. Named for the large magnolia tree in the middle of town, Magnolia was known as the "Little St. Louis of the Trinity." It boasted a population of 800 citizens at its peak in the early 1860s. After the railroad came to the county, Magnolia's population declined rapidly. Today the only evidence of the once magnificent port are a historical marker and stone foundations. The Magnolia Cemetery is near the old town site.

For those willing to work hard, life in the new county was going well. Palestine had become a boomtown, a true melting pot of people from other states and many foreign countries. Hardship was a way of life in any frontier town or county, but it was worth it to fulfill the dream of prosperity.

Just 15 short years after the new county was established, the Civil War began. While Anderson County escaped the devastation suffered by the southern states to the east, the absence of fathers and sons in the households made life extremely difficult. Between 700 and 1,000 men left their newly established homes to serve the Confederate cause. Congressman John H. Reagan became postmaster general of the Confederacy. He was later promoted to secretary of the treasury near the end of the war. The men from Anderson County formed several companies to join the fight for the Southern cause for state's rights. Those who were unable to serve in the fighting contributed to the cause by working in the cloth mills, the iron works, and the Confederate salt works. Washington Mills at Mound Prairie supplied cloth for Confederate uniforms. Also at Mound Prairie was a manufacturer that supplied ammunition and gun parts. Women contributed by making uniforms and blankets and knitting socks for the troops.

The end of the Civil War brought a new and very different type of havoc to the county when the northerners arrived to enforce the Reconstruction legislation. Their methods were harsh, bringing both economic and physical hardships. Another significant change came about by the shift from an agricultural economy to an industrial economy. In an effort to bring industry to the area, Palestine raised $150,000 in bonds and contributed land to obtain the International and Great Northern Railroad.

The coming of the railroad in the 1870s spelled the end of the steamboat trade on the Trinity. It provided a cheaper, more efficient way to ship the cotton and other crops to more diverse locations across the country. Life in the vicinity began to change, particularly in the county seat of Palestine.

After the turn of the 20th century, even more changes occurred. This era witnessed the coming of the automobile to Anderson County. Outlying communities became more accessible. Oil was discovered, and soon wells sprang up throughout the area, bringing unthought-of prosperity to Anderson County.

One

Early Anderson County

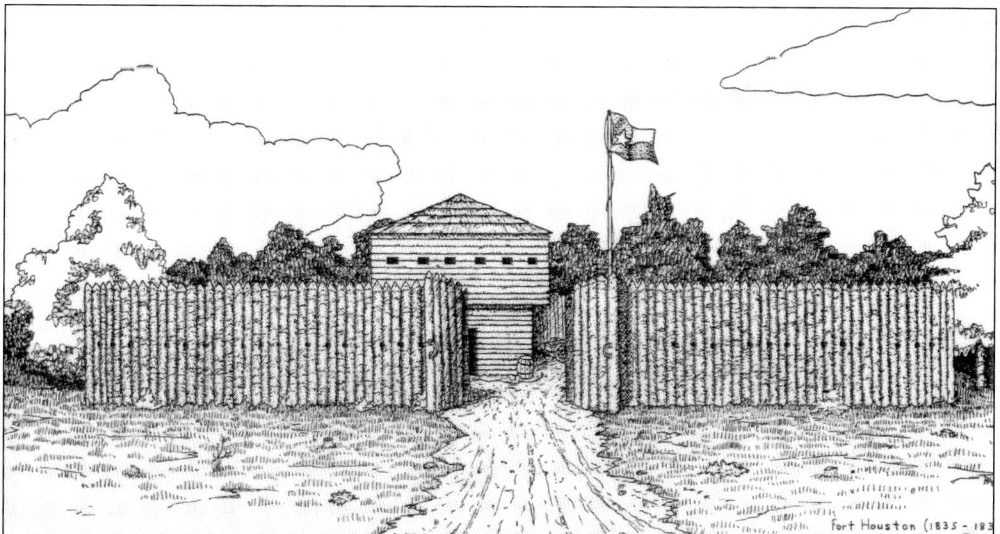

In summer 1835, a number of settlers and their families moved from the Nacogdoches District and established homes 2 miles west of what is now Palestine. First called Houston, the new town was renamed Fort Houston. There are not any pictures of the fort, but there is this Robert Howarton sketch, which gives an idea of how the area was laid out. (Courtesy of METC.)

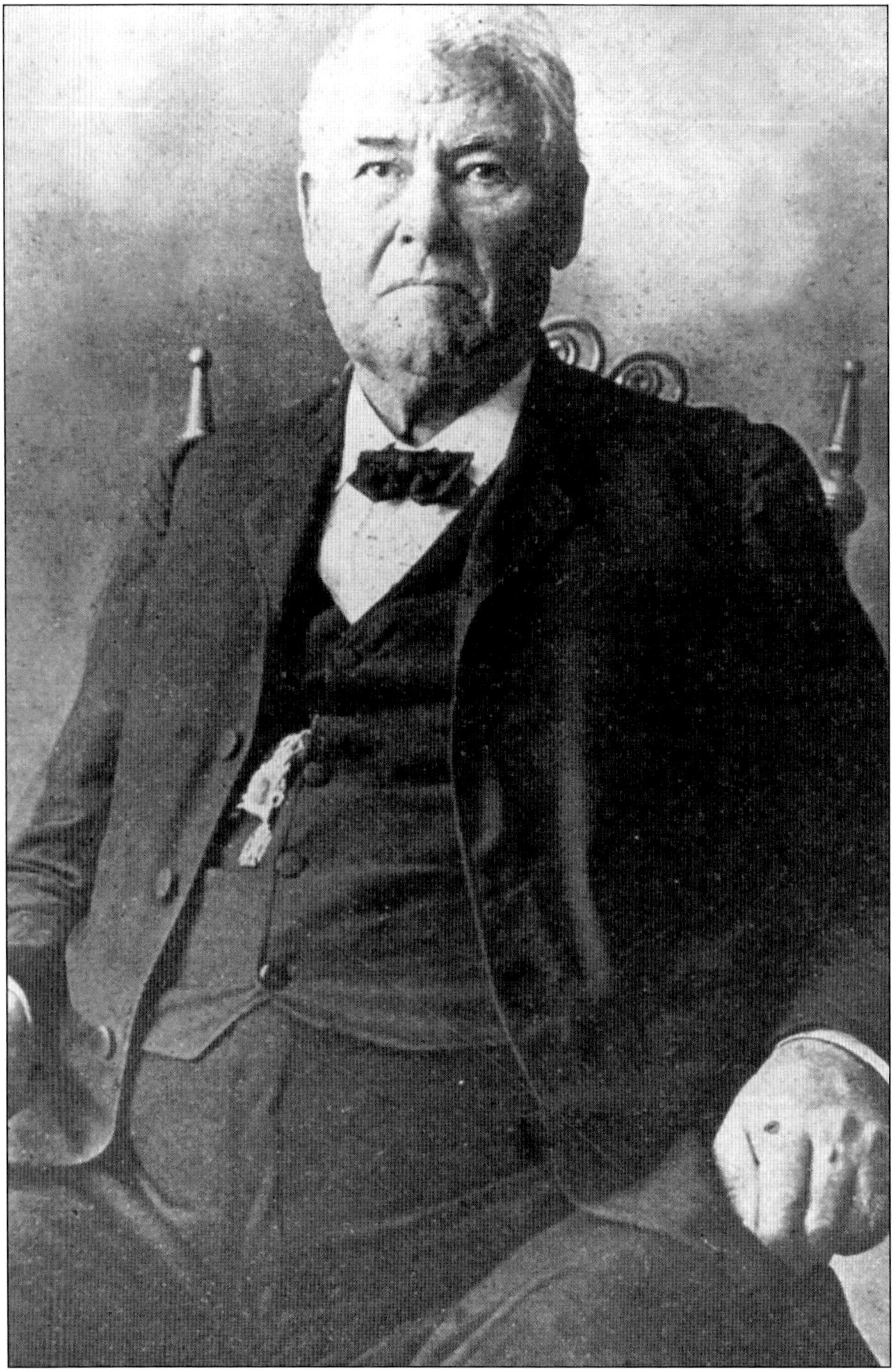
John H. Reagan was born on October 8, 1818, in Sevierville, Tennessee. He arrived in the Republic of Texas about 1837. He served as deputy state surveyor of public land and as justice of the peace in Nacogdoches County. He was admitted to the bar in 1848. He practiced law in both Palestine and Buffalo, Texas. After being elected to the Texas House of Representatives, he moved to Palestine in 1851. After the war, he served in both the U.S. Congress and the U.S. Senate. He died in Palestine March 6, 1905. (Courtesy of METC.)

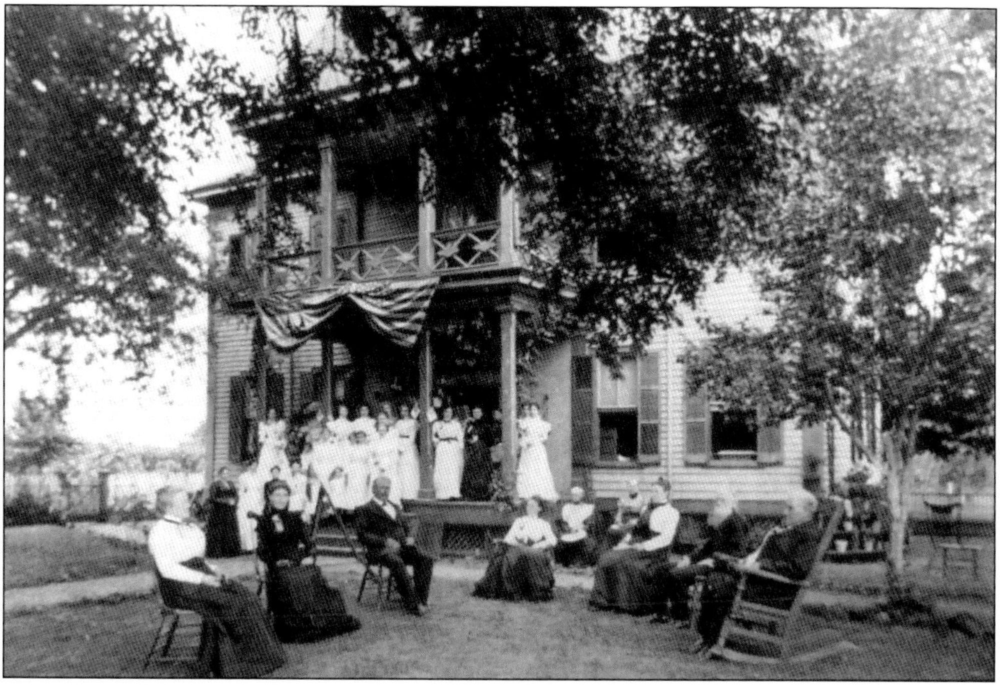

In the photograph above, Judge John Henninger Reagan relaxes with his family and friends on the front lawn of his home. He is in the rocking chair on the right. Below, he is shown in the study of his home on West Reagan Street. He came to the Republic of Texas about the age of 19. In 1838, he settled in Nacogdoches, where he joined local militia during the Cherokee War. In 1851, he became a citizen of Palestine and established a home with a law office in front on the old Rusk Road (now 900 Lacy Street). He later bought a farm west of Palestine on the old Fort Houston site. After a very active political life, he retired in 1901 to write his memoirs, with special emphasis on Secession and the Civil War. (Both, courtesy of METC.)

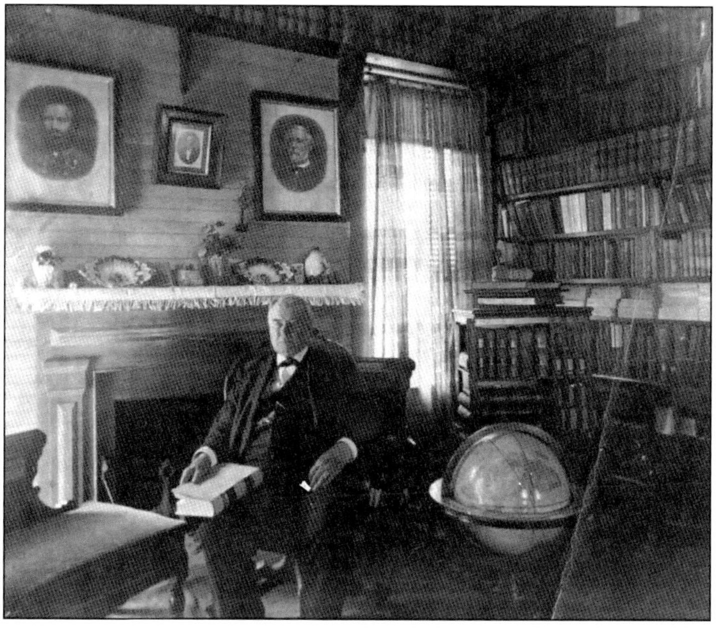

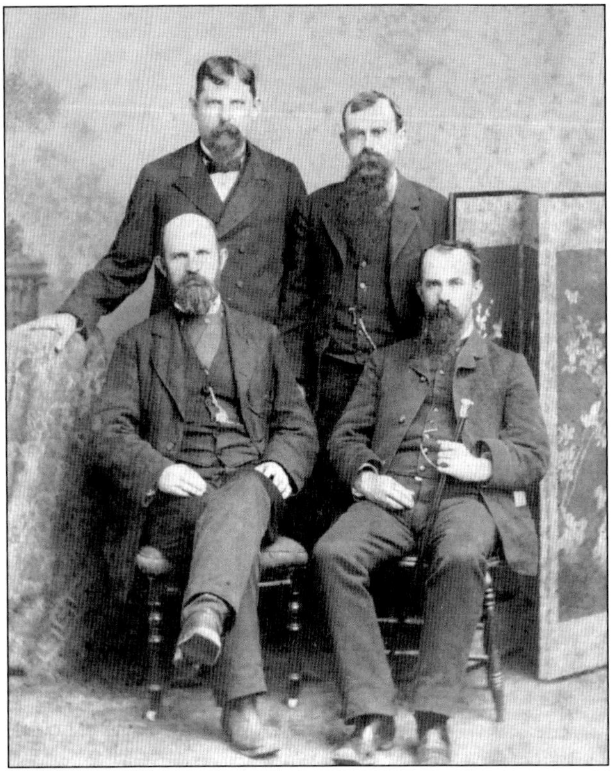

The man sitting on the left was N. W. Hunter, the son of the pioneer Dr. James Hunter, who came to Texas in 1838 and lived in Fort Houston. N. W. Hunter is the father of Kate Hunter, Maude Hunter, and Pauline Hunter. He is also the great-grandfather of Malcolm Hunter. Standing to the left is Gideon Gooch, with J. P. Allen standing on the right. The gentleman seated on the right is unidentified. (Courtesy of METC.)

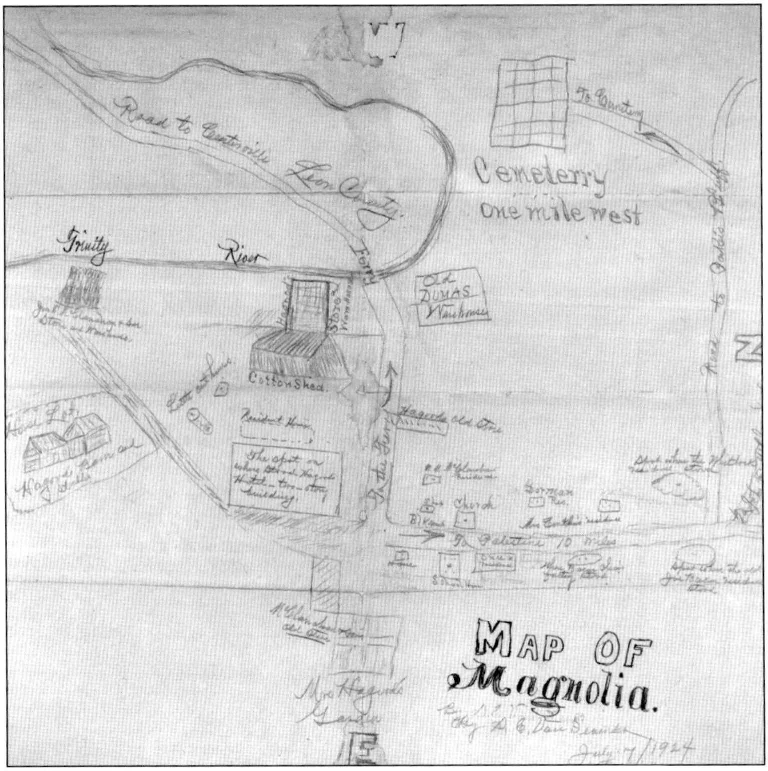

Magnolia, a ghost town 10 miles southwest of Palestine, was established in the early 1840s as a port on the Trinity River. It was named for a large magnolia tree in the center of the town. At one time, the town had a population of 800. When Palestine acquired a railroad, Magnolia declined rapidly. This map of Magnolia was drawn in 1924. (Courtesy of METC.)

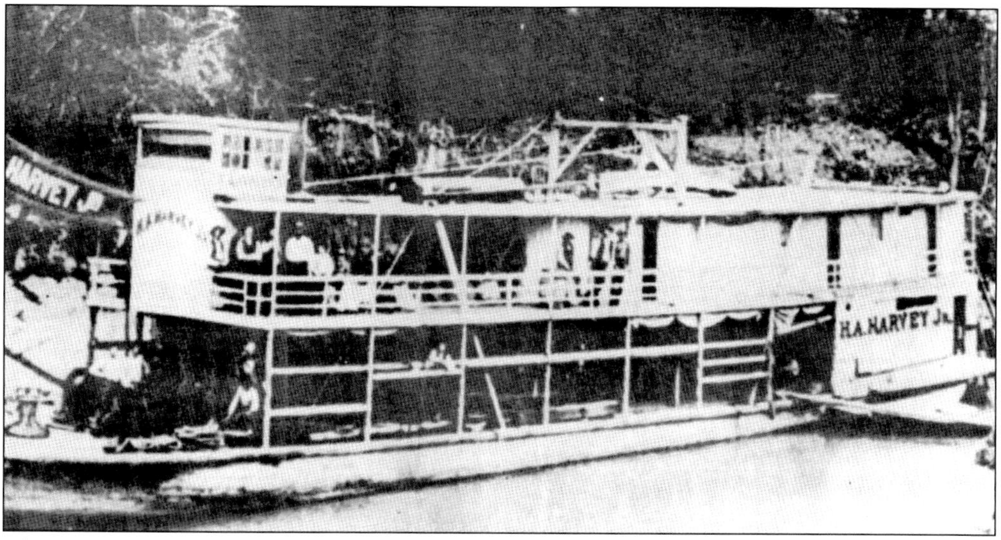

The stern-wheeler *H. A. Harvey Jr.* set a speed record of four days for completing the trip from Magnolia to Galveston while fully loaded with cotton and other freight. The steamboat is shown tied up at Commerce Street in Dallas. After plying the Trinity River for several years, it was sold and sailed to Louisiana in 1898 when the Trinity River navigation died out.

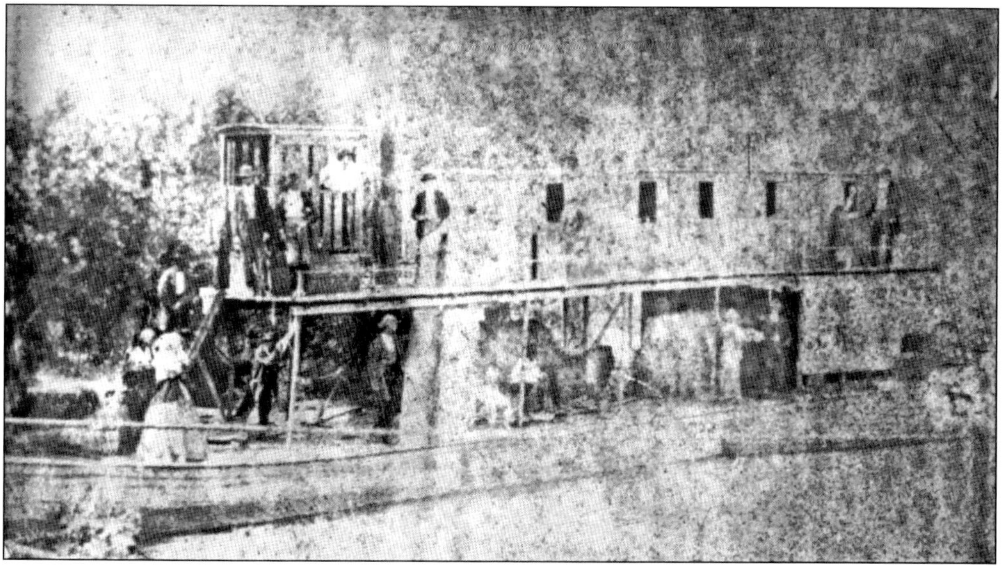

Pictured here is the steamboat *Job Boat No. 1*. The Trinity River between 1840 and 1872 became the Mississippi of Texas, a heavily traveled artery of trade between Magnolia and the booming port of Galveston. (Courtesy of METC.)

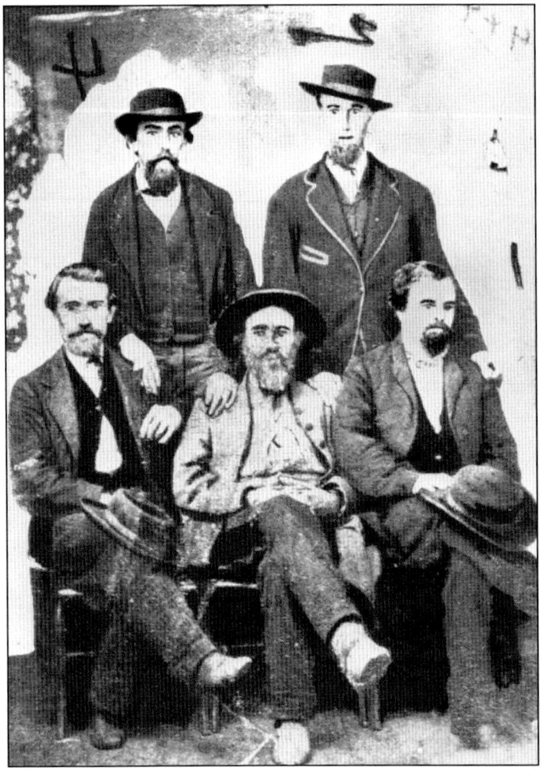

These are five of the early pioneers of old Magnolia. From left to right are (first row) Alex McCoffin, Q. A. Hagood, and Charles Boniselle (or Bonvill); (second row) W. B. Van Devender and J. H. McGarney. Hagood owned a hotel there. (Courtesy of PPL.)

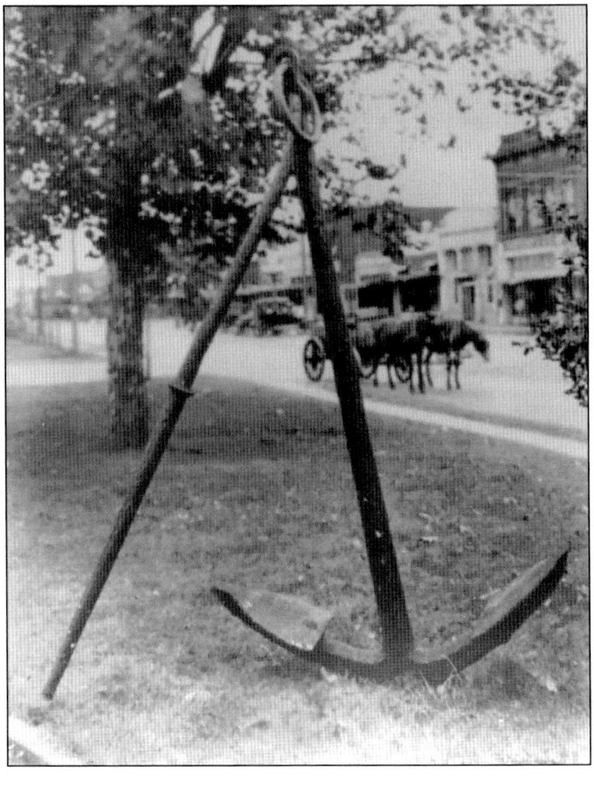

The steamboat *A. S. Ruthven* was built on the Ohio River. It traveled between Galveston, Magnolia, and Parker's Bluff in Anderson County carrying both cargo and passengers. After the coming of the railroad, the boat was dismantled in 1872 at Parker's Bluff. Fifty years later, the anchor was recovered. It is located between Spring Street and the railroad tracks near the site of the old depot, a reminder of the glorious days of steamboating on the Trinity River.

Two

Government and Military

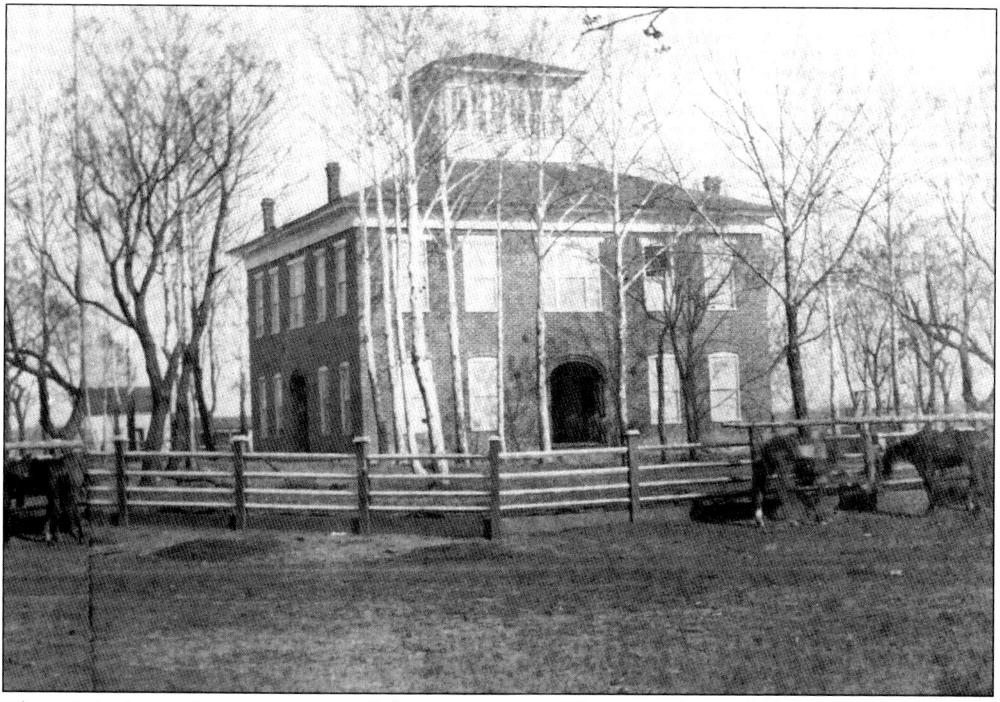

The original courthouse was a small frame structure. The second courthouse, a two-story brick building, 50 feet square, was completed in 1856. A cupola was erected and a lighting rod put in place. The original courthouse was sold and became a store. In 1884, the second courthouse was deemed unsafe and it was ordered that a new courthouse be built. The courthouse lawn became a place to sit and visit with friends.

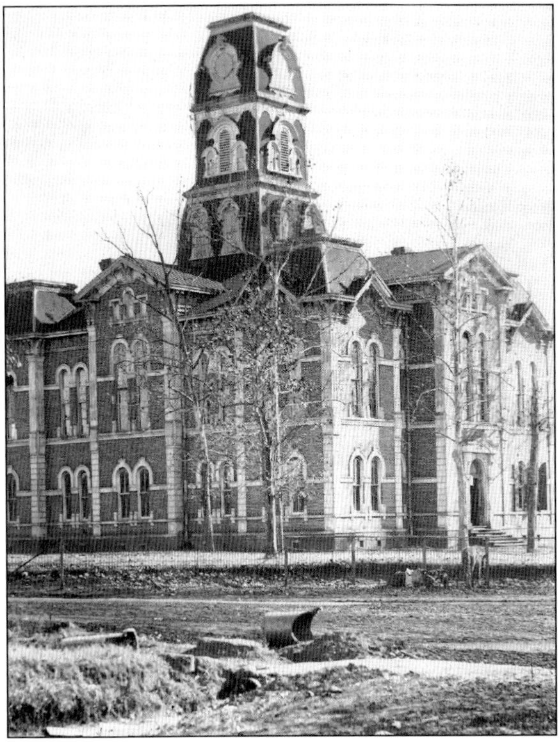

The third courthouse was built in 1886. This courthouse was built of brick with stone trim. On January 6, 1913, this courthouse was destroyed by fire. The fire was set by a young man who had a criminal charge pending against him. It was rumored that he was trying to destroy the records.

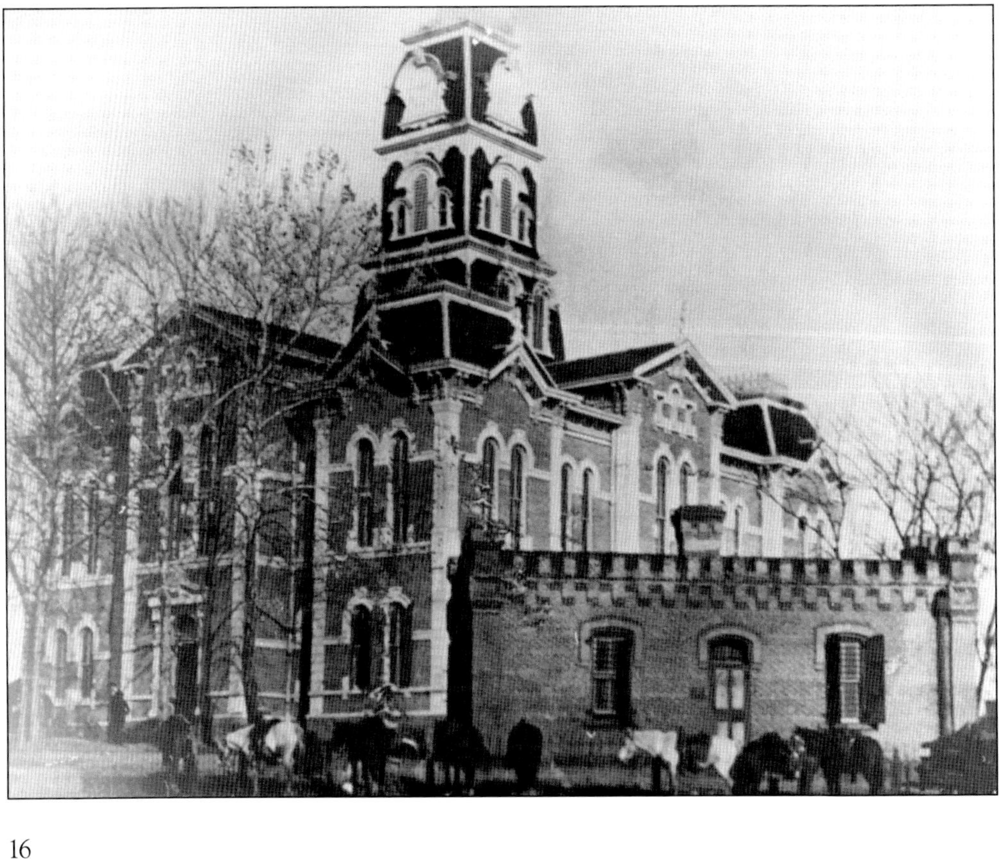

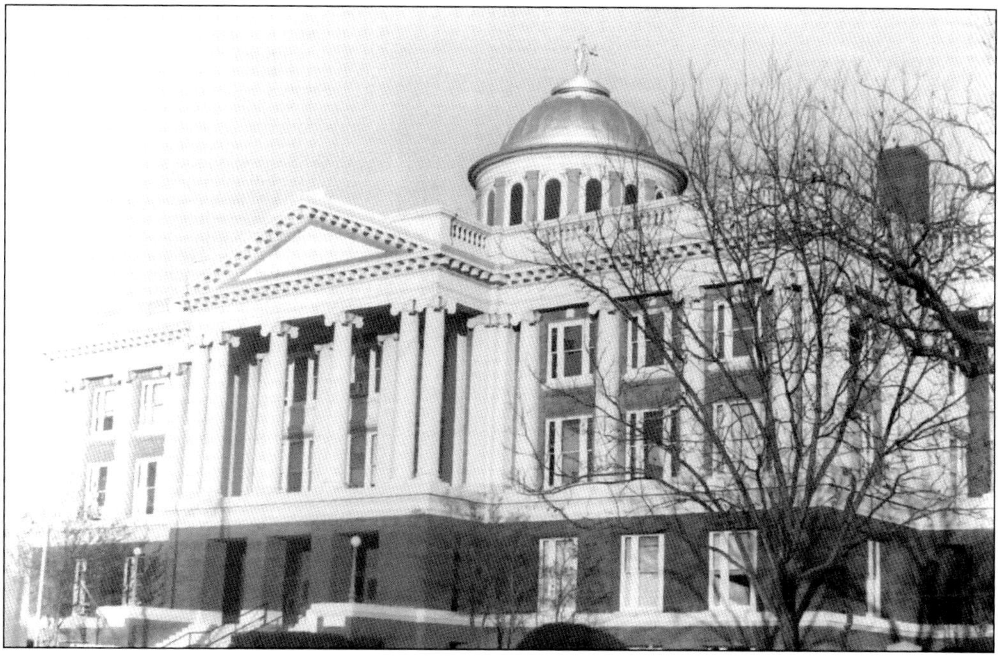

Construction on the current courthouse, the fourth one, began in 1913 when the third courthouse burned. It was mostly completed in December 1914, at a cost of $250,000. In April 1915, $1,600 was spent on curbs and sidewalks. The elevator was installed in 1945. These two photographs show the beautiful structure of Grecian architecture by night and by day. The silver dome is topped by a statue of Justice balancing her traditional scales. It is said that the county clerk's office is a fire-proof, burglar-proof room.

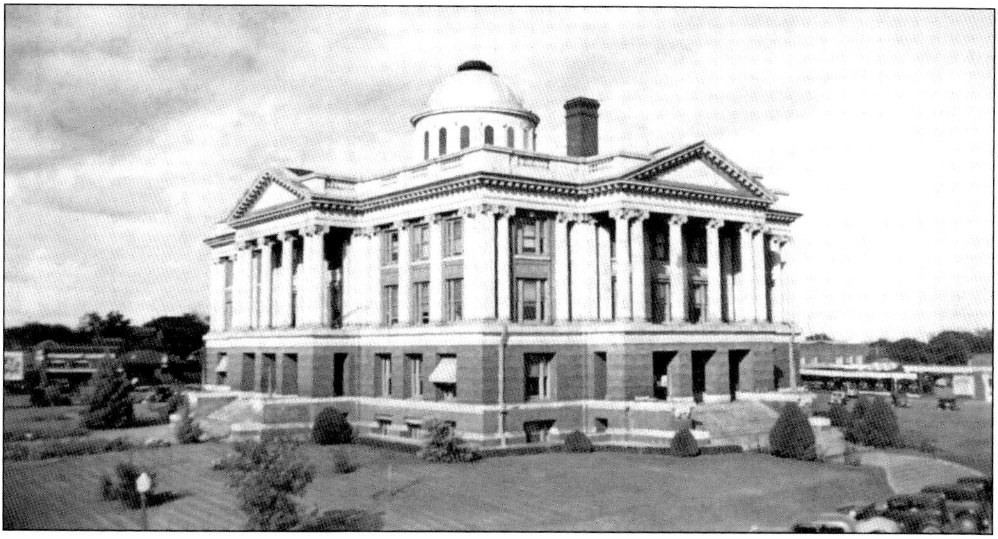

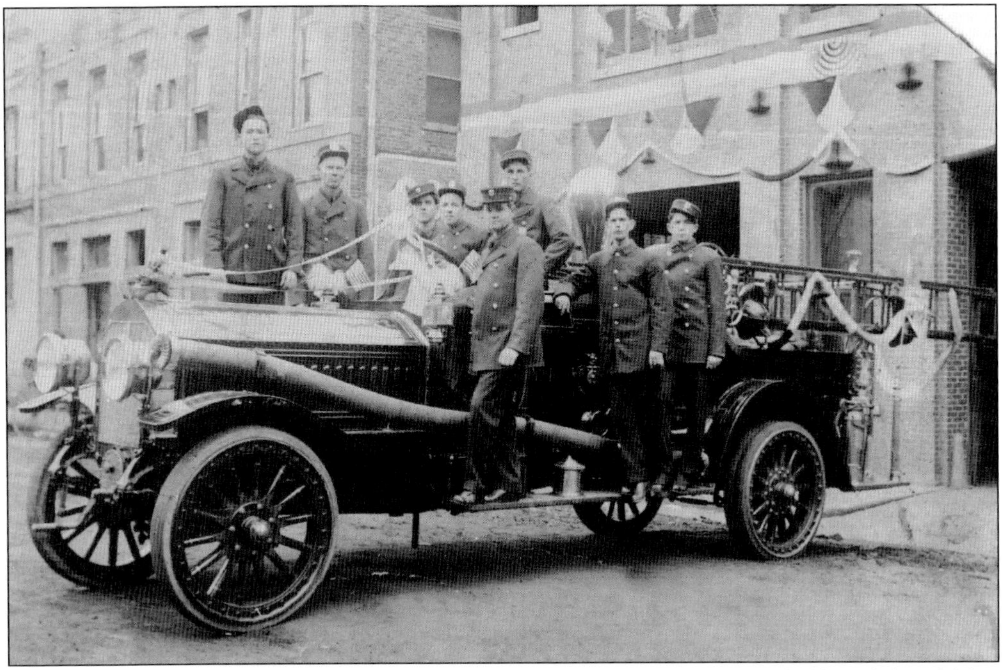

Pictured here is the fire wagon leaving the firehouse. The fire bell in the belfry of the old fire station tolled the alarm in the day of horse-drawn firefighting equipment. After being stored in the basement of the Carnegie Library for a time, the bell was returned to the belfry during World War II to toll the alarm should Palestine come under attack by German forces.

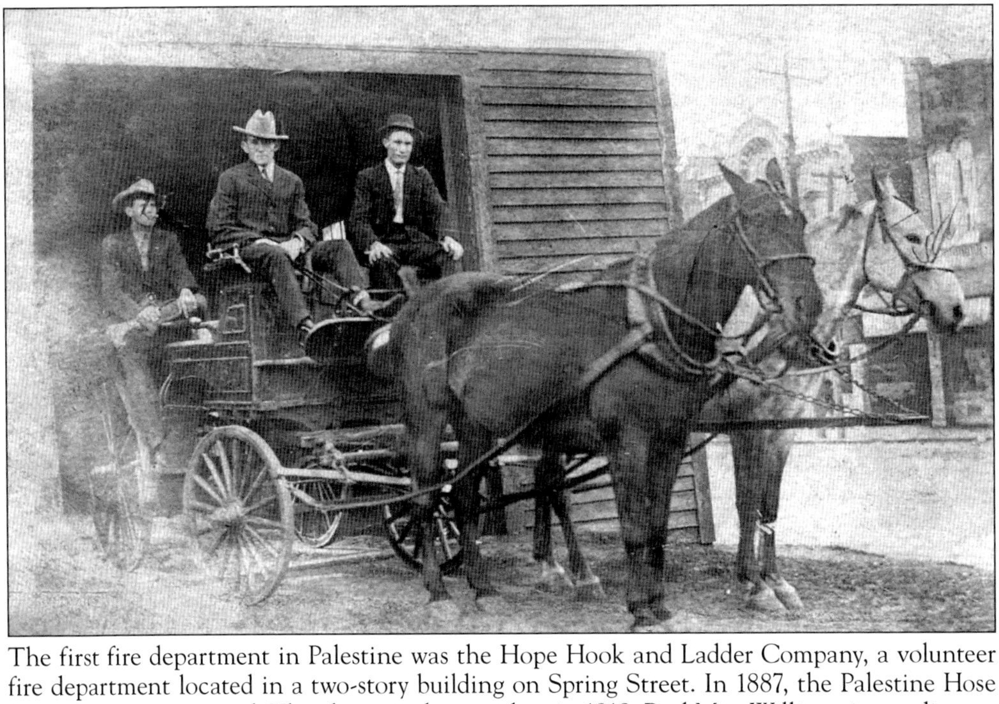

The first fire department in Palestine was the Hope Hook and Ladder Company, a volunteer fire department located in a two-story building on Spring Street. In 1887, the Palestine Hose Company was organized. The photograph was taken in 1918. Paul Max Williams is standing on the left end of the running board.

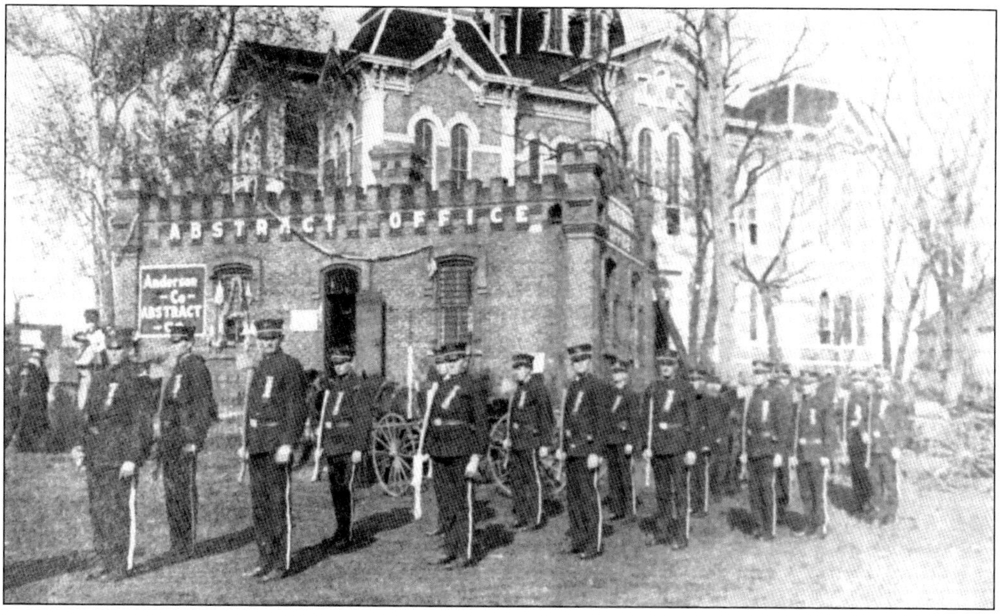

In the photograph above, the Palestine Rifles are standing at attention on the courthouse square. This may be the same group as the Dilley Rifles. The Anderson County Abstract Office and the third Anderson County Courthouse are in the background. The Dilley Rifles, shown below, were organized after 1875. There were between 50 and 75 young men in the drill team, all crack shots. The captain of the team was Warner Williams. Their headquarters were in the home on South Sycamore across from the Dilley home. Drill practice was held upstairs in Bailey Hall on Avenue A.

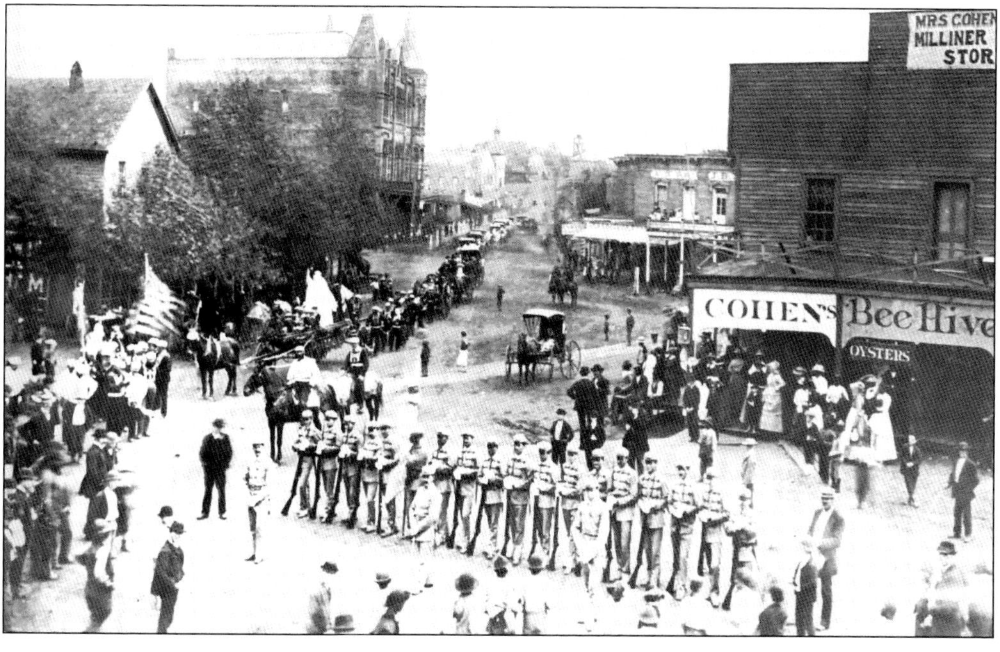

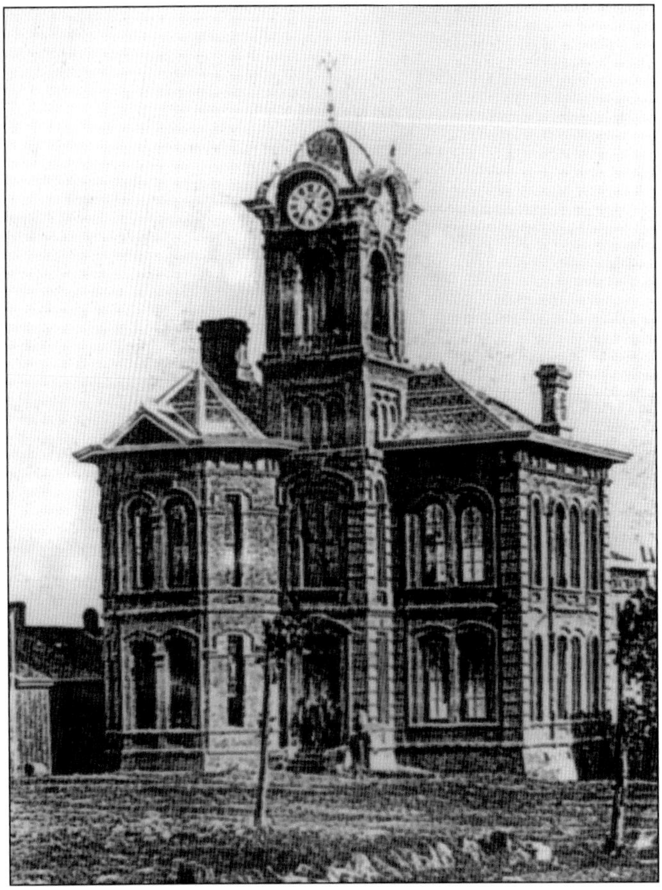

In the 1870s, the citizens realized that the rapidly growing county needed a new, larger jail. In 1879, work began on a new, two-story limestone building located on Avenue A at the southwest corner of the courthouse square. The new jail was an impressive building with a clock tower. The clock was a gift from George Wright. That building was replaced in 1931 with the three-story jail pictured below. That jail was built on the same site as the old one. It served as the county jail for almost 55 years until it was replaced by a new, modern one on East Lacy Street.

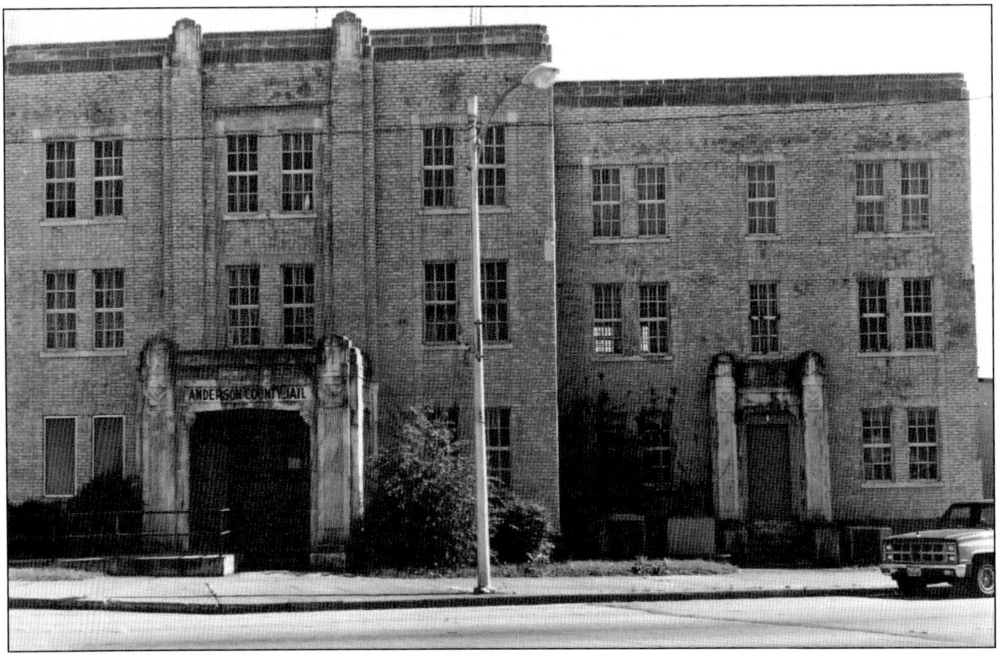

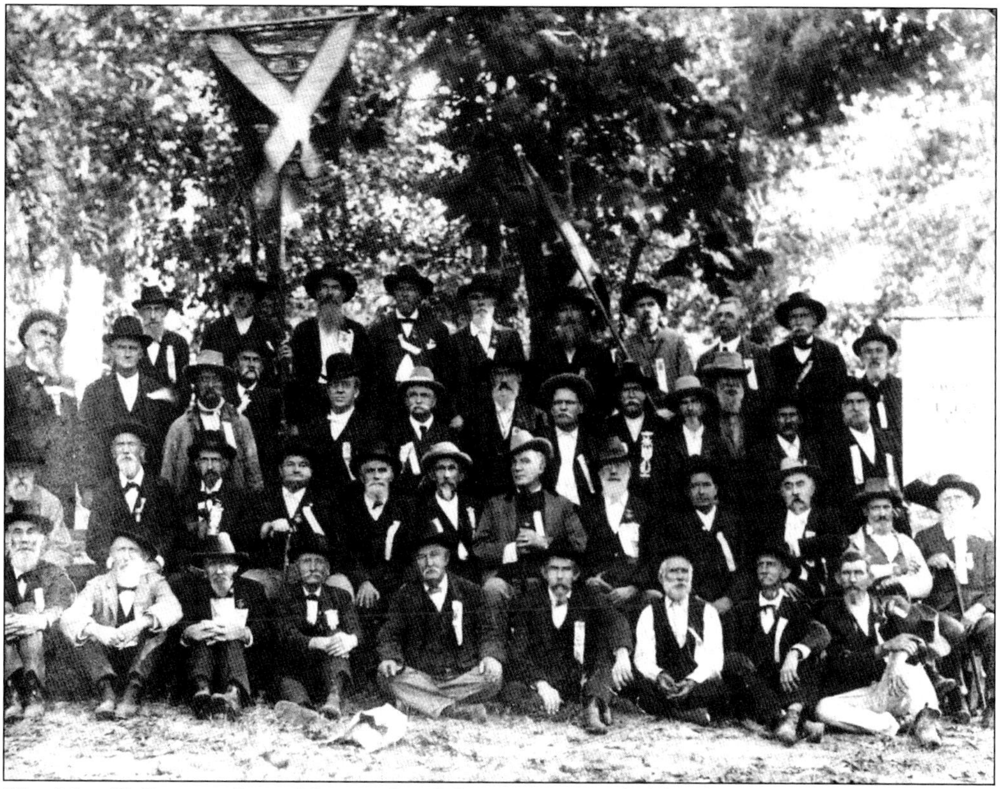

The John H. Reagan Camp No. 44, Confederate veterans, held a three-day meeting beginning on August 20, 1902, at Matthews and Strickland Park. Confederate veterans came from all over Texas to the meeting. The governor-elect, Samuel Willis Tucker Lanham, was present for the festivities. He was the last confederate veteran to serve as Texas governor. The only veteran identified above is A. L. Huddleston, second from the right in the first row.

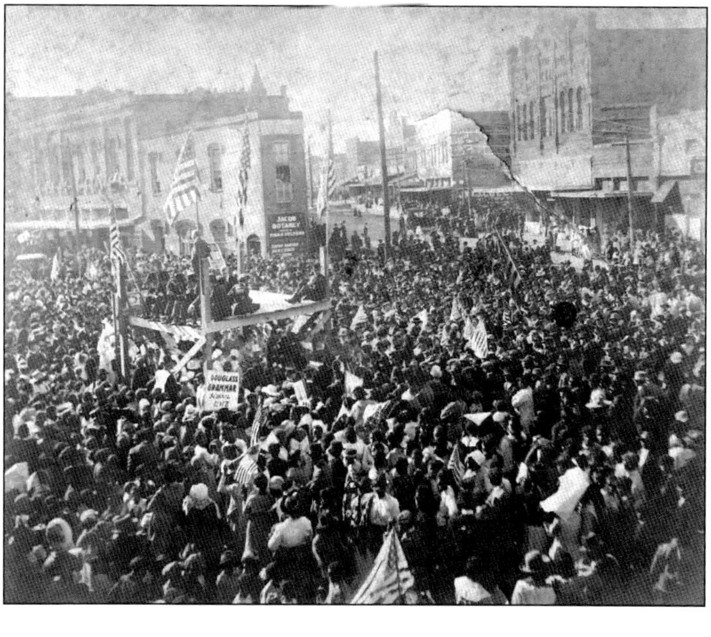

McKnight Plaza on Avenue A is shown during the parade celebrating the armistice signed between the allies of World War I and Germany at Compiegne, France. The armistice for the cessation of hostilities on the Western Front went into effect at 11:00 a.m. on November 11, 1918, "the eleventh hour of the eleventh day of the eleventh month of 1918." Former Gov. Thomas Mitchell Campbell of Palestine was the speaker.

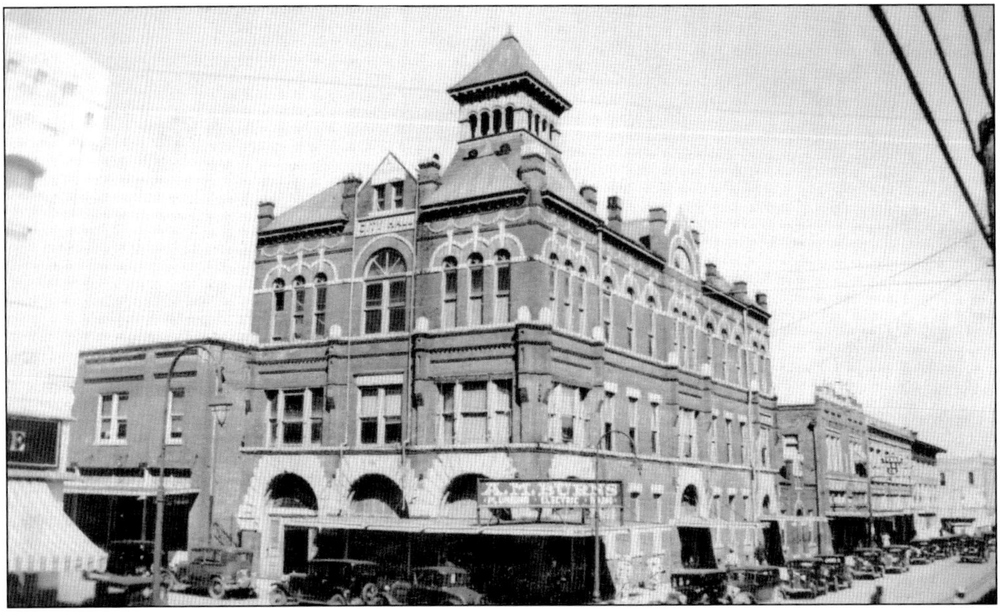

This new city hall was built in 1899 at the corner of West Oak and North Magnolia Streets. The grand opening was held on August 22, 1899. It replaced the old city hall on Avenue A. A. L. Bowers was mayor at that time. The Honorable Thomas Mitchell Campbell, later governor, delivered the opening address. In 1940, this building was razed and a new municipal building was constructed on the same site.

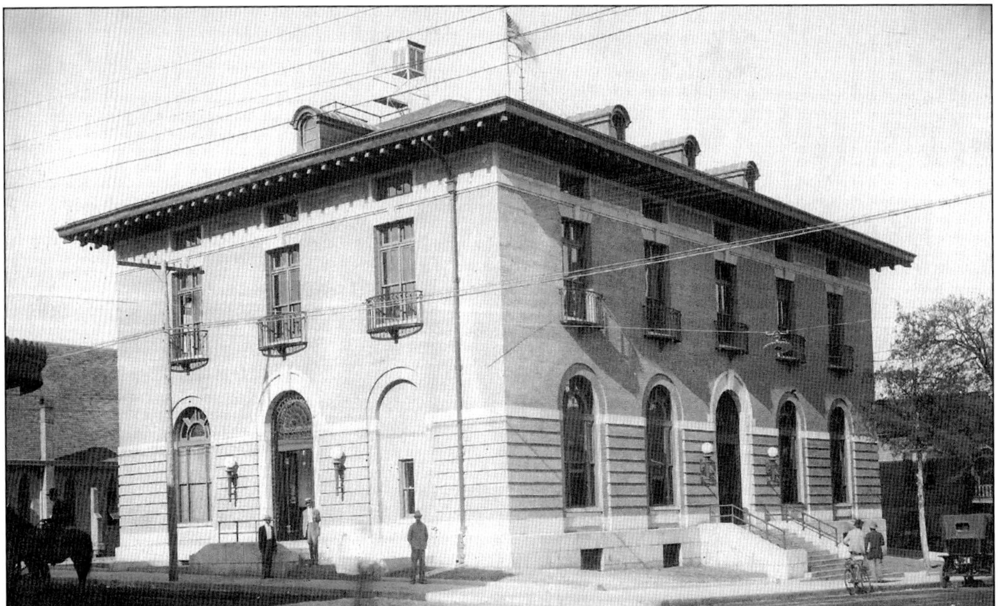

The land for the federal building was purchased in 1907 from St. Philip's Episcopal Church. It was located in the commercial district of Palestine on East Oak Street at North Sycamore Street. For many years, it served as the post office. It has been the home of the Selective Service Office and the National Weather Bureau's reading station. It currently houses the Anderson County Extension Service and Anderson County Historical Commission.

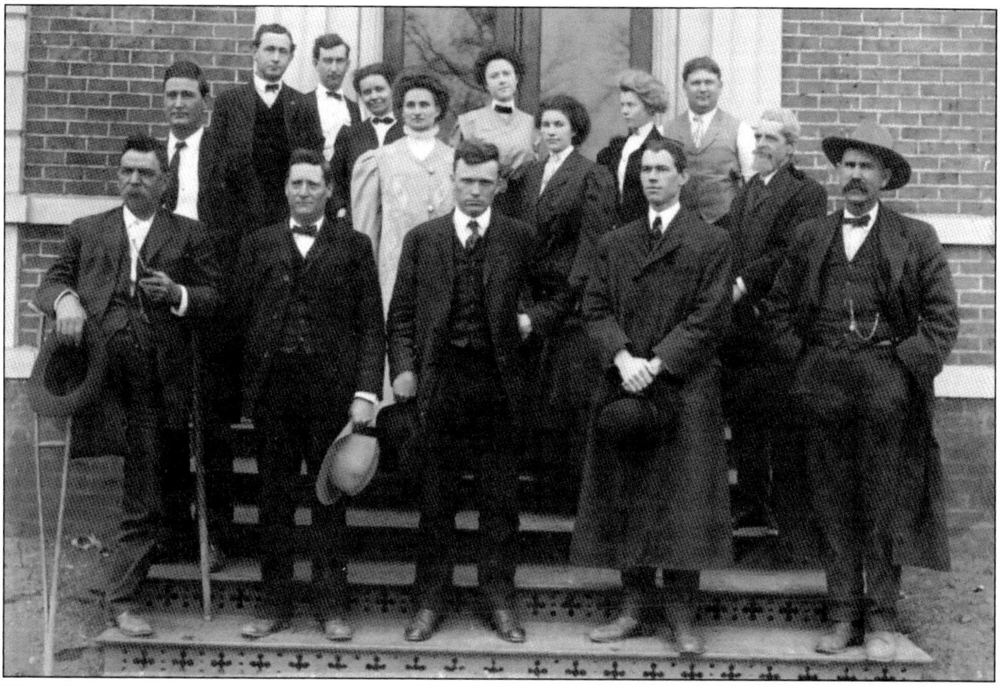

This photograph was taken about 1909–1910 in front of the third Anderson County Courthouse. From left to right are (first row) Z. A. McReynolds, tax collector; H. C. Williams, county treasurer; O. C. Funderburk; Ben Jackson, tax assessor; and Bill Black, sheriff; (second row) John Moore, district clerk; Ed Erwin, county judge; Walter Rogers, clerk; Maggie Wright; unidentified; Maud Greer; Sally Wolf; Ella McReynolds; Jim Britton, county clerk; and Major Phillips, justice of the peace. (Courtesy of Anita McReynolds.)

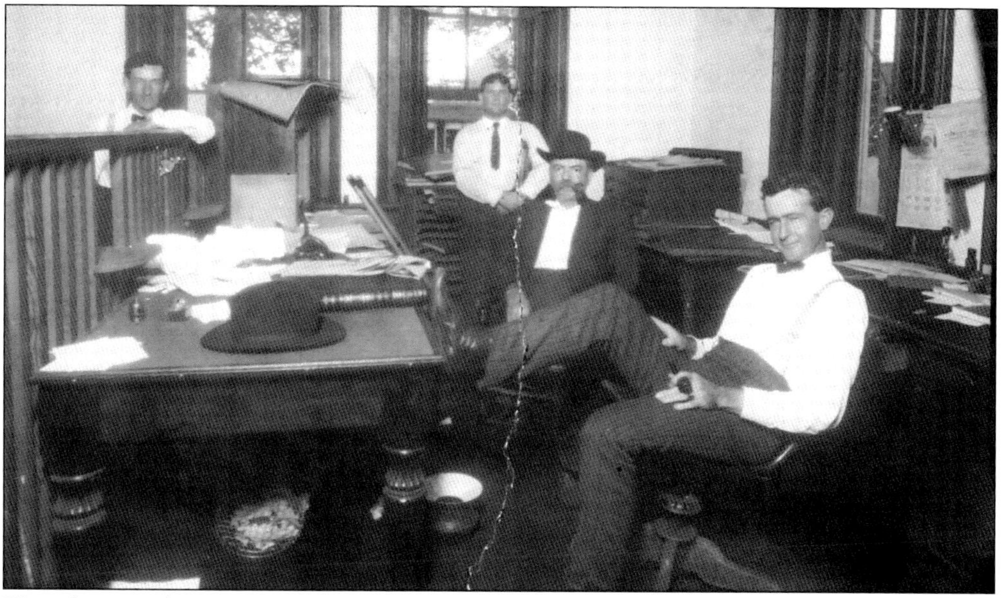

This photograph was taken about 1909–1910 in the tax collector's office of the third Anderson County Courthouse. Pictured from left to right are Walter Rogers, clerk; Jim Britton, county clerk; Z. A. McReynolds, tax collector; and Ed Erwin, judge.

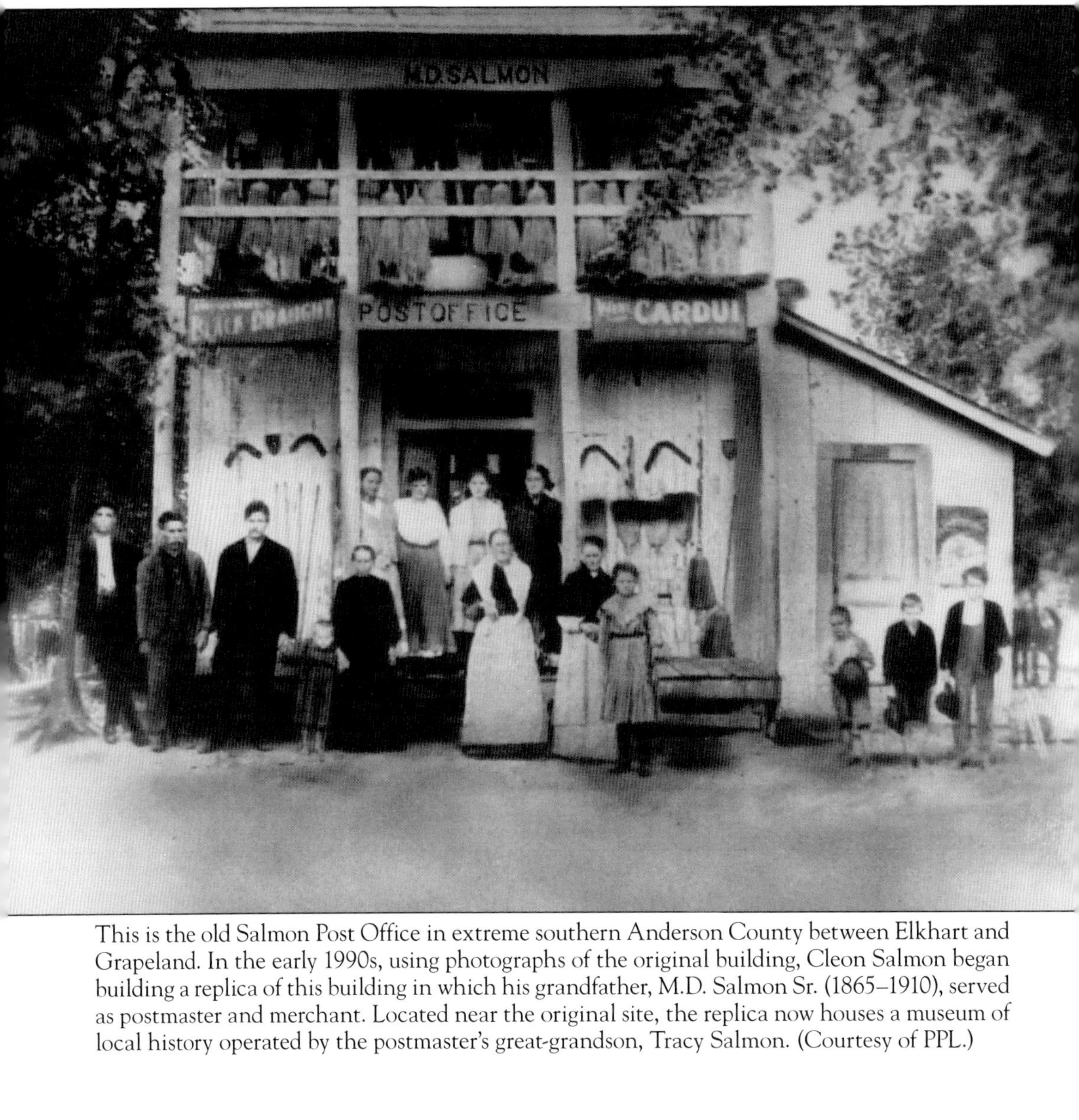

This is the old Salmon Post Office in extreme southern Anderson County between Elkhart and Grapeland. In the early 1990s, using photographs of the original building, Cleon Salmon began building a replica of this building in which his grandfather, M.D. Salmon Sr. (1865–1910), served as postmaster and merchant. Located near the original site, the replica now houses a museum of local history operated by the postmaster's great-grandson, Tracy Salmon. (Courtesy of PPL.)

Three

Business and Industry

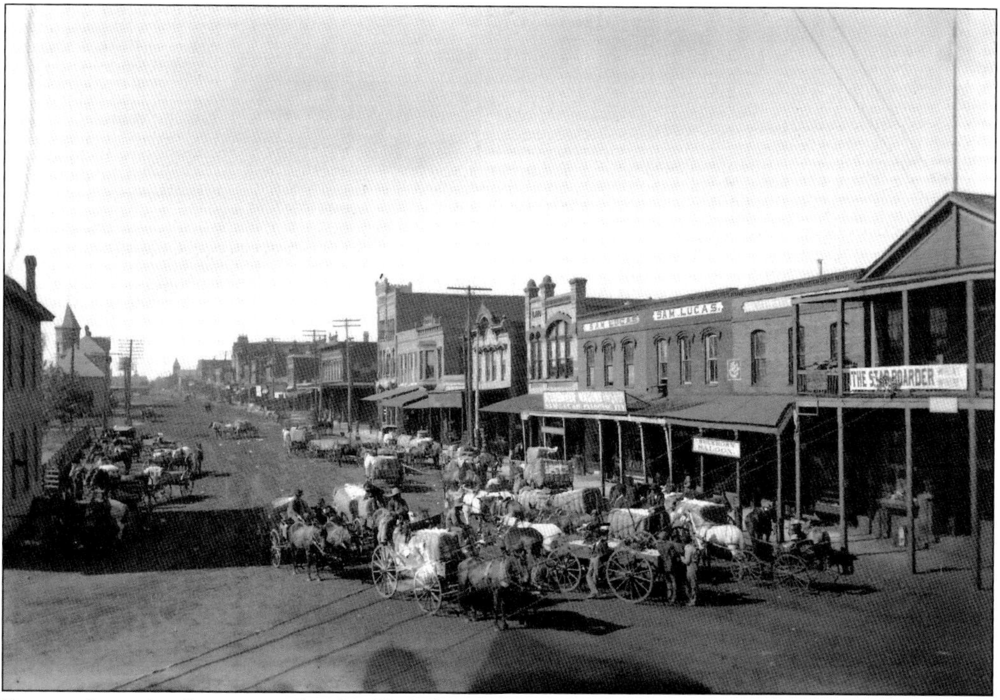

Farmers brought their wagonloads of baled cotton to Front Street (now Spring Street) in the late 1890s. On Front Street, cotton buyers took samples from each bale and bid on them. The steeple at the far end of the street is from the Congregational Church. The tall building on the corner of Front Street and Magnolia is the new Royall Bank building. It was constructed after the old building was destroyed by fire.

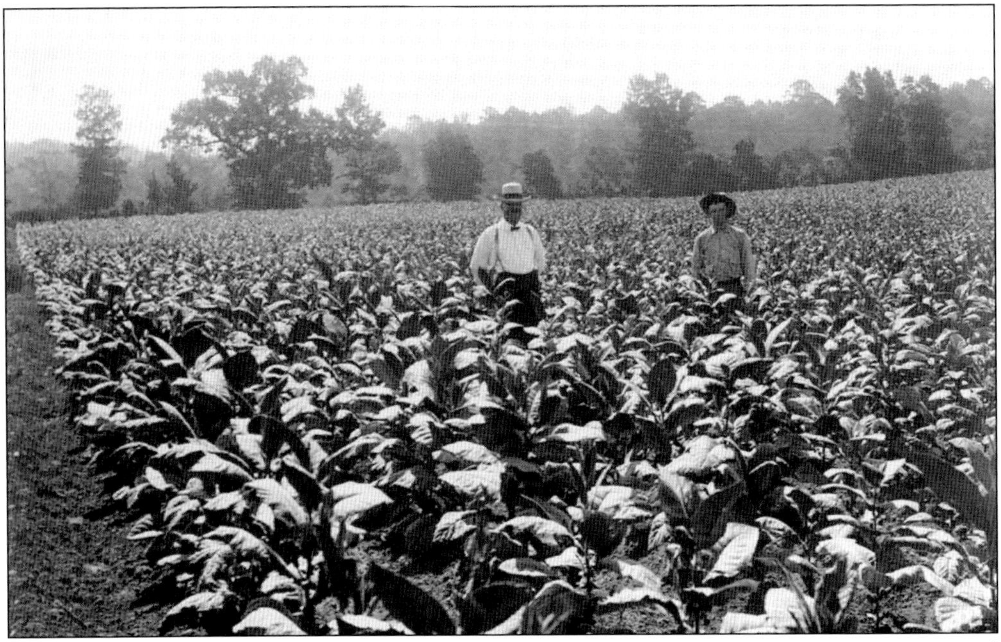

The tobacco industry in Anderson County began in late 1904. Chief tobacco expert McNess and state expert Hinson of the U.S. Department of Agriculture became satisfied that the Orangeburg loam soil here would produce a good quality of both the Cuban wrapper and filler leaf used in the manufacture of the finer grades of cigars. Encouraged by the conclusion, several local businessmen and farmers began growing it. A small company was organized to test the paying qualities of the new cash crop. Five acres were planted under cheese-cloth shade in 1906, and the result was a success, yielding 5,000 pounds, which sold for 40¢ per pound. (Both, courtesy of CA.)

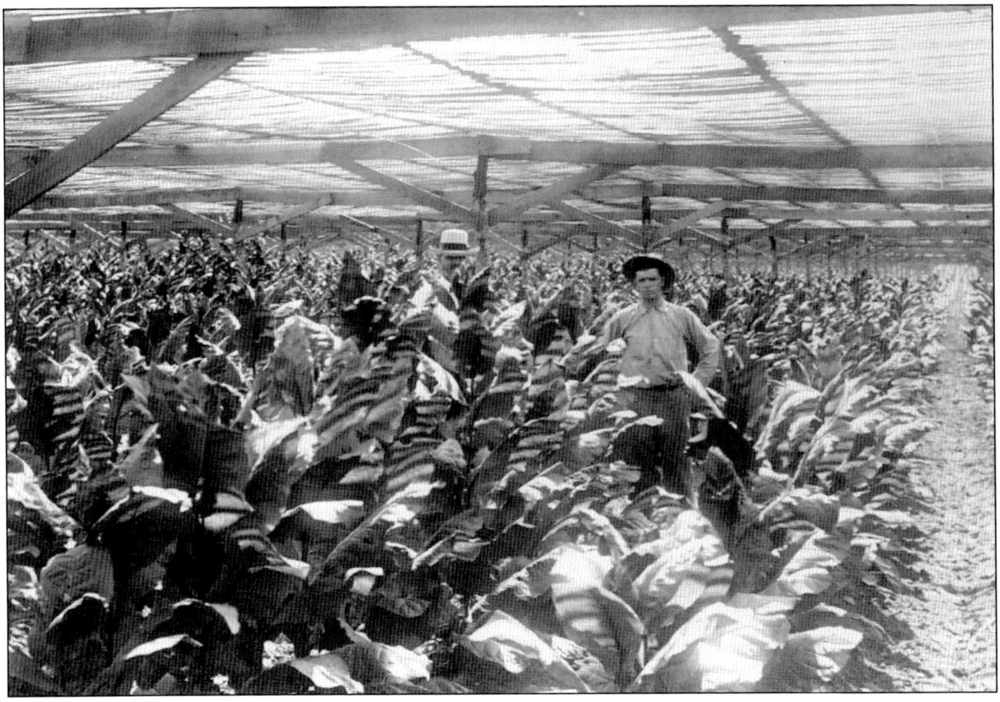

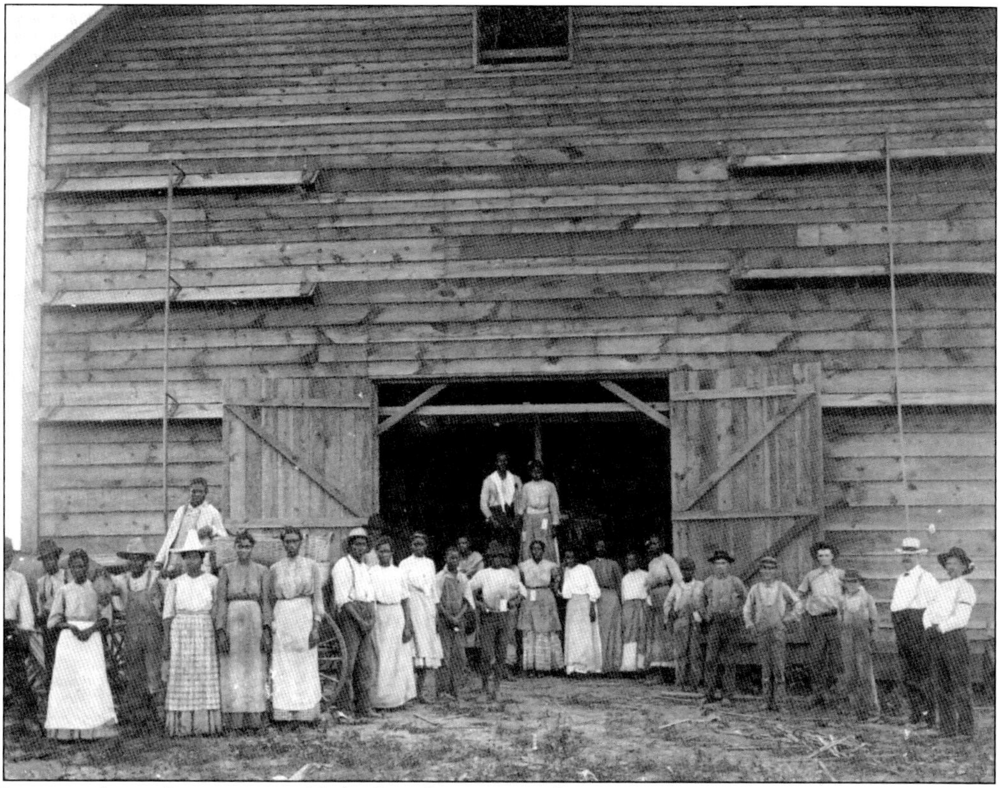

Later a tobacco barn was established, and prominent businessman John R. Hearne had a crop as late as 1928. (Courtesy of CA.)

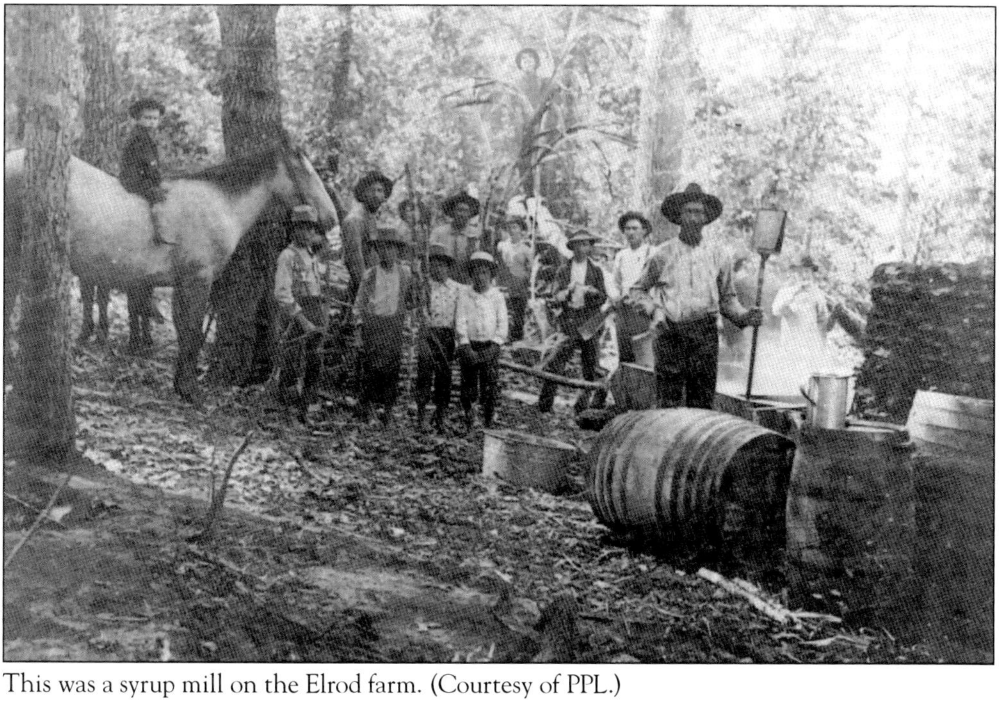

This was a syrup mill on the Elrod farm. (Courtesy of PPL.)

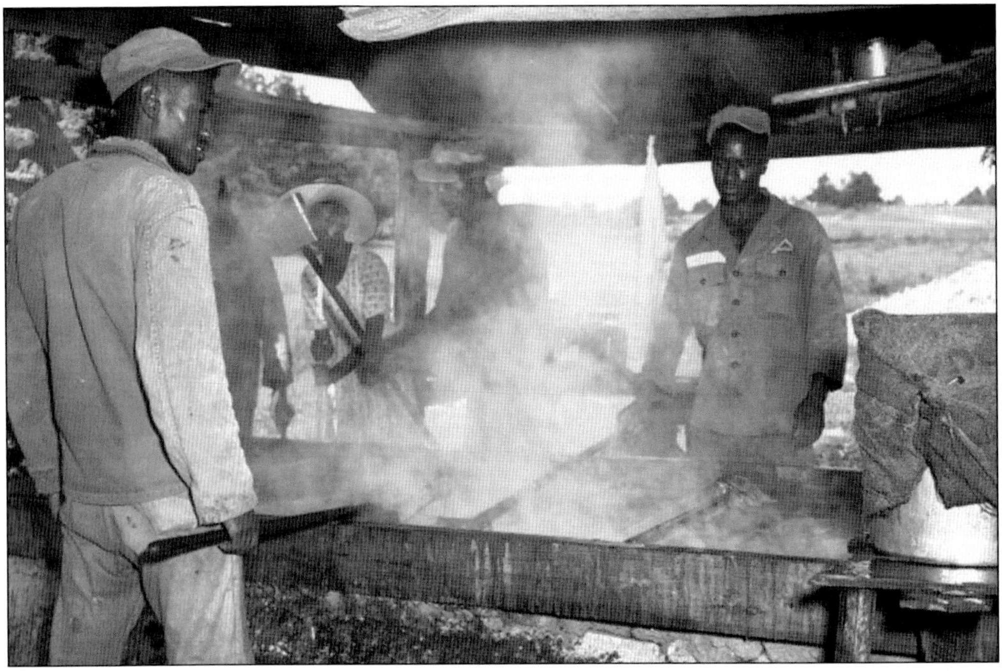

After 18 months of growth, the cane is ready to be harvested. Sugar Cane stalks would be fed into the maw of crushing rollers. The cooking syrup had foam that needed to be skimmed off. The foam consists of cane wax, dirt, and other impurities. What is left is good old ribbon cane syrup, country made. It is not known where these pictures were made, but they are reflective of life in this county. Just imagine on a chilly morning having a breakfast of fresh pork, home-churned butter, and homemade hot biscuits flavored with fresh ribbon cane syrup. What a treat! (Both, courtesy of PPL.)

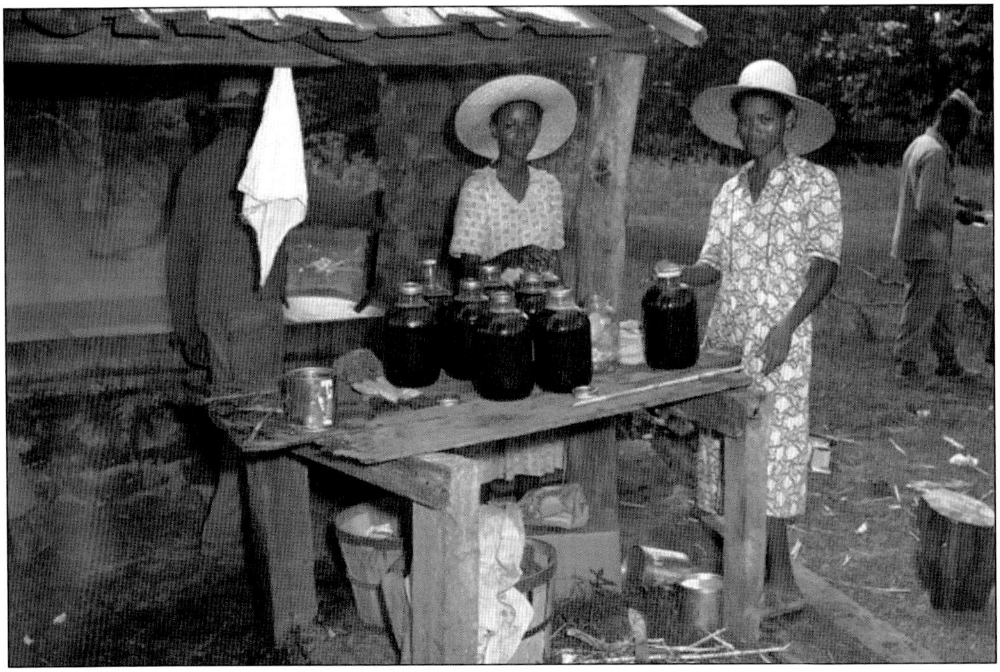

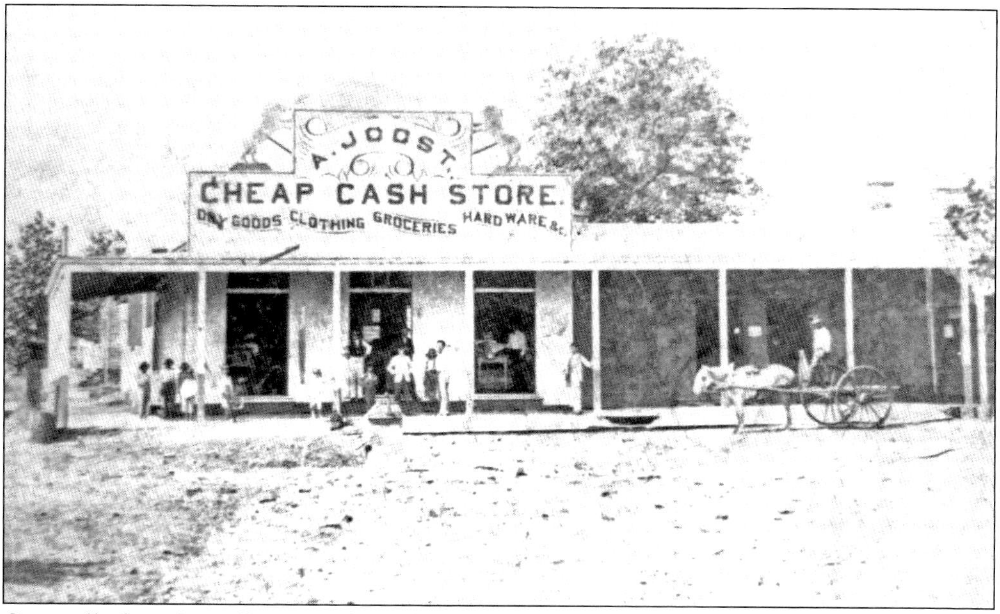

Originally from Paris, France, Alexander Joost moved from Fort Houston to the new town of Palestine in 1846. He opened A. Joost Cheap Cash Store on the northwest corner of the old town square. It is believed to be the first business in Palestine. It was built of rough logs, later replacing it with a store of finished lumber. It stood where Jackson Hanks' law office is now located.

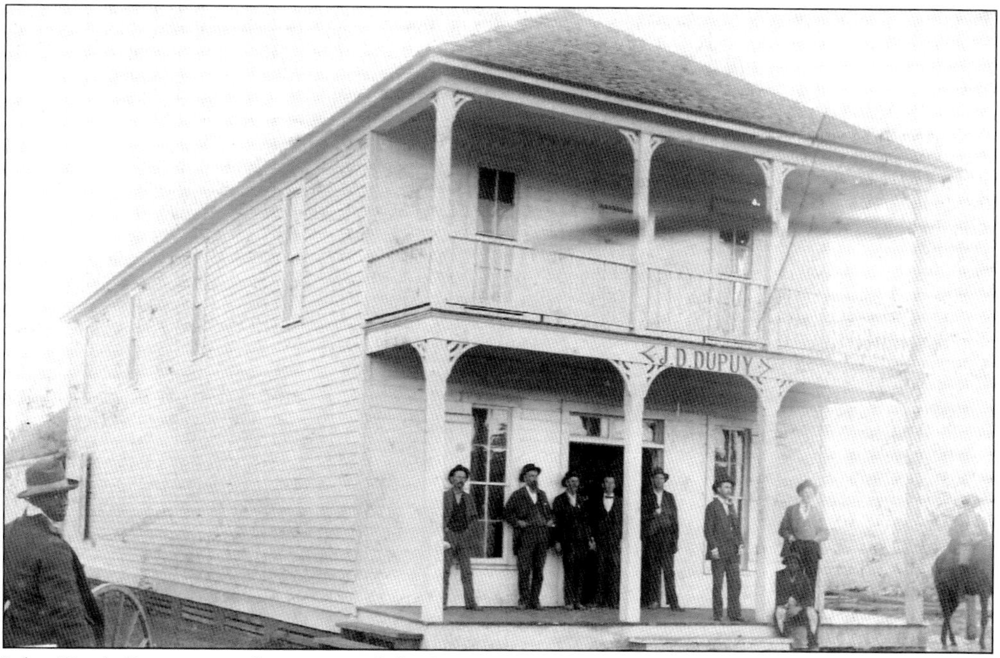

John Dock Dupuy was the owner of the J. D. Dupuy Store in Elkhart. He had a large business until the boll weevils hit in 1904. He sold the business and moved to San Antonio. In 1908, he returned to Anderson County, making his home in Palestine. (Courtesy of Scott Fitzgerald.)

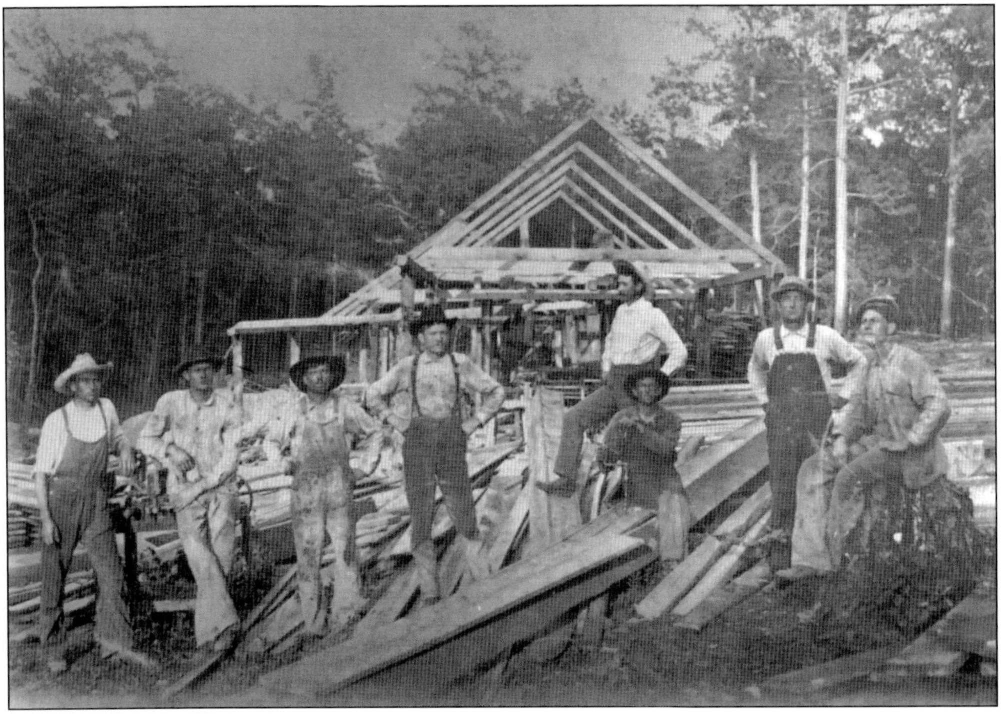

Logging and sawmills were important industries in East Texas in the late 1800s and well into the 1900s. When the logs had to be hauled a distance to a sawmill, mule teams were the usual method of transportation. These photographs were taken near Elkhart. (Both, courtesy of CA.)

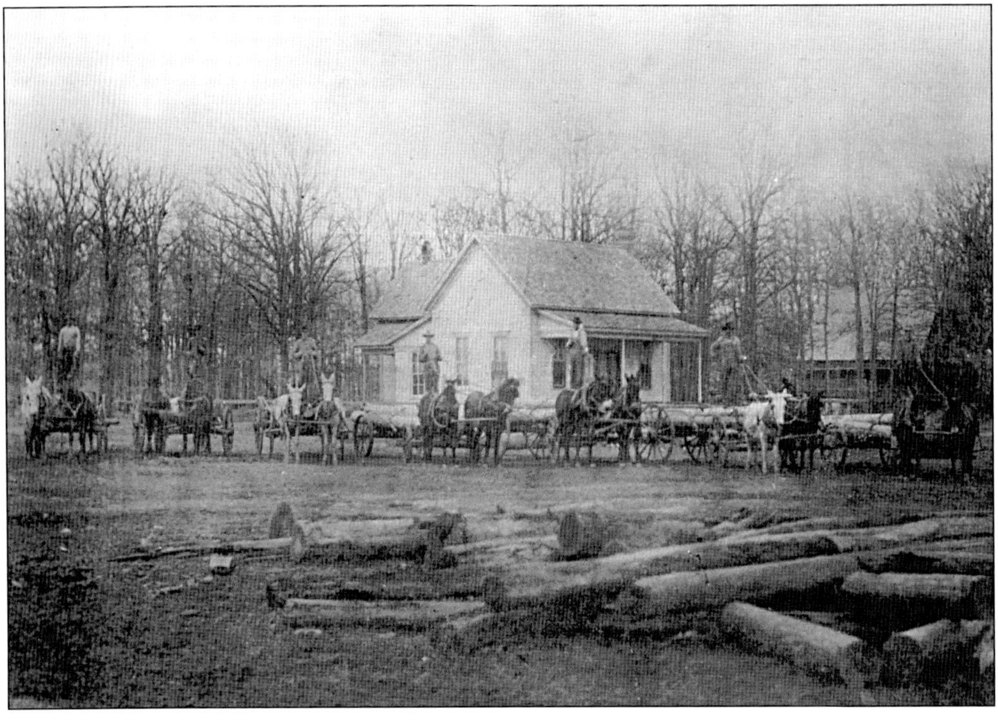

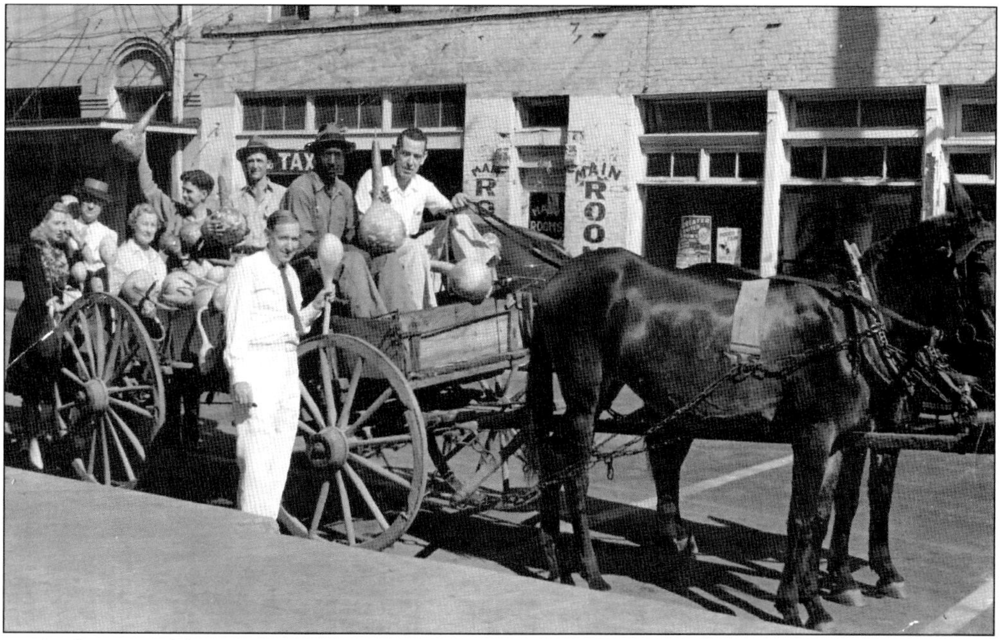

In the horse-and-buggy days, farmers would bring their produce and other crops to town to sell them. Pictured here, a farmer is selling gourds. Those were the days before running water, and they used dippers to retrieve the water from buckets. The gourds made excellent dippers.

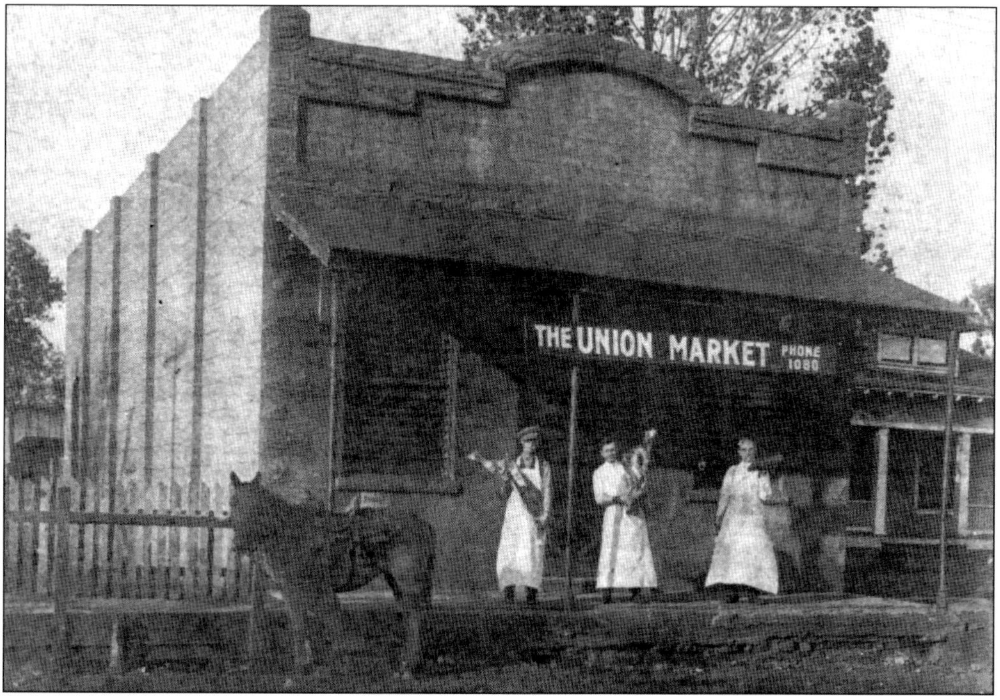

Anthony Nelson "Tony" Spaith owned the Union Market at 1009 West Lacy in Palestine. It closed before 1921. Previously he and his half-brother, Charles Bodden, owned the City Market on West Main. At one time, Tony owned Washington Market at 106 Main Street and Charles owned the Model Meat Market at 608 Main Street. (Courtesy of Louise Spaith.)

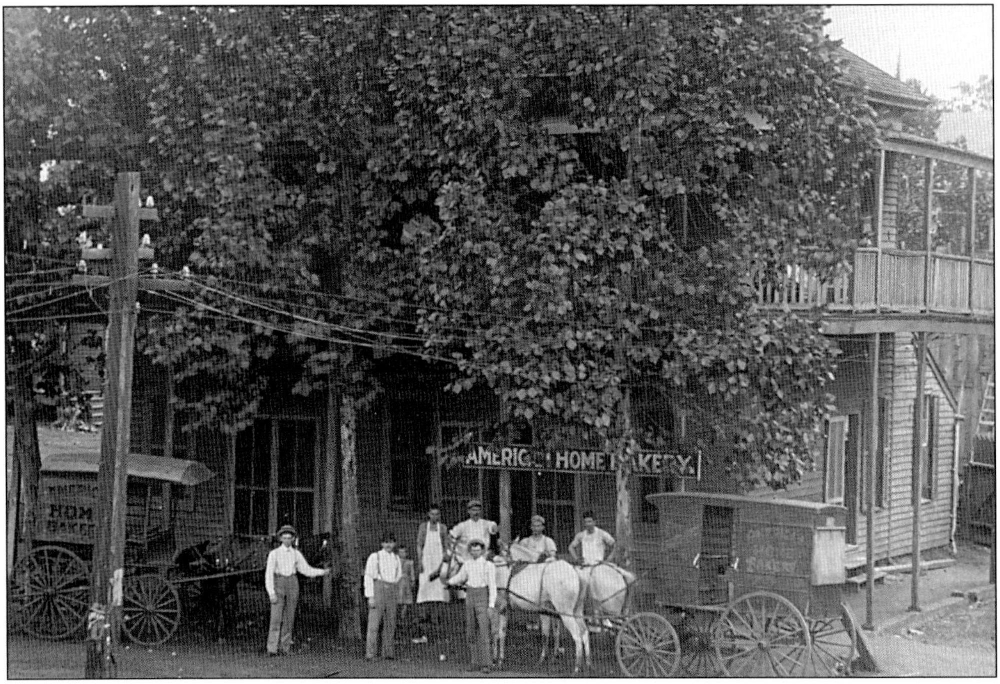

When he was three years old, F. H. Eilenberger's family immigrated to Fort Worth, Texas, from their home in Leipzig, Germany. He learned the baking trade in Galveston and Fort Worth. The photograph above was taken in 1898, when he first came to Palestine and opened the American Home Bakery at the corner of West Oak and John Streets. His goal was to provide the best quality products. Later he moved one block north to the corner of Crawford and John Streets. Known worldwide for their fruit cakes, the bakery is still operated by a member of the Eilenberger family. The second photograph was taken in 1919.

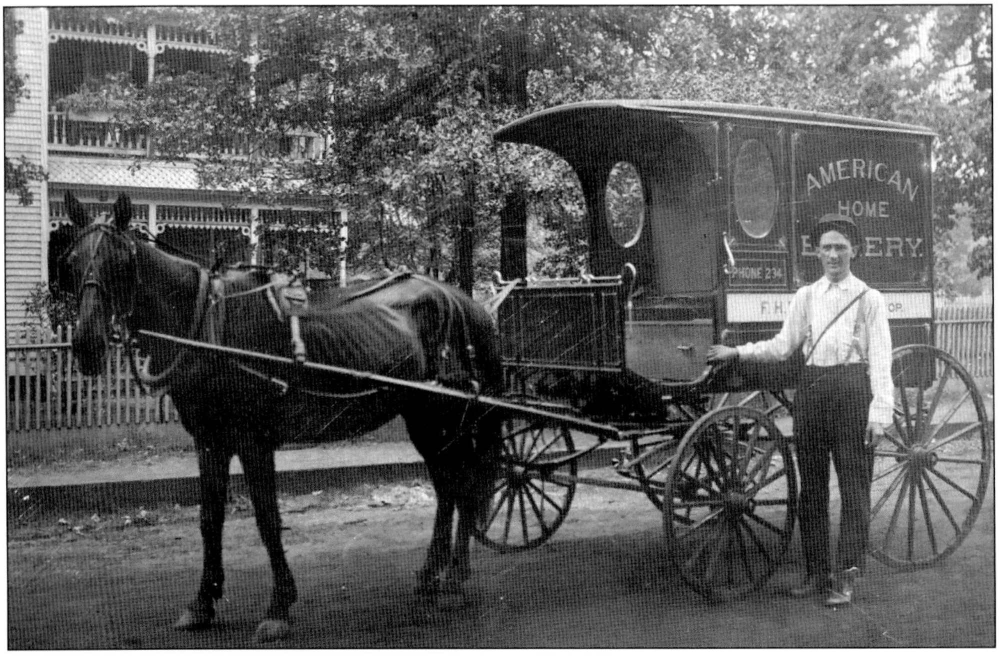

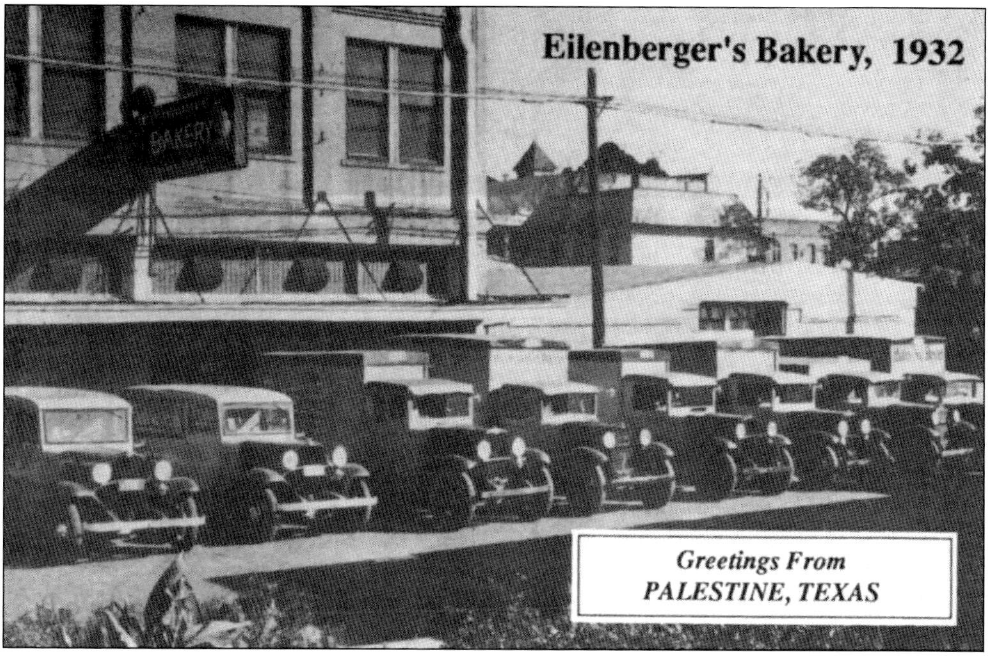

After the original bakery burned in 1918, Eilenberger's Bakery purchased the brick building on the corner of John and Crawford Streets from William H. and Dora Lee Reese. An A&P grocery store had formerly occupied the building. At that time, they also opened a retail bakery in the front of the building facing Crawford Street. Until 1920, all products were delivered by horse-drawn delivery wagons. Later they purchased a fleet of trucks to deliver their baked goods. Eilenberger's Butter-Nut bread was a familiar word in many East Texas homes for over 60 years. No one who lived in Palestine during those years can forget the wonderful aroma of freshly baked goods wafting throughout downtown.

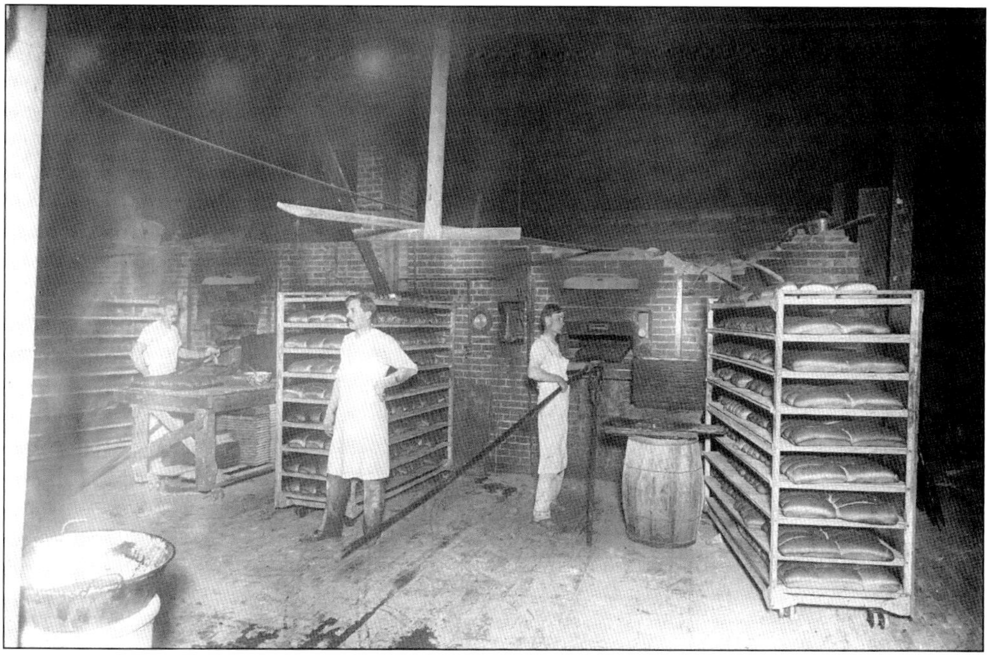

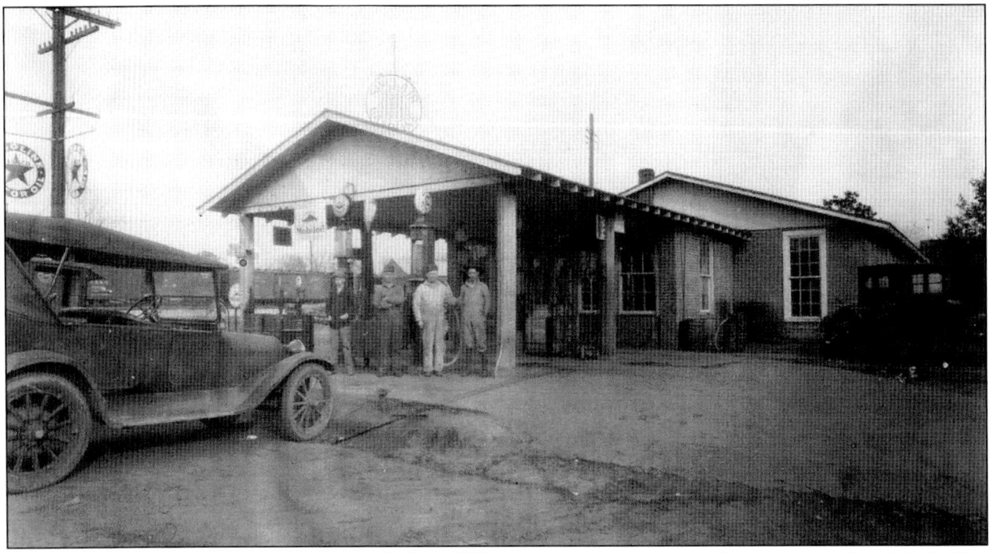

Chan Jefferson "C. J." Moran operated this Elkhart service station until sometime after 1940. The station was located at the corner of Parker and Main Streets on land that is now the parking lot for the Elkhart State Bank. (Courtesy of Karren Jones.)

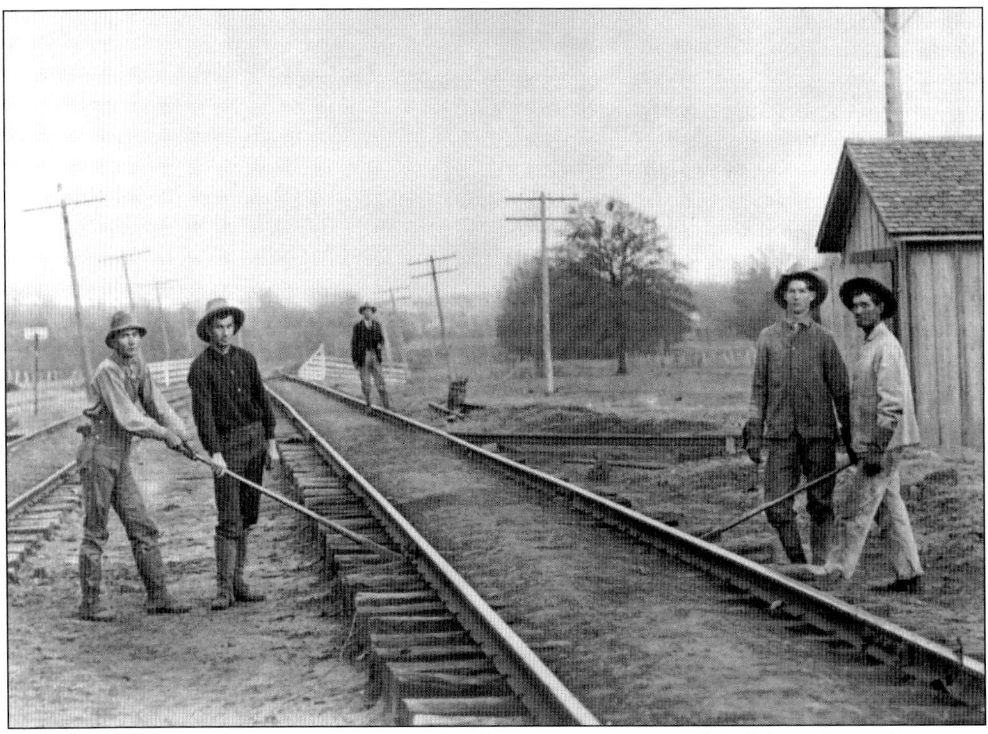

Foreman Ned Corley oversees track repairs by the section crew near the Elkhart depot. (Courtesy of CA.)

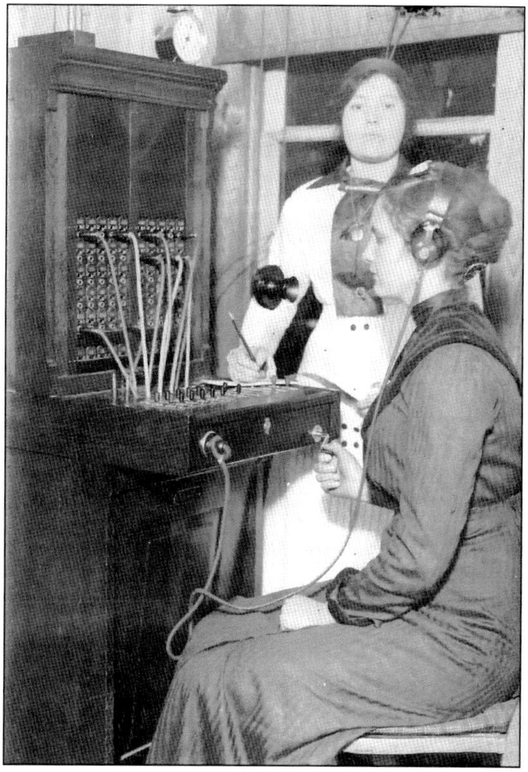

The Elkhart Telephone Exchange building, around 1916, was located on what is now Church Street. The telephone operator is believed to be Cora Parker. Atop the pole are Charles Arthur Page and Gord Bowdoin. The others pictured are, from left to right, Will A. Montgomery and his daughter, Zelma; Cora Parker; Tom O'Brian; and Tony Holcomb. (Both, courtesy of Wilda Page Collection.)

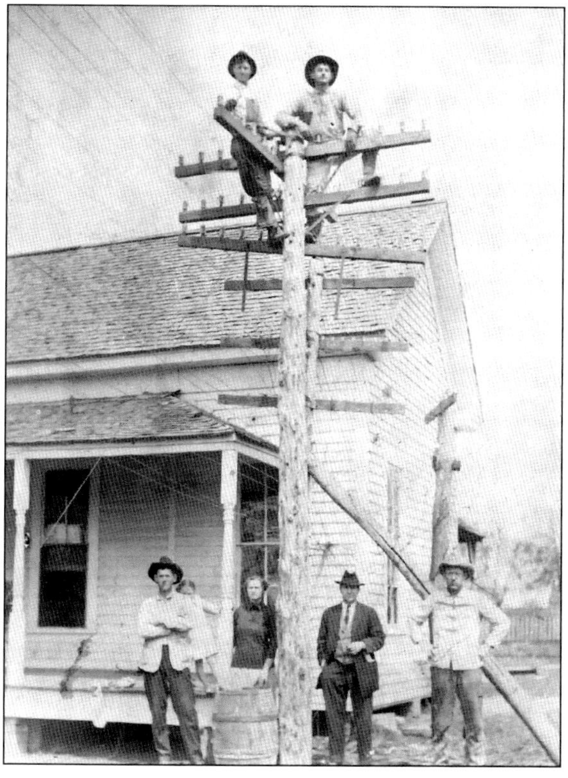

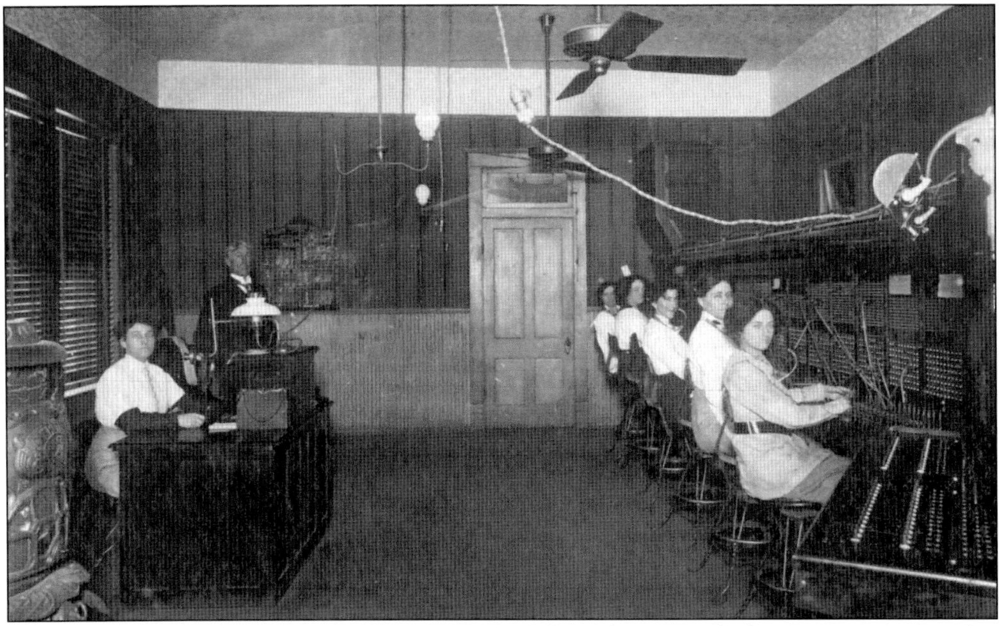

James Wisdom Ozment was one of the owners of the Palestine Telephone Company. In this photograph taken around 1912, he stands beside the desk of the chief operator, Marie Rawls. On the right side of the room, the other operators are, from front to back, Cora (Moser) Roberson, Mary Lou (White) Jenkins, Mable Culver, Minnie (Britton) Nash, and Mary Starnes.

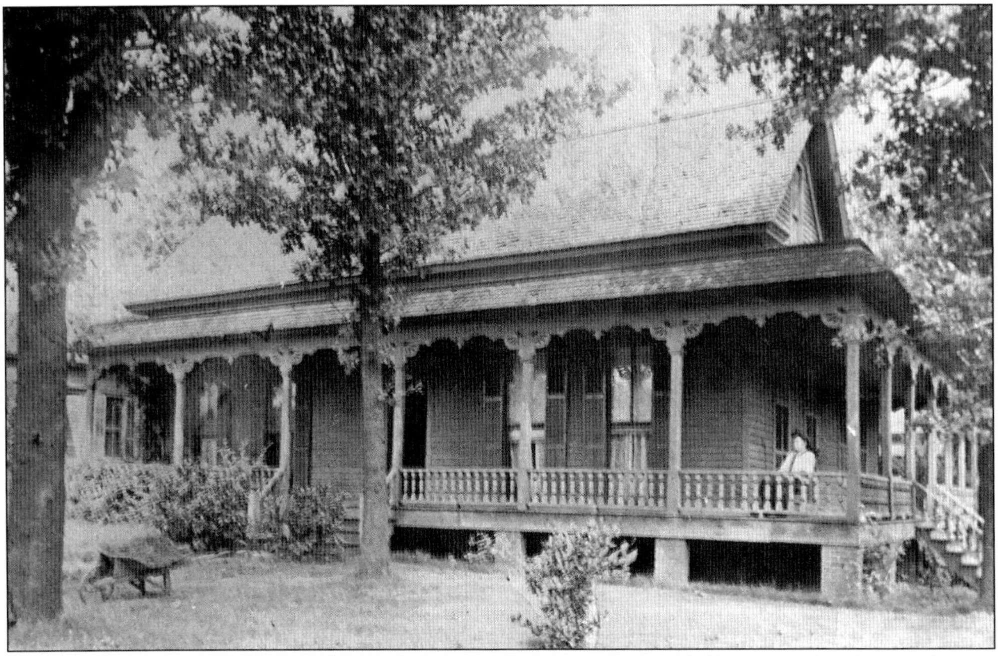

In 1873, George M. Dilley established Palestine's first industry, Dilley Foundry, for producing gray irons and brass castings for the railroad. Dilley's son, George Edward Dilley, and grandson, C. V. Dilley, each managed the foundry in turn. C.V. Dilley operated it until his death in 1937. The foundry employed up to 25 people. It closed its operations in the late 1930s, but the office building pictured above still stands today.

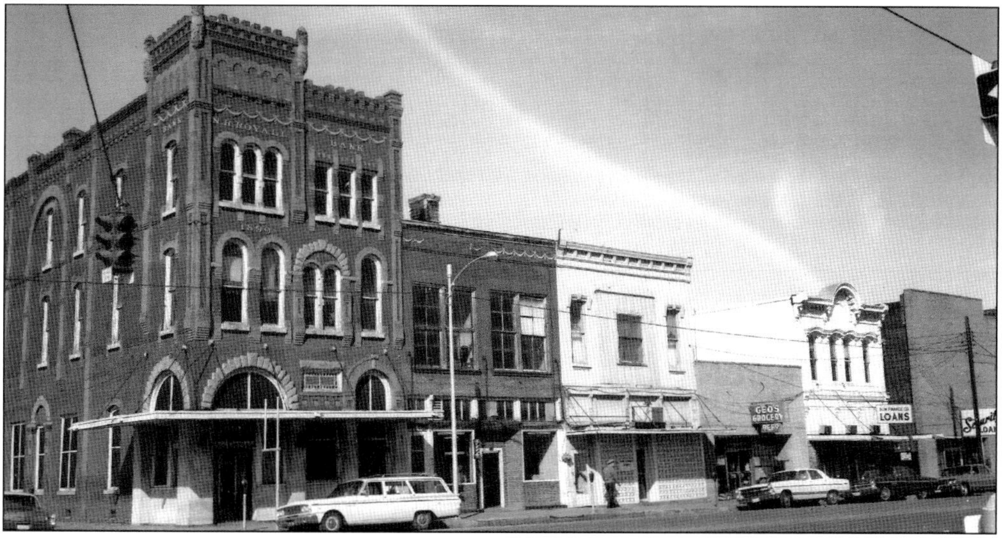

N. R. Royall opened his first banking facility in Palestine in 1873 on the corner of Spring and Magnolia Streets. When this building burned in 1899, he constructed a beautiful Victorian-style building at the same location. On April 1, 1904, the private bank became Royall National Bank. It operated at the same location until moving to its last location at 519 North Sycamore Street. It merged into Compass Bank in 1996.

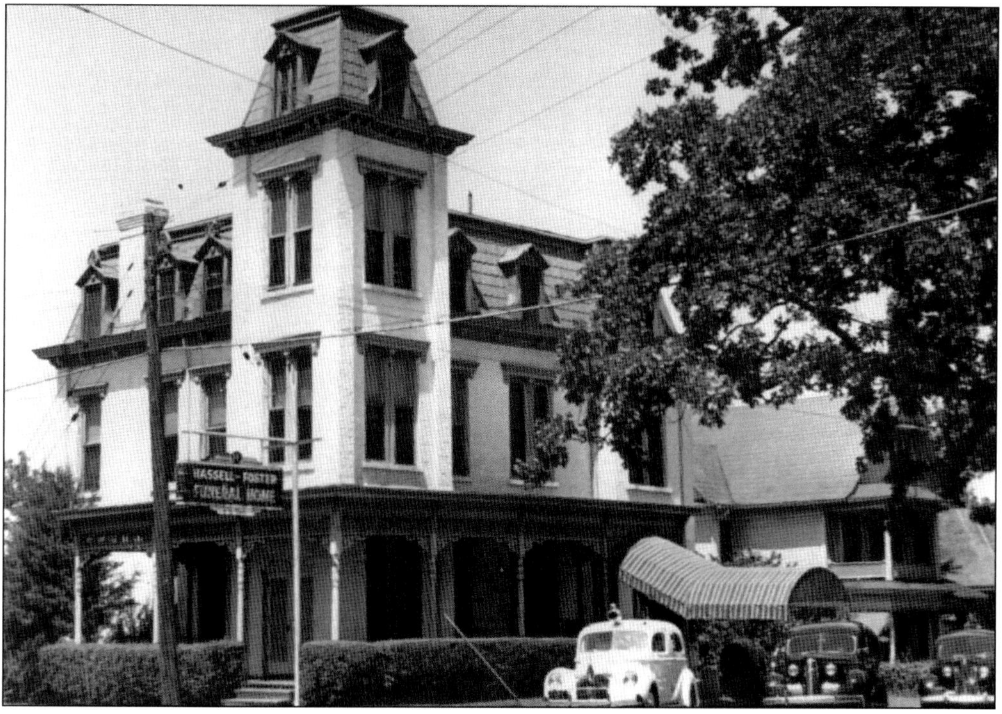

Hassell and Foster Funeral Home was originally South-Hassell Funeral Home. It was located at the corner of North Sycamore and East Crawford Streets. This photograph was probably taken in the late 1930s. In February 1948, Hassell and Foster moved into a remodeled home at 207 South Magnolia Street. In 1985, the business merged with Bailey Funeral Home and continued operating at the Magnolia Street location under the name of Bailey and Foster.

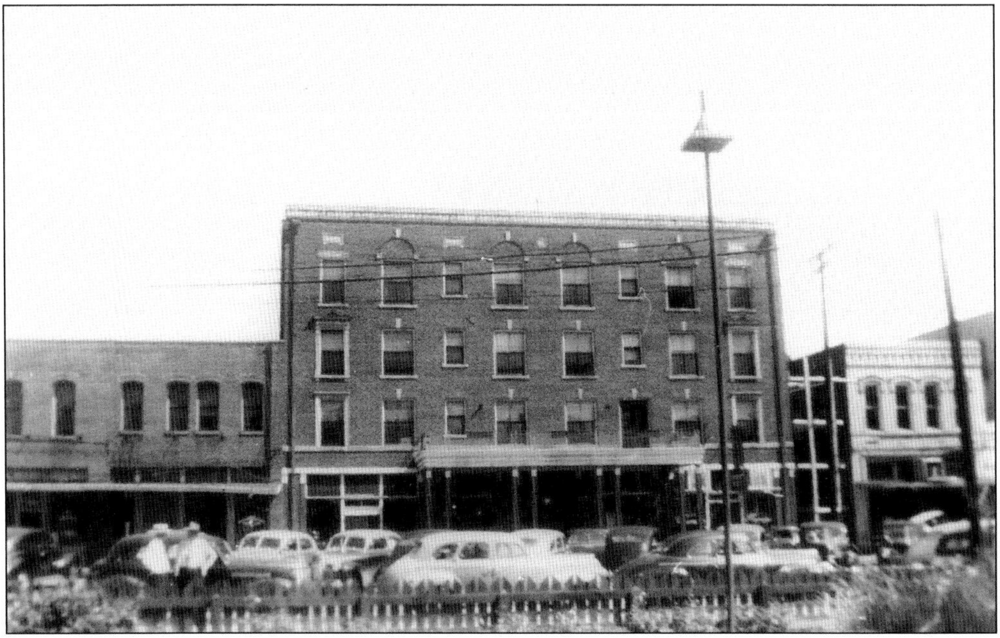

The O'Neill Hotel opened June 1, 1923, on Spring Street across from the railroad depot. It was owned by George W. Burkitt, who named the hotel for his mother's family in Ireland. The new hotel had four stories and a basement. Each of the 75 rooms had hot and cold running water. The hotel boasted an Otis Electric Elevator. The O'Neill Coffee Shop, a barbershop, and the O'Neill Drug Store adjoined the hotel. From April 1942 through December 1945, the Palestine Service Men's Club operated off of the lobby on the west side of the hotel. It was a place for soldiers passing through on trains to rest and enjoy refreshments, music, dancing, and conversation before heading to war. It was operated by local women who volunteered their services around the clock. They met every troop train that came through Palestine during the war years.

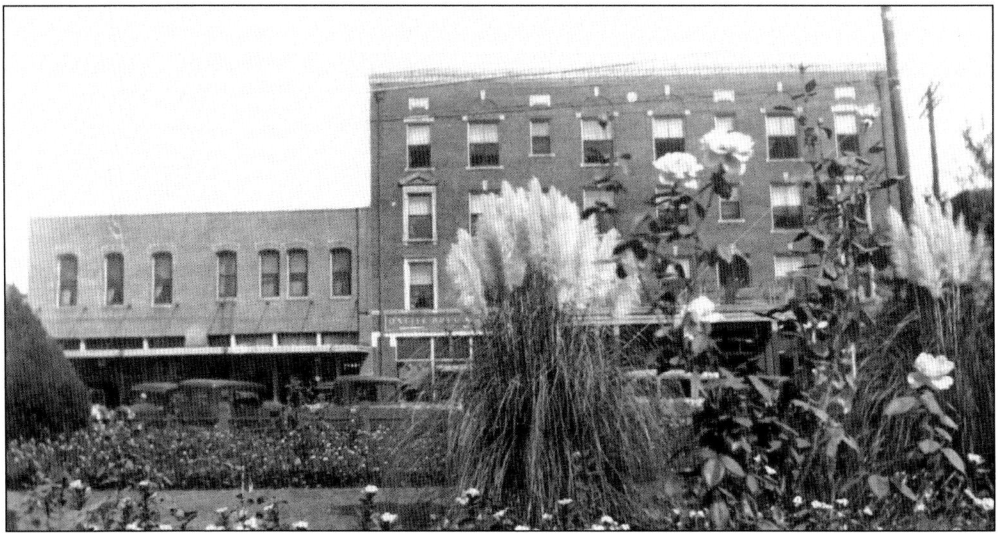

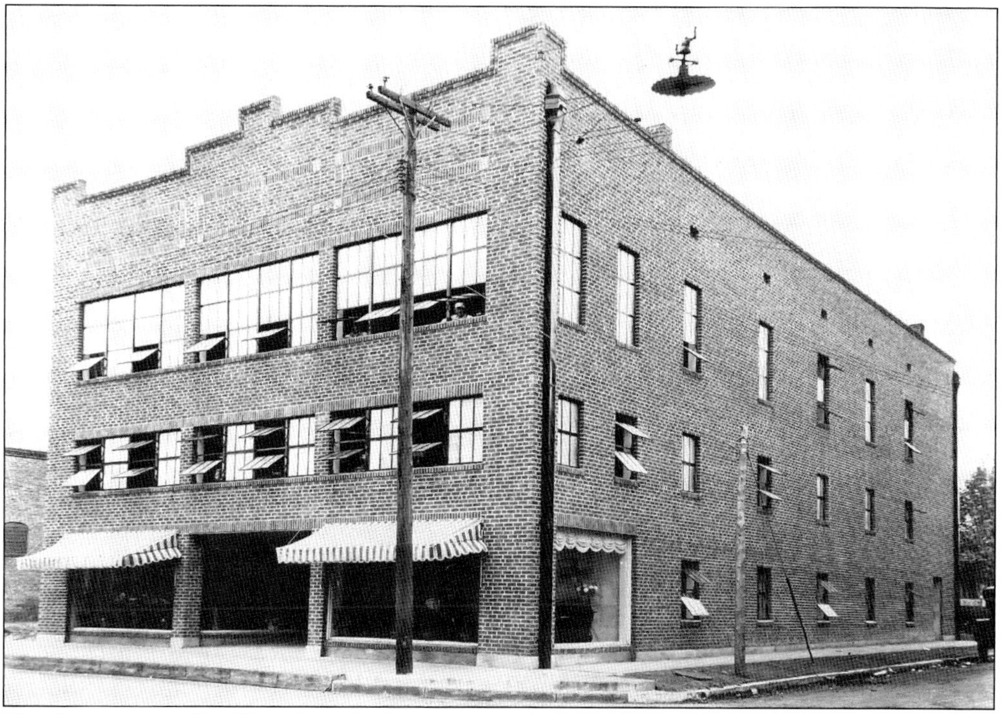

This building at 201 West Crawford Street in Palestine was built in 1935. It was designed by prominent Palestine architect Theodore S. Maffitt. It was McInnis Furniture Company, which was owned by Vergil McInnis, who lived on Fowler Street. It later became Denby Furniture Company. It was added to the National Register of Historic Places, building No. 98000694. The photograph above shows the exterior of the building. The interior of the store when it was McInnis Furniture is shown below. (Both, courtesy of Connie Lenore Glenn.)

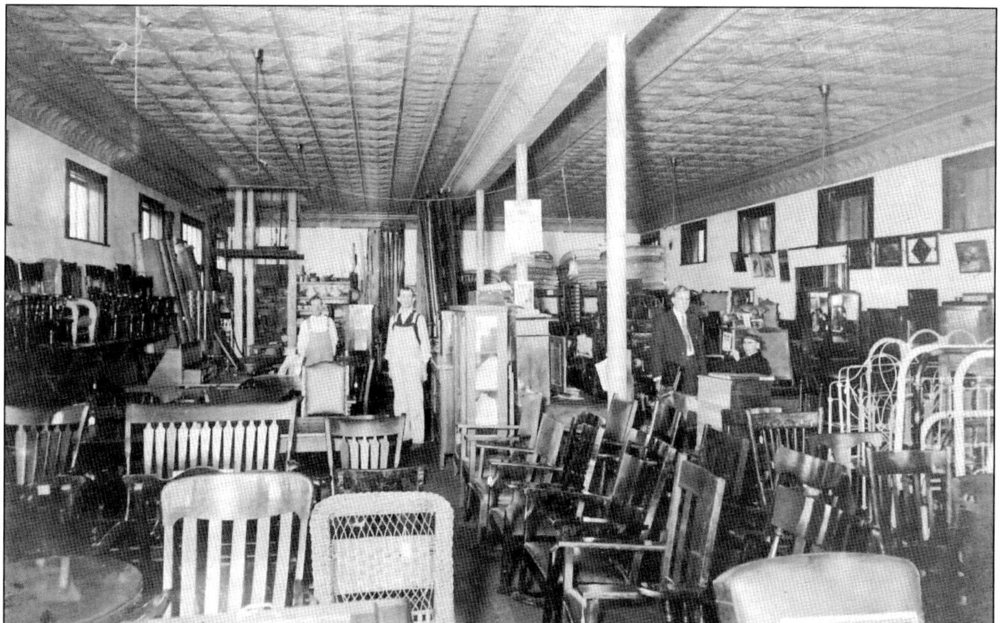

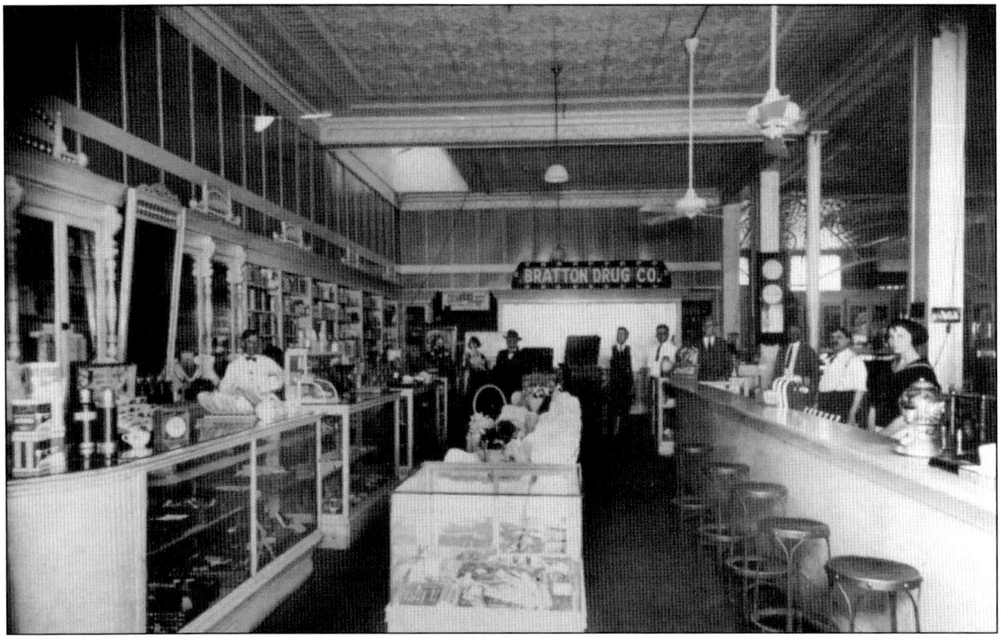

Bratton Drug Company was established in 1894 by Dr. C. S. Bratton at a location on Spring Street. The location is now a part of the East Texas National Bank site. Bratton's moved to the corner of Oak and Sycamore Streets in 1907. Later this location was called "Big Bratton's" when "Little Bratton's," shown above, was opened at the corner of John, Oak, and Main Streets. Little Bratton's was managed by Vernon Burnett.

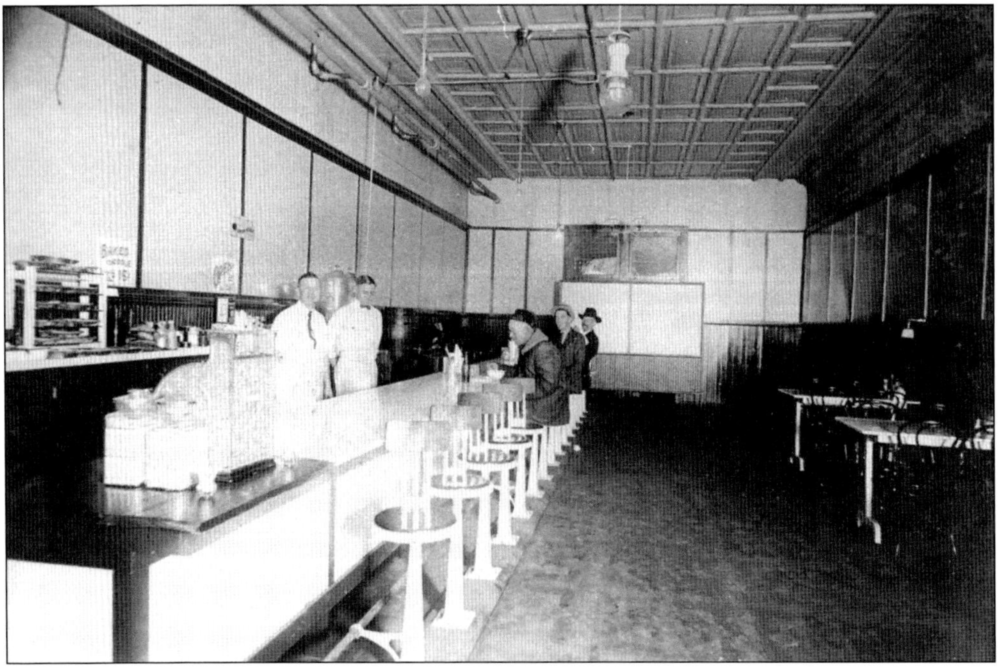

The Continental Trailways Bus Station was on Spring Street between Spring and Main Streets. The photograph above shows the Terminal Café, which occupied the north end of the lobby of the bus station.

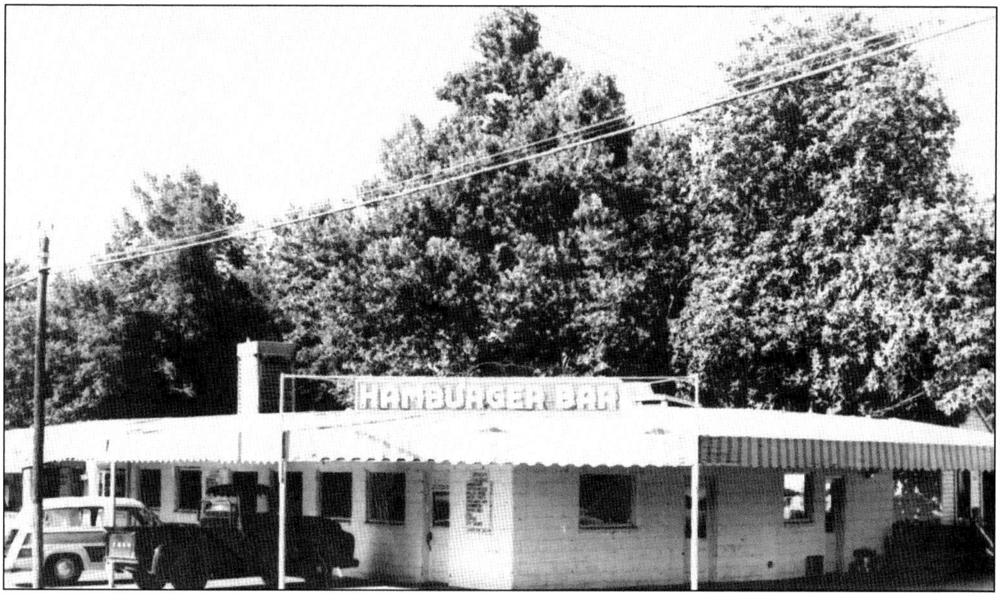

In October 1958, Henry Cody "H. C." Redwine purchased the Hamburger Bar at 502 North Tennessee Avenue from May Berry Hill. B. J. Porter opened the original café in a small trailer located between the current building and the brick house next door. At that time, hamburgers were 5¢ each. In 1967, H. C. Redwine sold the business to a Mr. Durrette, who sold it to Mary Beth Beason in 1982.

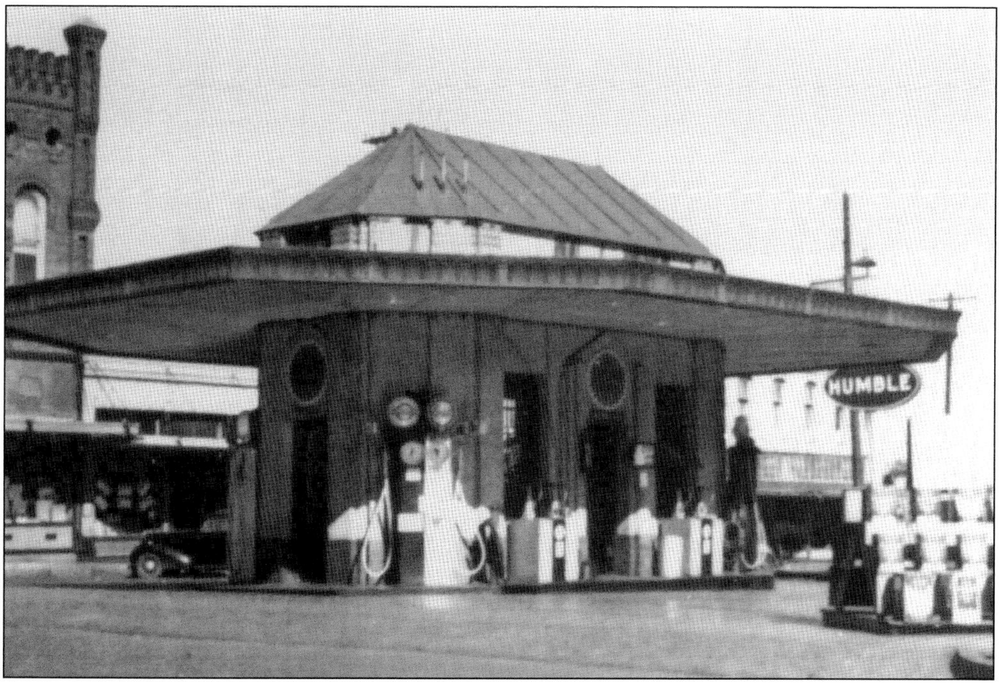

This is the Triangle Humble Service Station on Avenue A at North Sycamore Street. Humble Oil and Refining bought this property in 1929 from Tucker Royall, W. L. Welborn, and George F. Pessoney. In 1935, it was managed by James Teel. Johnnie Herrington bought it in 1957. He demolished the service station and built Johnnie Herrington Insurance office.

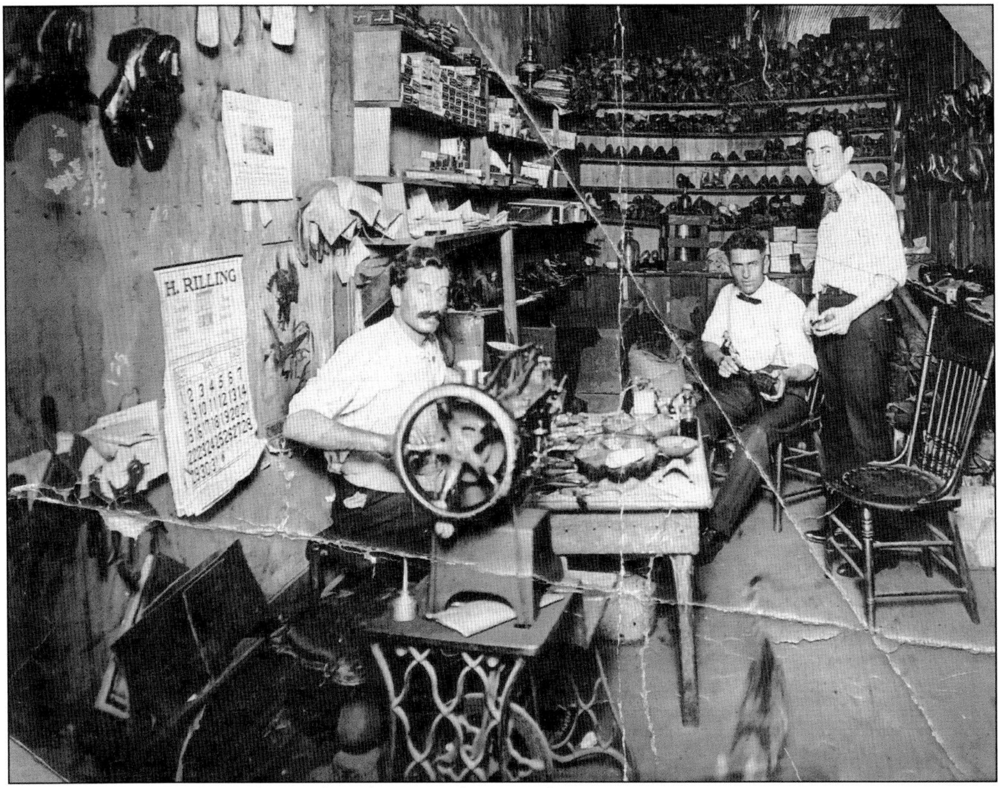

Pictured here is a shoe shop. The photograph was taken in May 1921.

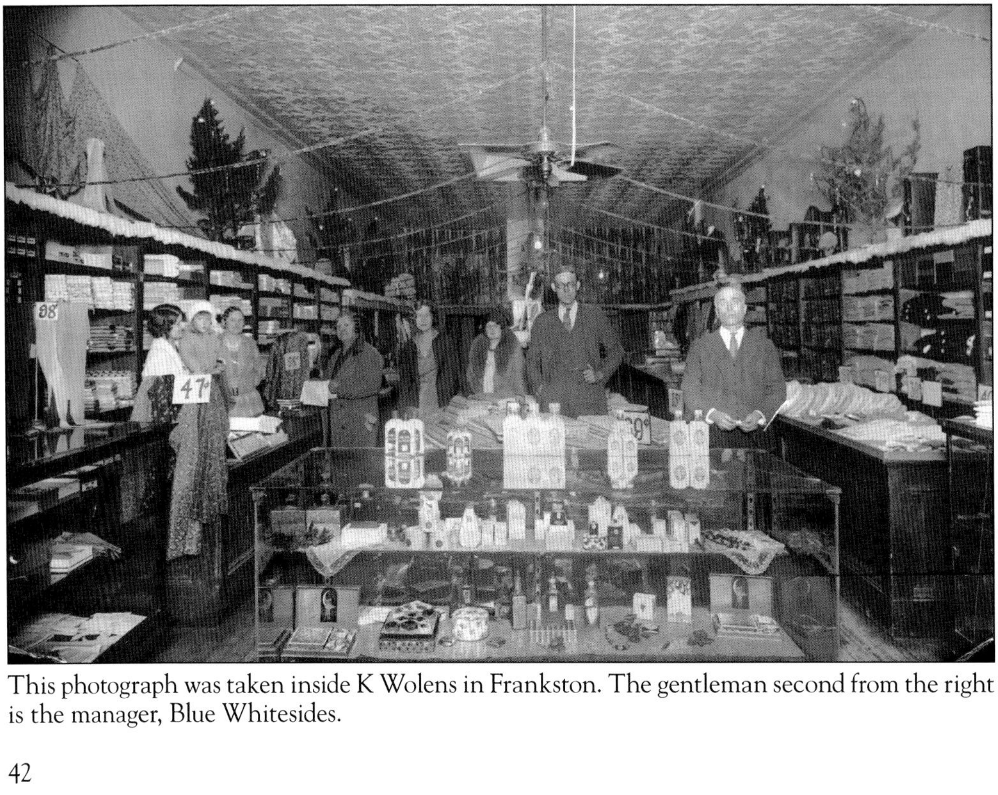
This photograph was taken inside K Wolens in Frankston. The gentleman second from the right is the manager, Blue Whitesides.

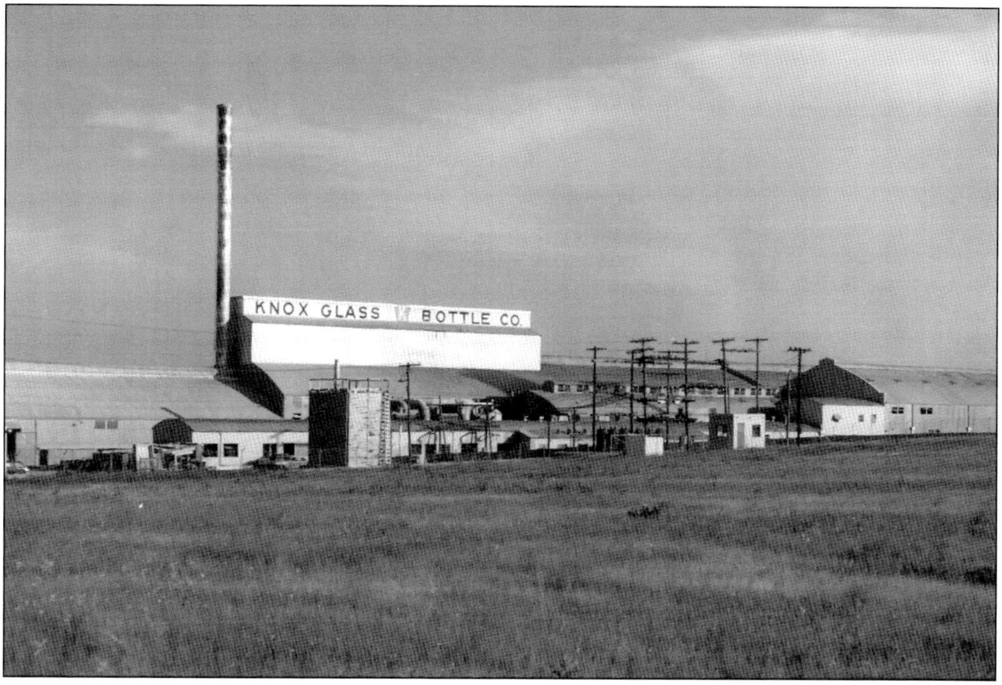

The photograph above of Knox Glass Bottle Company on West Oak Street was taken about 1954. The plant started production on July 5, 1941. It maintained its own fleet of trucks, below, from 1941 and 1951. The plant manufactured Knox canning jars, soft drink returnable bottles, Bama jelly jars, and other glass products. In 1969, Glass Containers Corporation bought Knox Glass. It maintained the name "Glass Containers" until the early 1980s, when it became Containers General, which it was called until the plant officially closed on December 20, 1984. (Both, courtesy of PPL.)

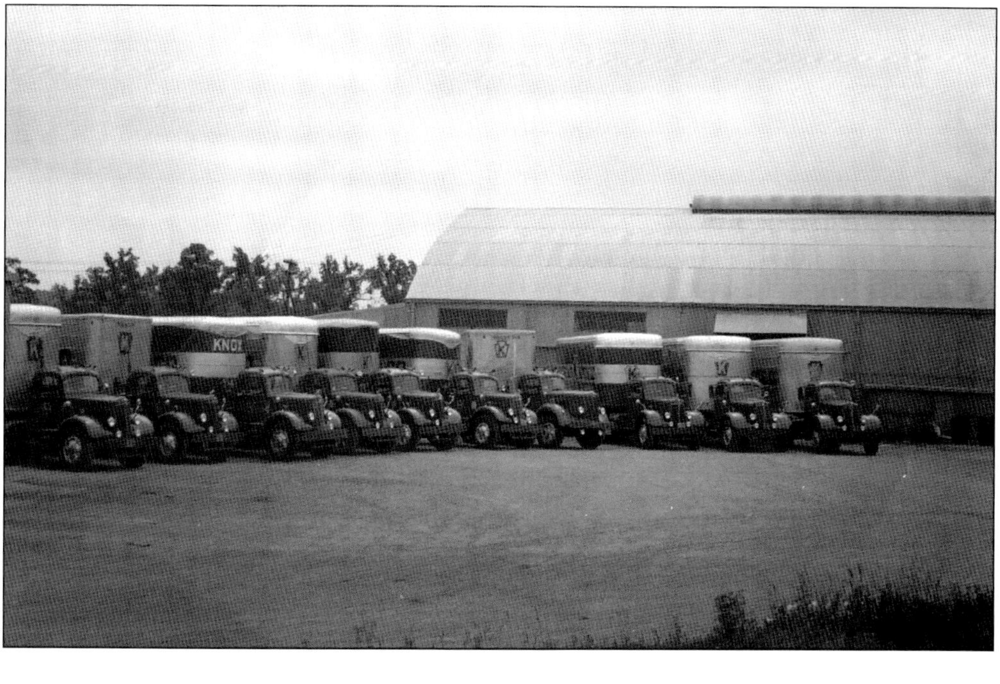

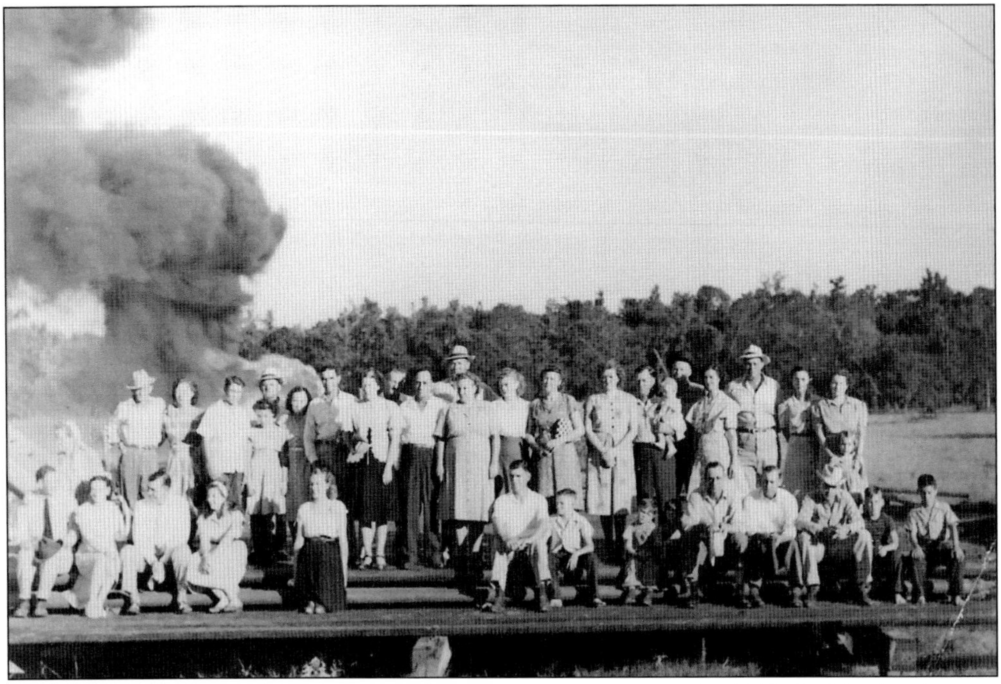

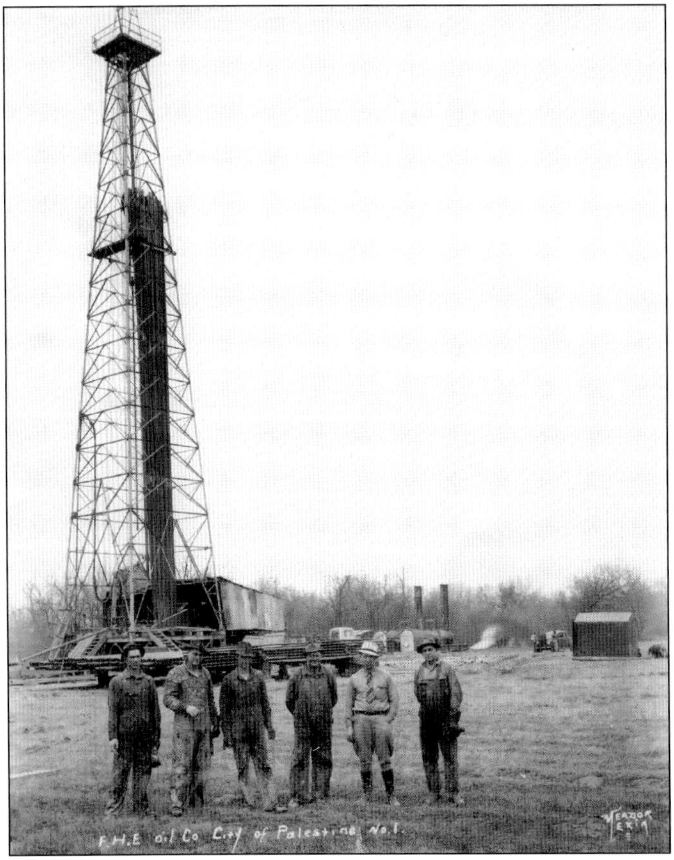

In 1947, the No. 1 R. F. Broadway Oil Well was drilled and completed in the Blackfoot field. A barbeque was given for everyone who had a part in drilling the well. This picture was taken at the barbeque. Hubert Schitoskey worked on the drilling crew. (Courtesy of Sue Schitoskey Miles.)

Early settlers of Anderson County used the scum from the oil seeps to treat sores on their animals. The earliest attempt to drill was in the late 1880s. The pipe was still visible in as late as 1921. M. A. Davey was instrumental in discovering the Boggy Creek Dome. (Courtesy of Louise Spaith.)

Four

TRANSPORTATION

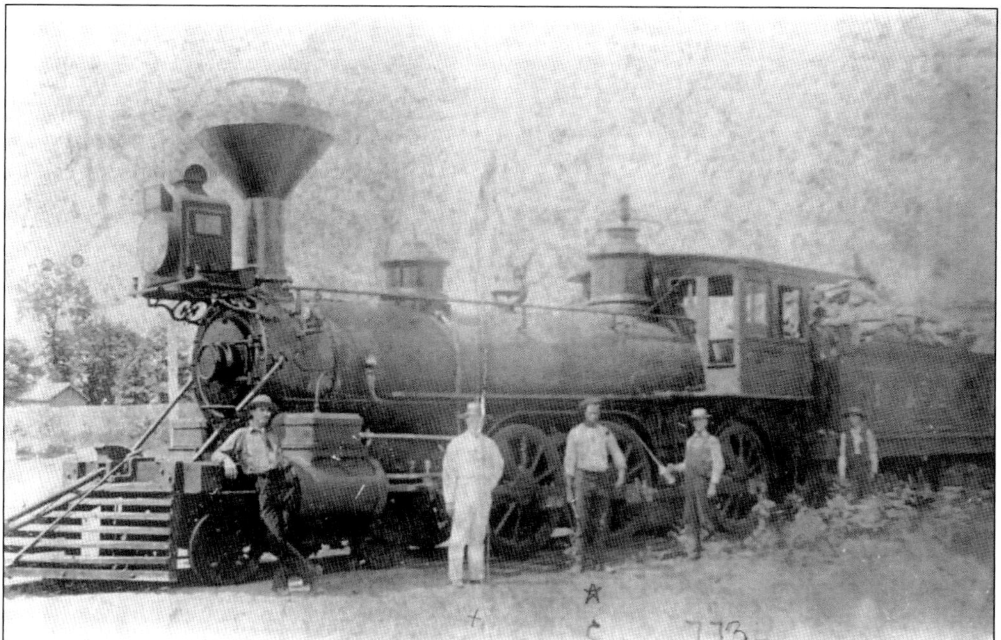

Palestine was a railhead for cattle being shipped north. There was a large holding pen for the cattle at the west end of Palestine near what is now DeBard and West Oak Streets. This photograph is of International and Great Northern Steam Engine No. 773 and crew.

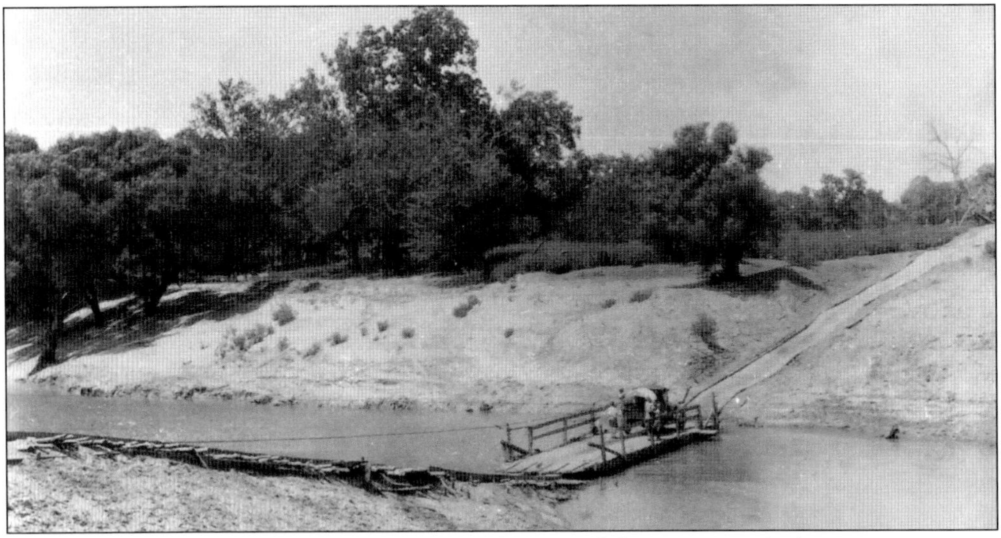

Travel was almost at a standstill during the Civil War, and there was very little immigration into the county. Toward the end of the war, travel by stage became almost impossible because of the risk of bandits on the road. All of the stages that left Palestine departed from the Hunter Hotel. There were stage roads to Crockett, Rusk, Alto, Fairfield, Tennessee Colony, and Tyler. There were no bridges that crossed the Trinity or Neches Rivers, and the use of ferries was the only effective means to cross these rivers. On the Neches were located Blackburn's Crossing, Cannon's Ferry, and Stemson's Ferry. On the Trinity, ferries were located at Magnolia Crossing, Parker's Bluff, Wildcat Ferry, Greens Bluff, and Bonner's Ferry. These are two photographs of the old Bonner's Ferry. (Above, courtesy of PPL; below, courtesy of METC.)

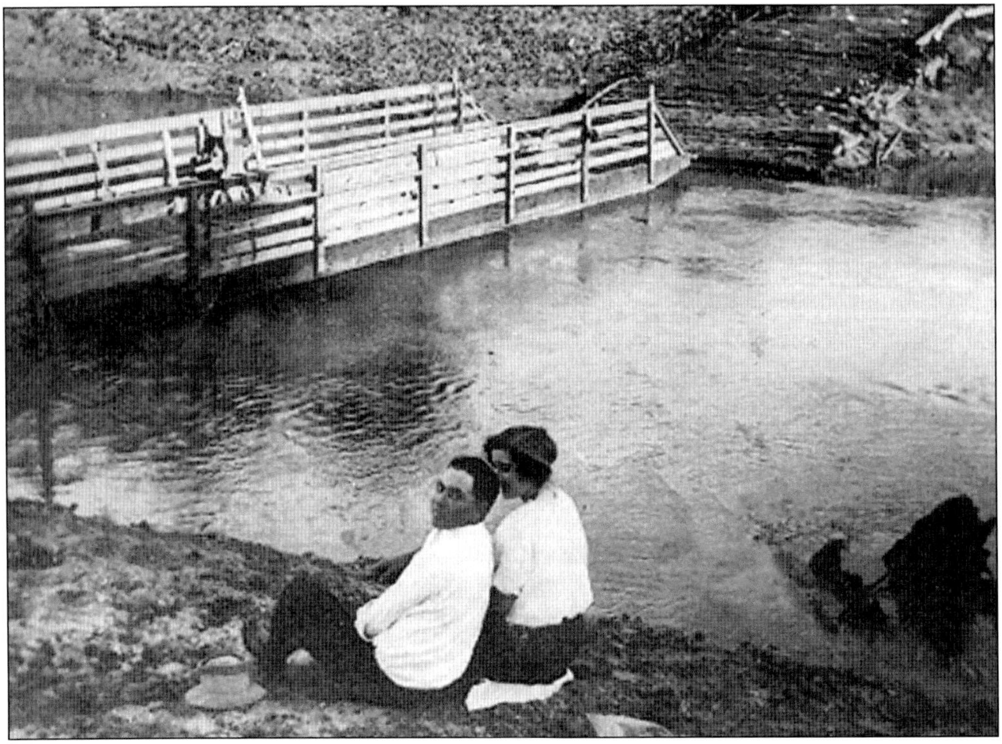

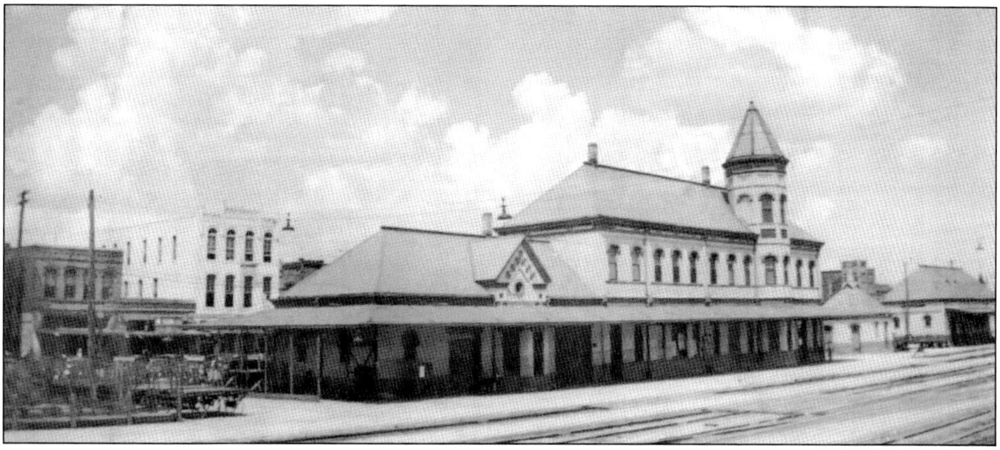

The Palestine Passenger Train depot was built in 1891. Both photographs were taken from the main line side. The photograph above is looking east, and the one below is looking west.

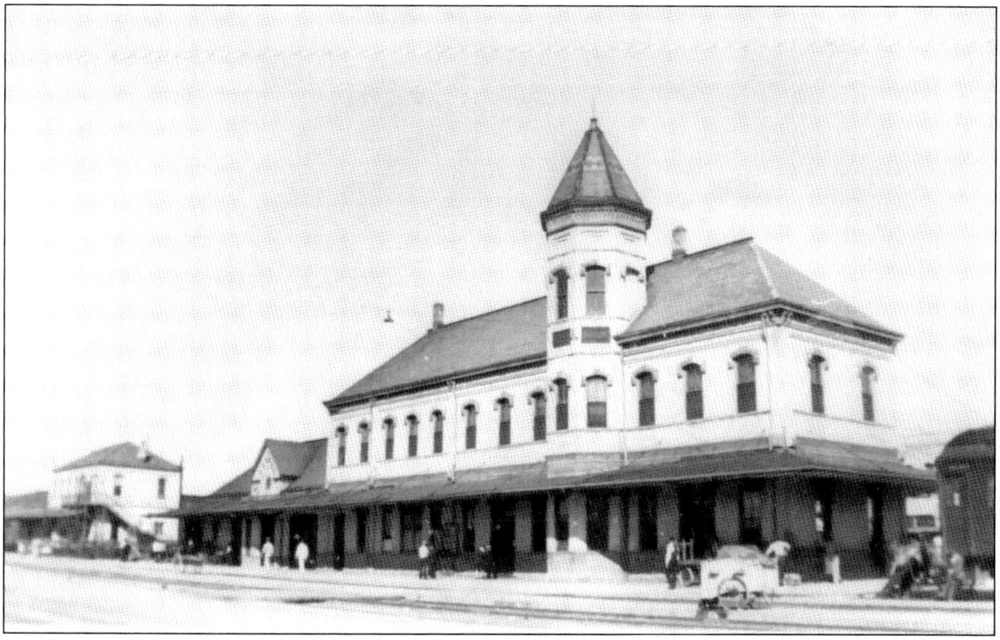

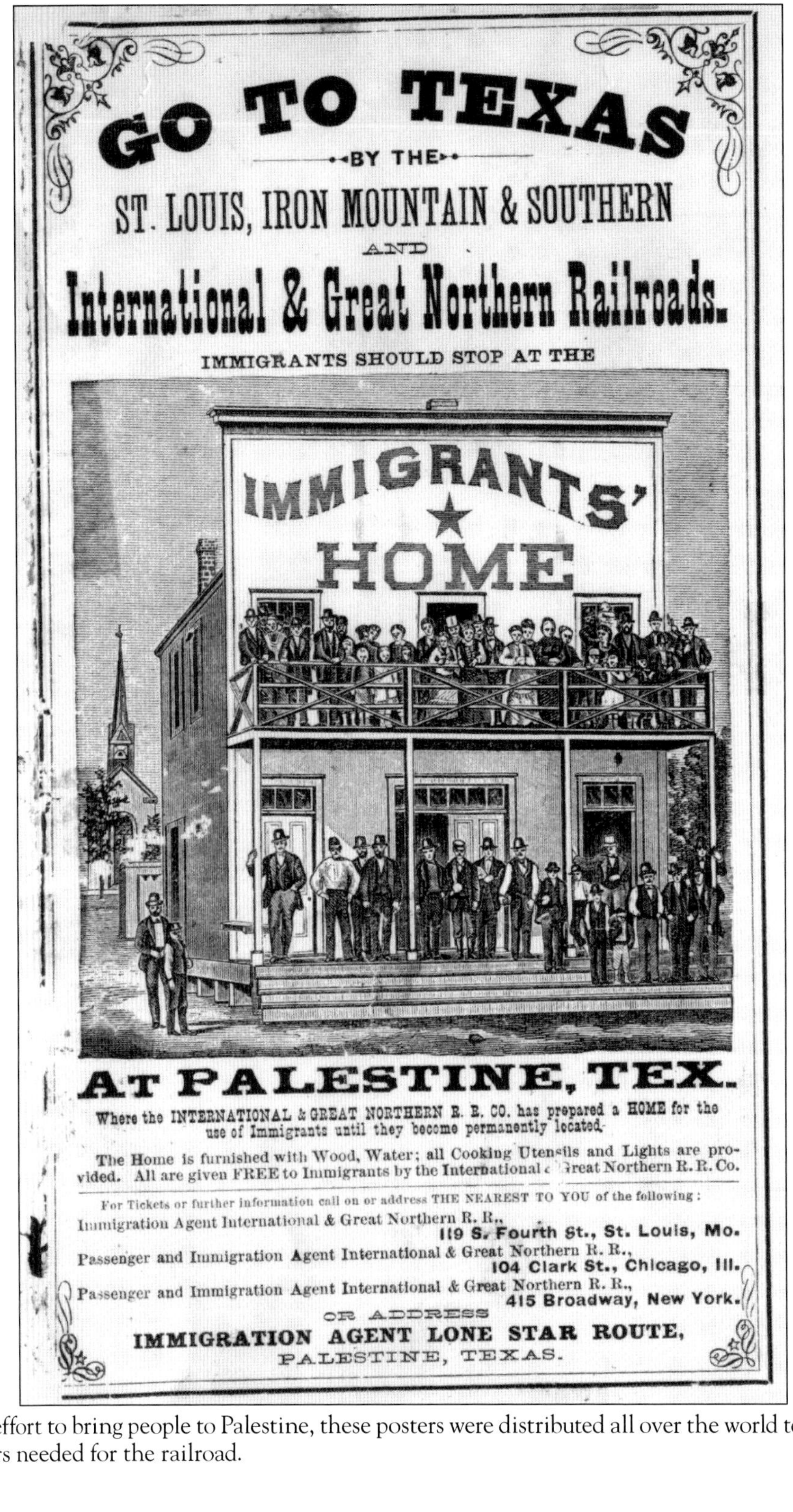

In an effort to bring people to Palestine, these posters were distributed all over the world to recruit workers needed for the railroad.

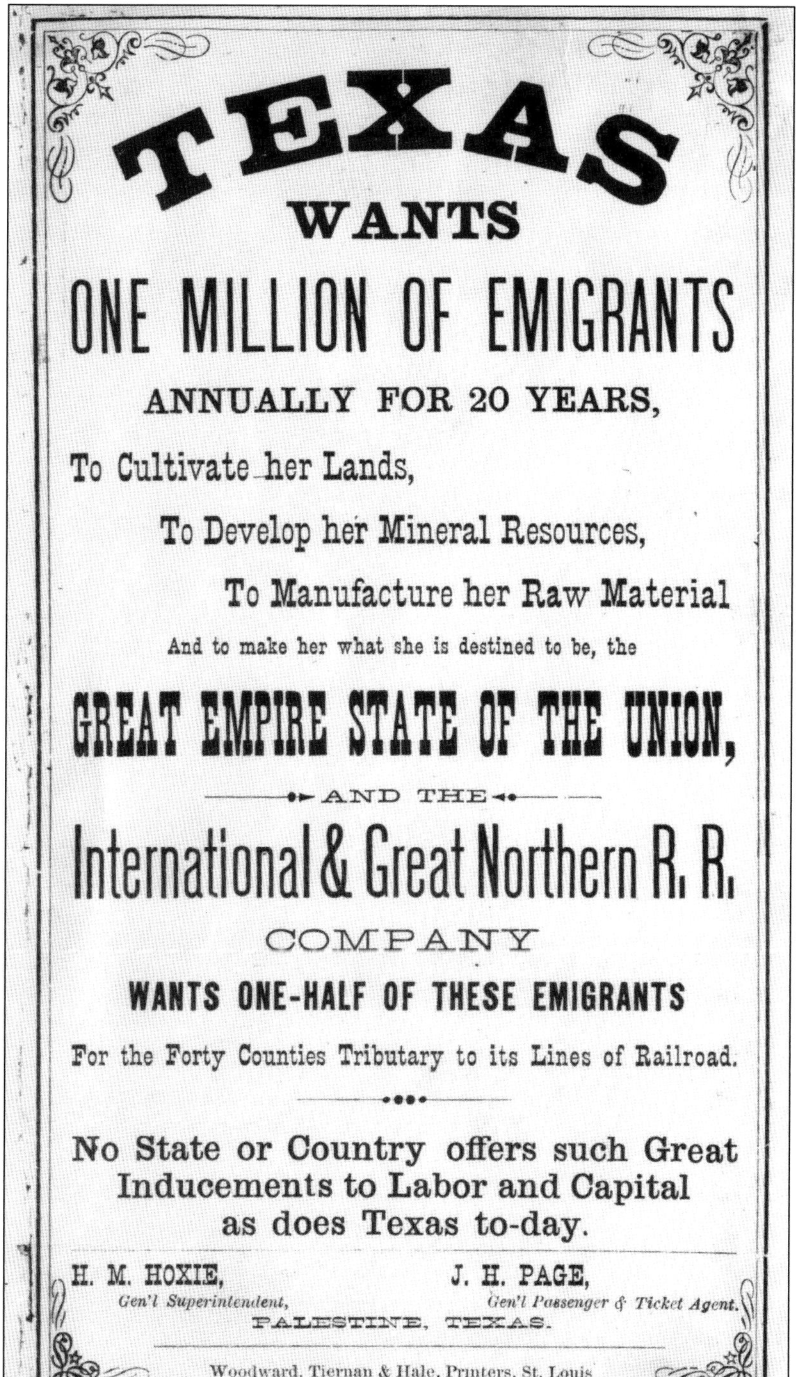

These posters offered information about the fertile prairies, the rich grazing lands, and the valuable timber in the area. They advertised the Immigrants Home, shown on the following page, which provided free use of stoves, cooking utensils, wood, water, and lights to the newcomers. Free maps and printed matter were available to anyone interested.

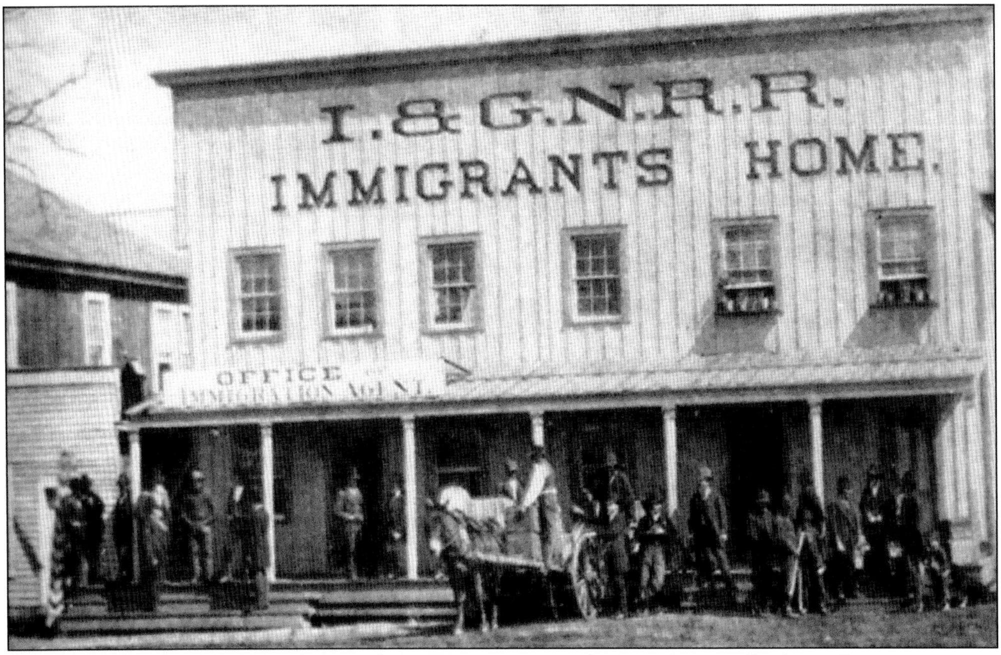

The posters on the previous pages brought many people to Palestine looking for a new start. The International and Great Northern Railroad built this home to aid the influx of the new immigrants by providing temporary housing facilities until they could build their own homes. It was located on Sycamore Street north of the railroad tracks.

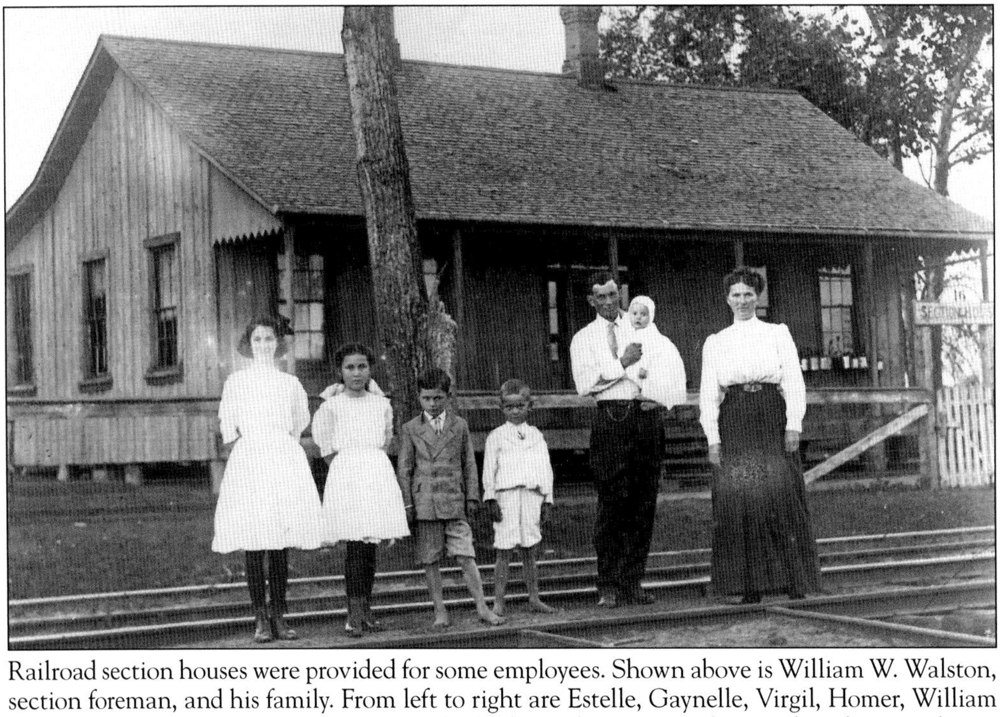

Railroad section houses were provided for some employees. Shown above is William W. Walston, section foreman, and his family. From left to right are Estelle, Gaynelle, Virgil, Homer, William holding Y. B., and William's wife, Mary Elizabeth Featherstone Walston. This photograph was probably taken in early 1912.

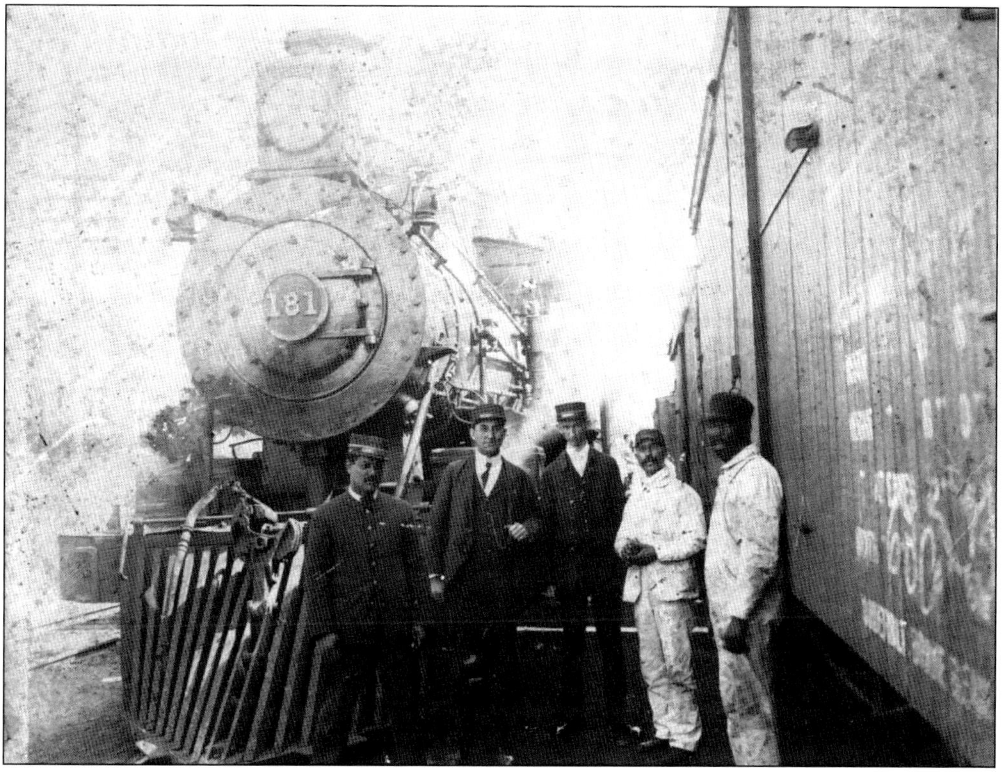

This photograph shows a train crew consisting of, from left to right, a conductor, a brakeman, a porter, and two firemen.

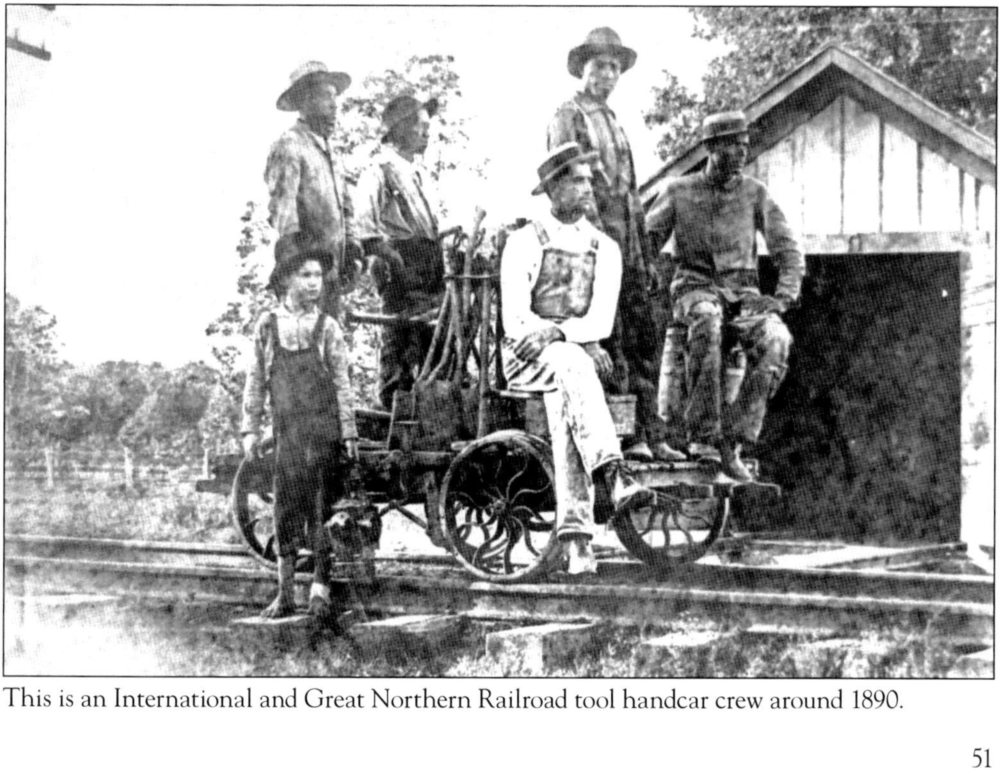

This is an International and Great Northern Railroad tool handcar crew around 1890.

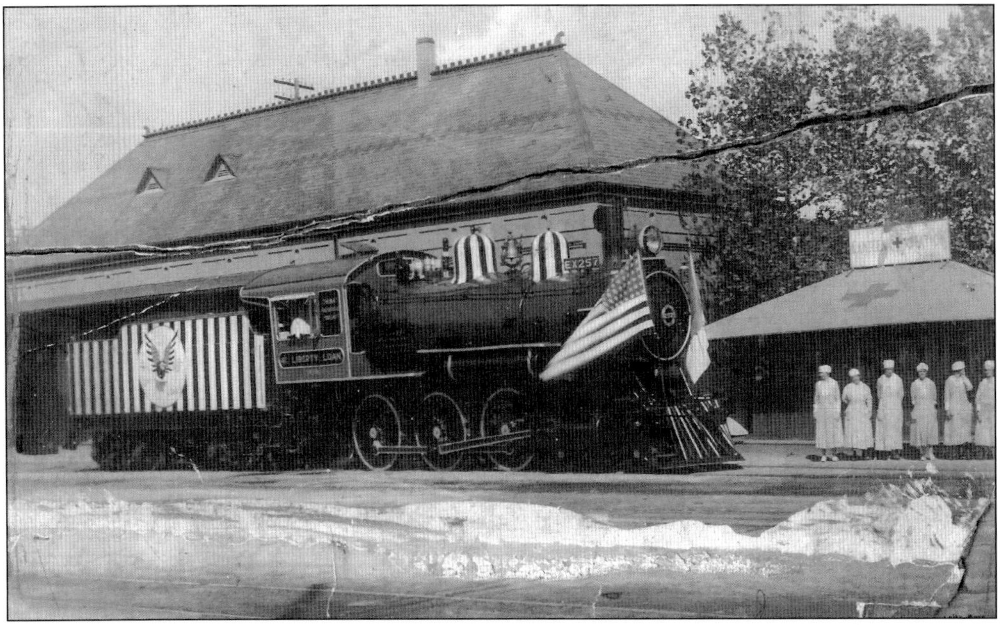

This photograph was taken at the International and Great Northern Station in Palestine in June 1918. The patriotically decorated Liberty Loan trains toured the nation encouraging citizens to buy liberty bonds issued to support the allied cause during World War I.

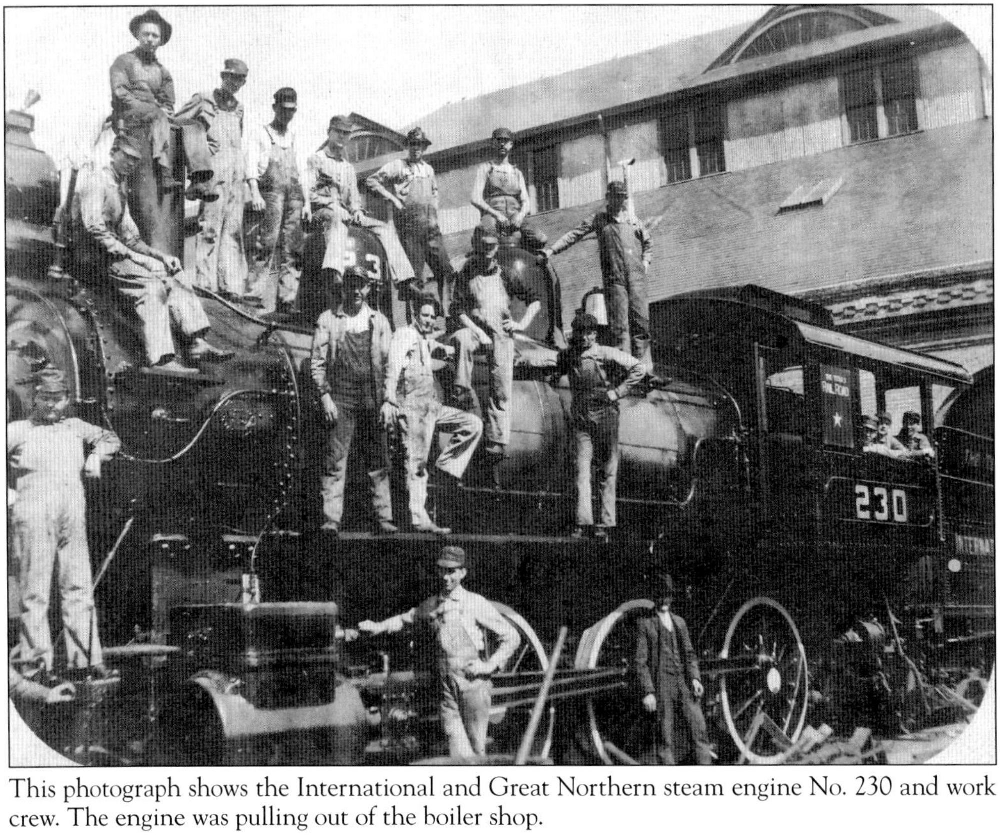

This photograph shows the International and Great Northern steam engine No. 230 and work crew. The engine was pulling out of the boiler shop.

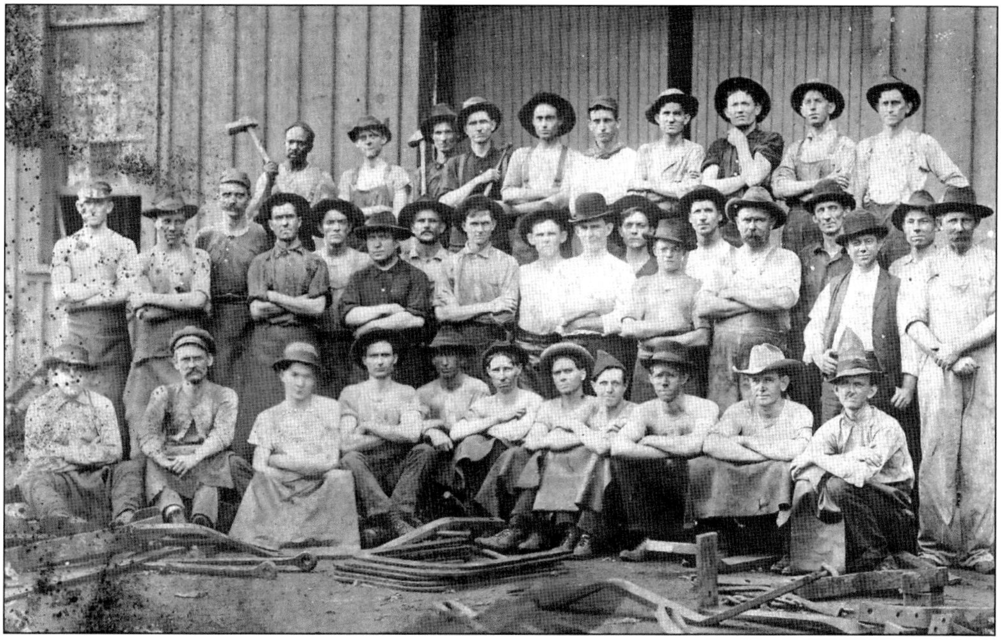

This is the International Brotherhood of Blacksmiths and Helpers, Local 273, "Holy City." Local 273 met the first and third Mondays at Macabees' hall on Main Street. Officers were Pres. D. R. Tompkins and secretary J. W. Brightman. One unidentified man's journal reads: "The boys here seem to be going along with but very little friction; the great trouble is they want more money, and they expect to get it, too."

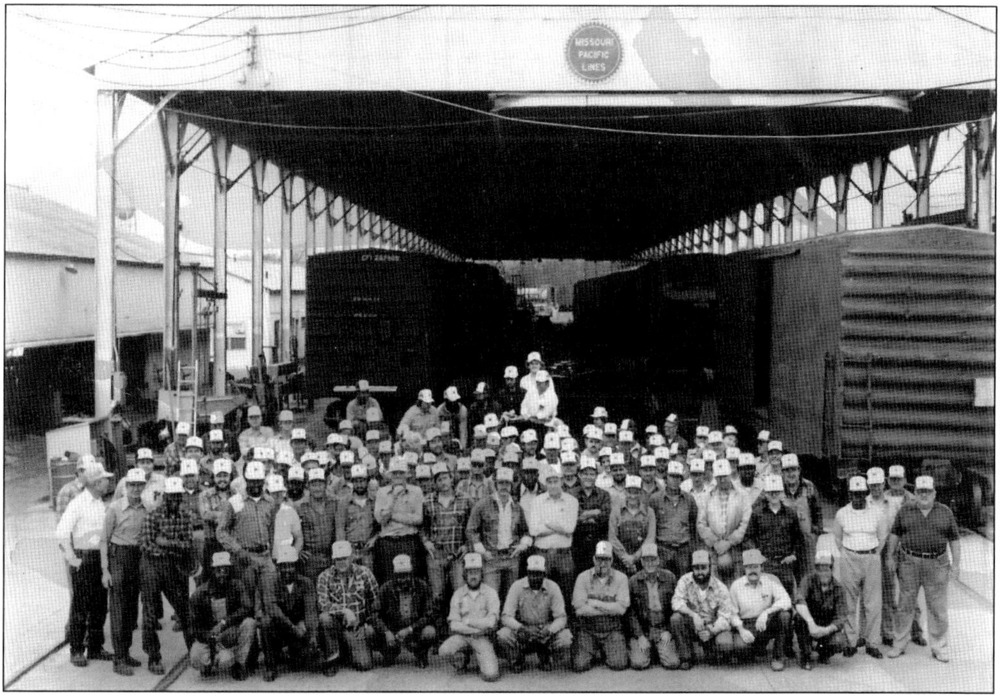

This photograph was taken in the late 1970s of the railroad car shop. (Courtesy of James W. Mosley.)

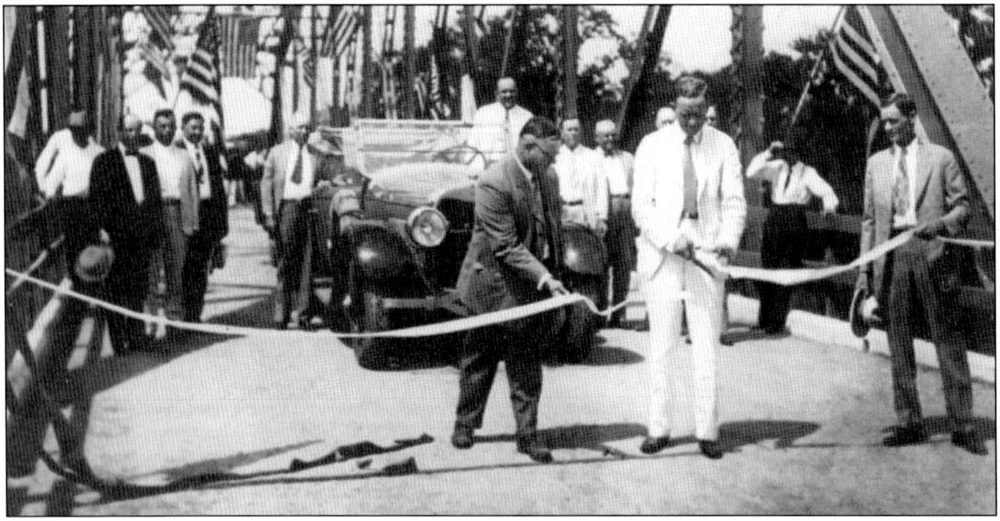

Texas governor Dan Moody cut the ribbon at the dedication ceremony of the new suspension bridge over the Trinity River at Long Lake in 1927. The Freestone County judge, on the left, and Anderson County judge E. H. Shelton, on the right, hold the ribbon. Virgil McInnis, Palestine Chamber of Commerce president, is on the left by the car door. Virgil was a successful furniture merchant and businessman in Palestine. (Both, courtesy of Connie Lenore Glenn.)

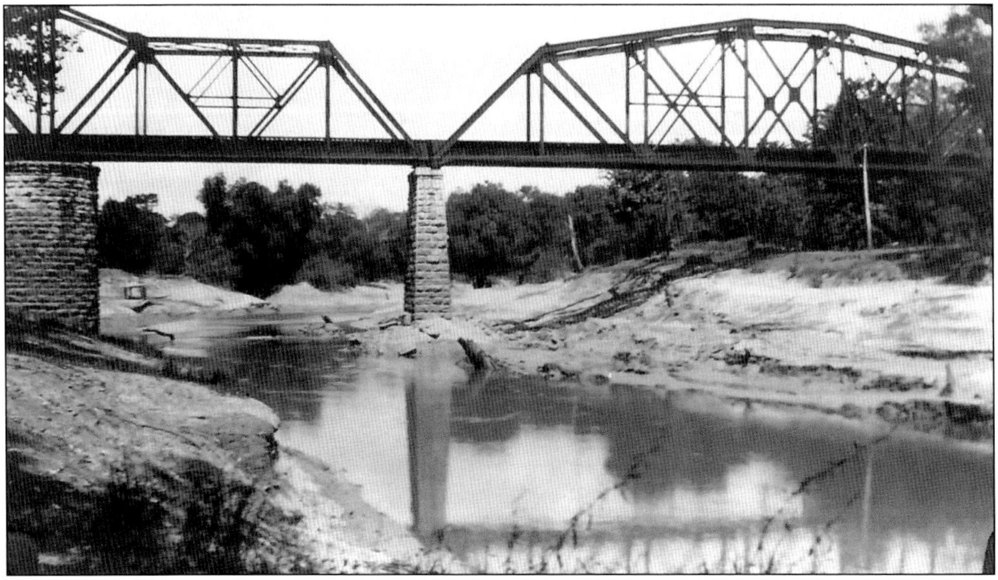

Five

Churches

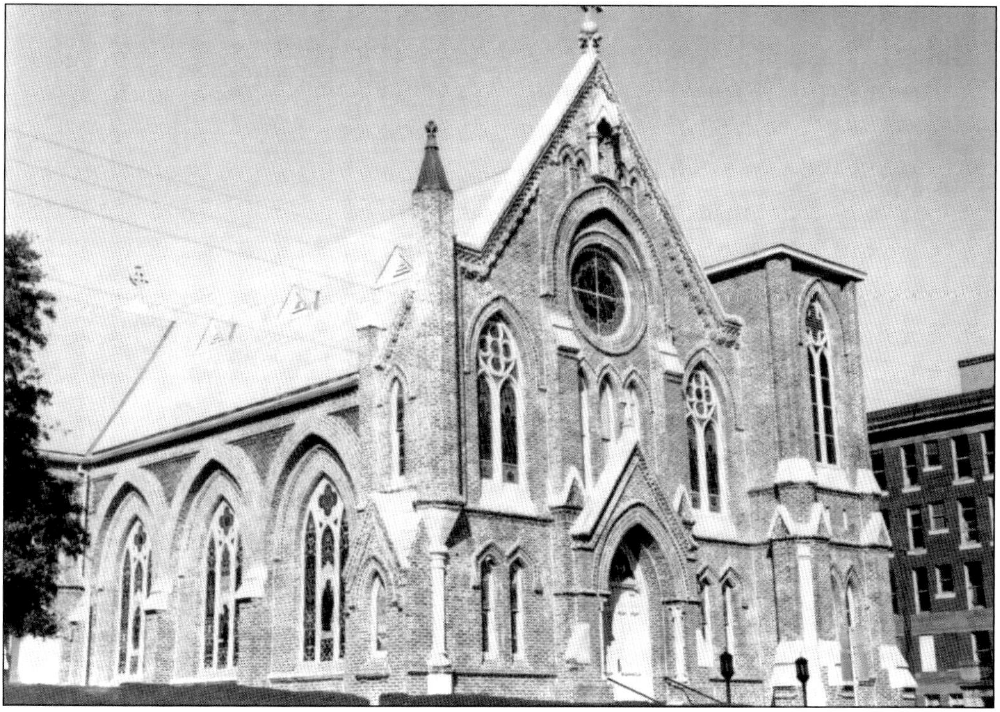

In 1874, the International and Great Northern (I&GN) Railroad deeded two lots to the Roman Catholic Church of Palestine. These lots were on Oak Street where the present church stands. The church acquired an additional 4 acres from the City of Palestine in 1884. Saint Joseph's Cemetery occupies most of this acreage. In May 1890, a fire destroyed the Saint Joseph Catholic Church and all church records. The present building, renamed Sacred Heart, was dedicated on June 18, 1893.

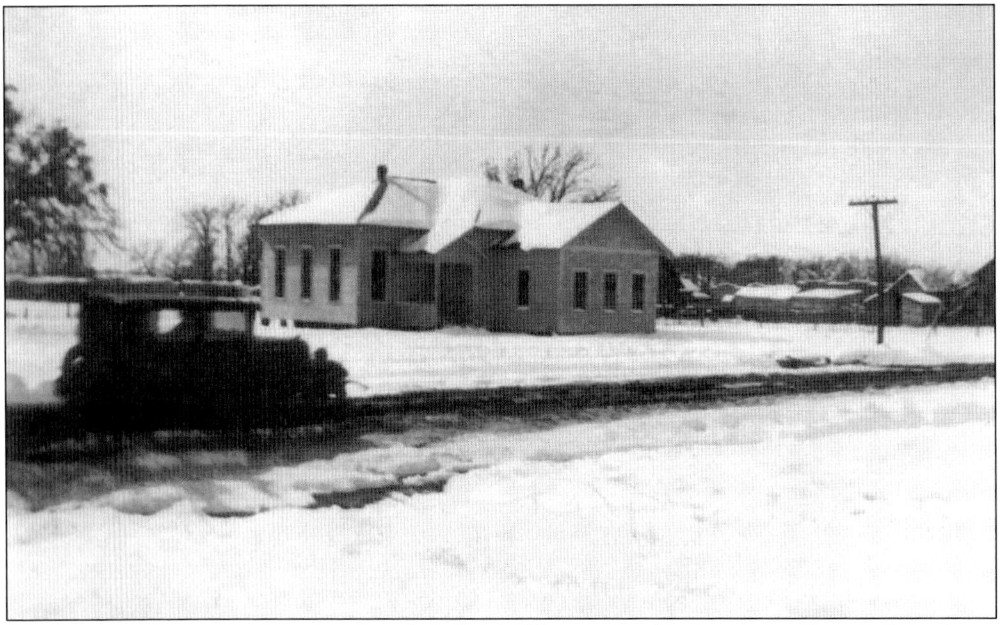

This snowy scene of the First Baptist Church of Elkhart was taken in 1919. This may have been the church building once located on Main Street behind where the Elkhart State Bank is currently located. (Courtesy of CA.)

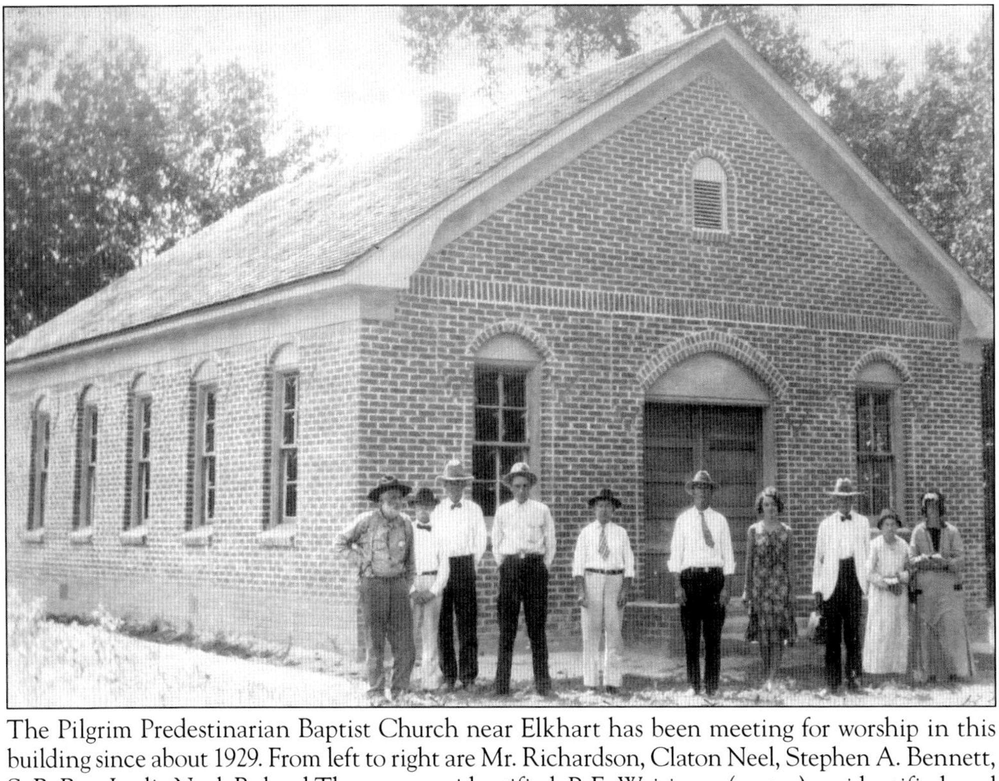

The Pilgrim Predestinarian Baptist Church near Elkhart has been meeting for worship in this building since about 1929. From left to right are Mr. Richardson, Claton Neel, Stephen A. Bennett, S. B. Ray, Leslie Neel, Roland Thurman, unidentified, P. E. Weisinger (pastor), unidentified, and Mrs. Ben Walston. (Courtesy of Dan Trigg.)

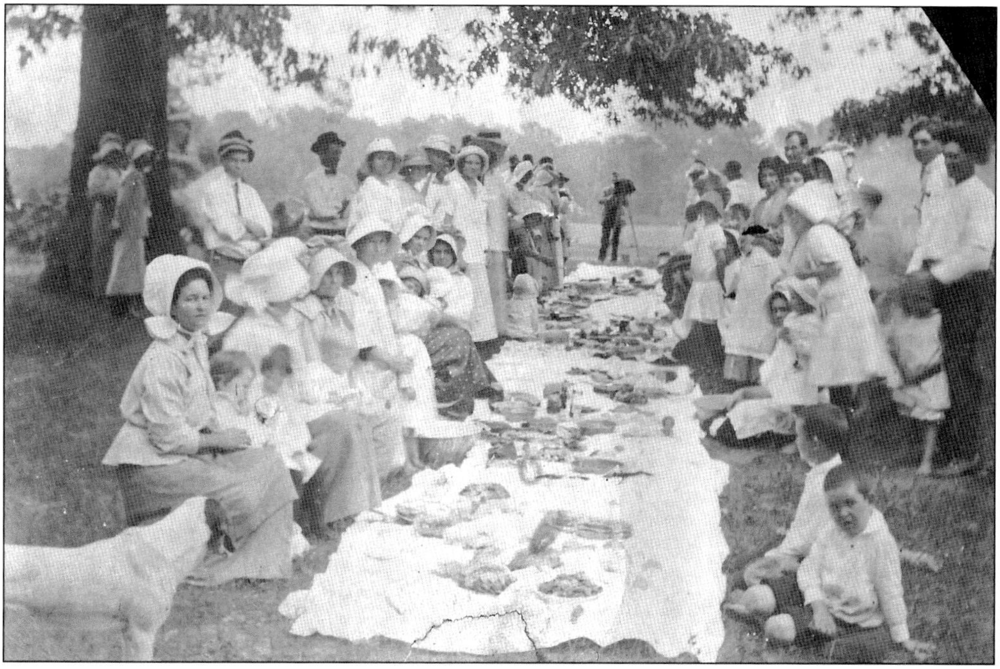

Dinner on the ground was a popular social activity of most church congregations of that era. Here the men, women, and children of Pilgrim Baptist Church at Elkhart have spread their picnic dinners on the ground to share with one another. Notice there were two photographers taking pictures, one at each end of the group. The wooden church building in the background of the first photograph is a clue that this picture was taken around 1920. William Robert Bennett can be seen on the right side of the picture below, standing behind the girl with the dark hair. (Both, courtesy of Wilda Page Collection.)

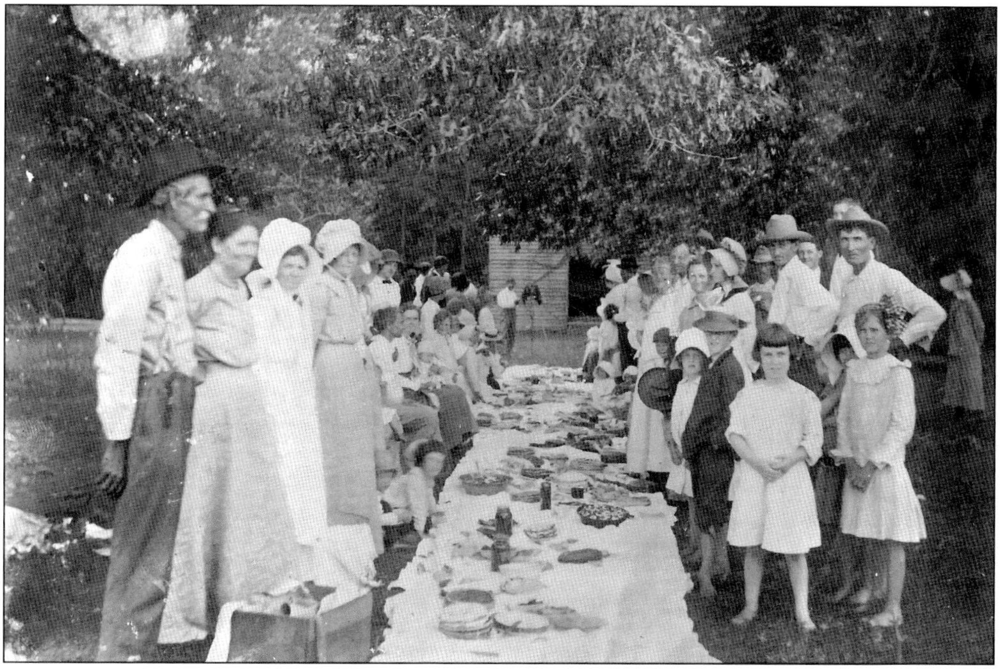

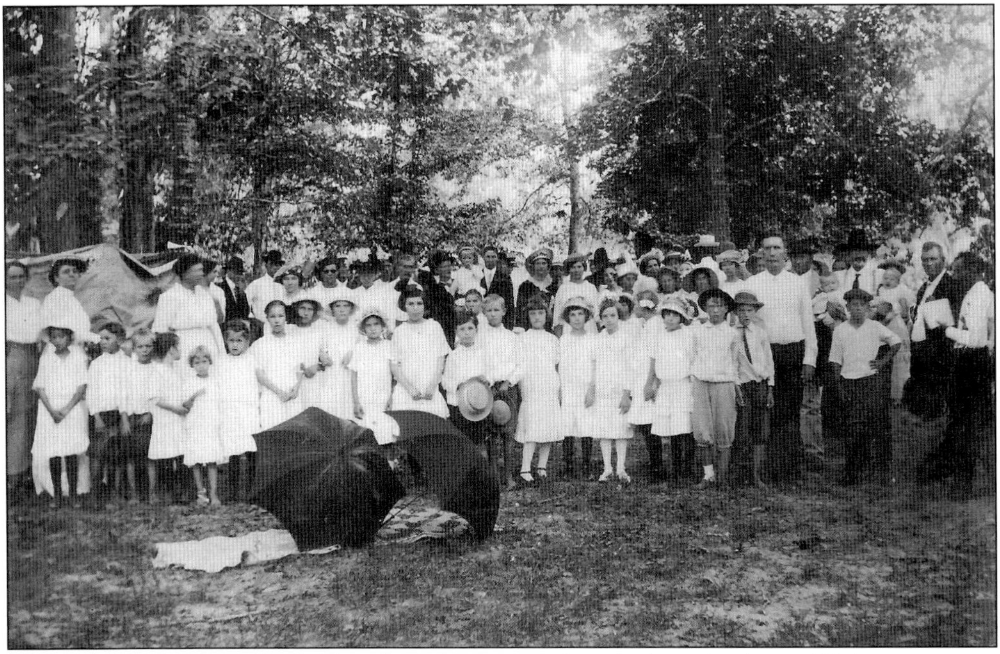

These members of the Elkhart Church of Christ are gathered at Box Creek near Elkhart to witness a baptismal ceremony. Baptisms in a creek required warm weather, so there were often multiple baptisms performed on the same day. (Courtesy of Wilda Page Collection.)

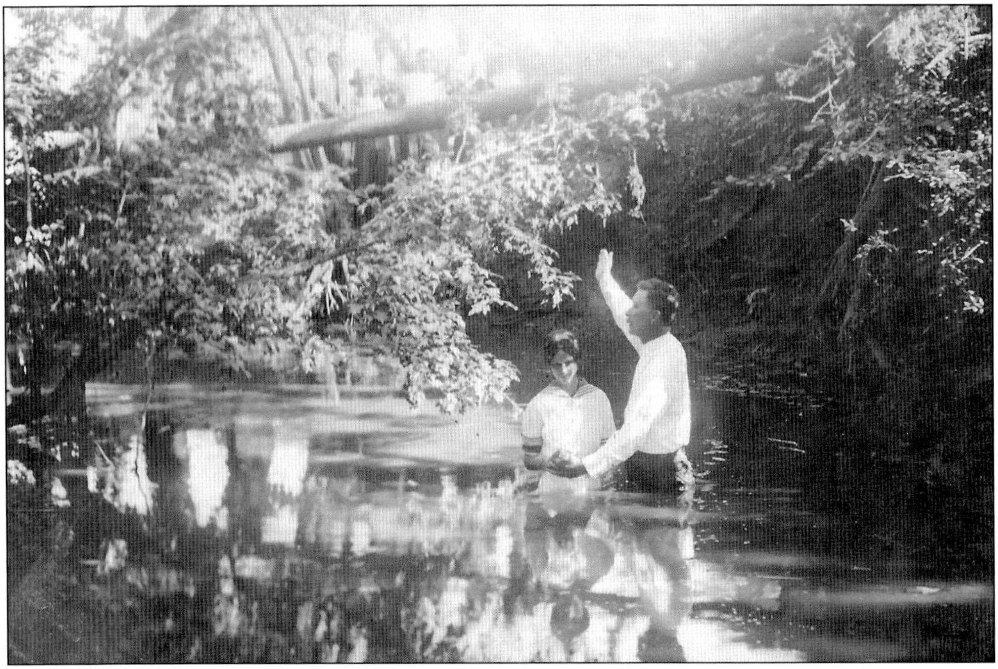

Box Creek was a popular choice of many Elkhart churches for baptisms. Here the Reverend Stovall is baptizing Eula Whitley. Notice the people in the background at the top of the picture. (Courtesy of Wilda Page Collection.)

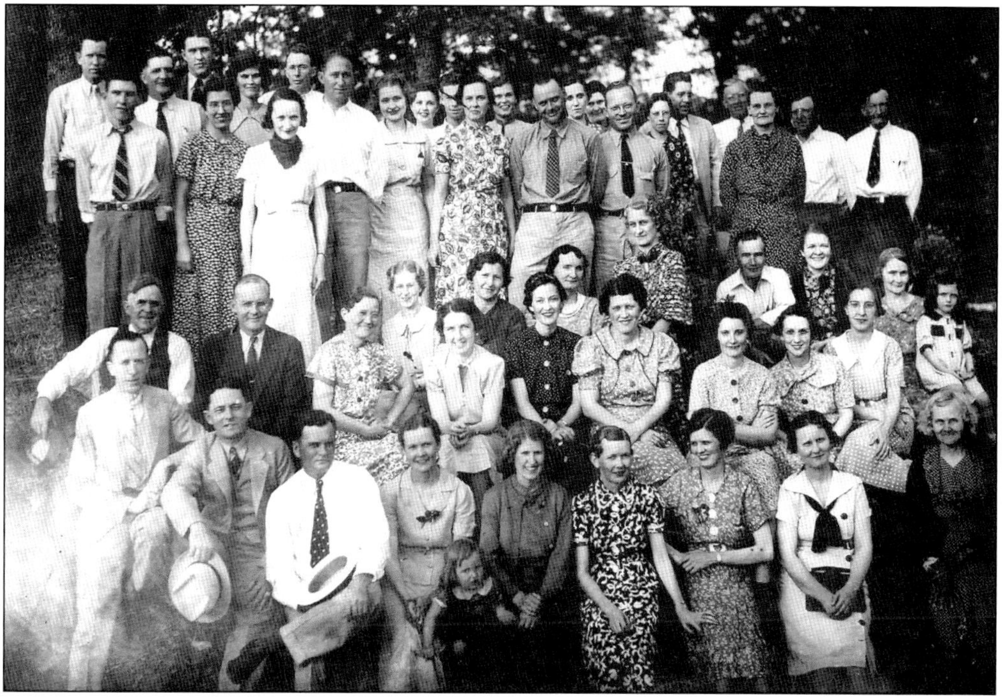

These are the Sunday school class members of Elkhart Methodist Church around 1936. (Courtesy of Wilda Page Collection.)

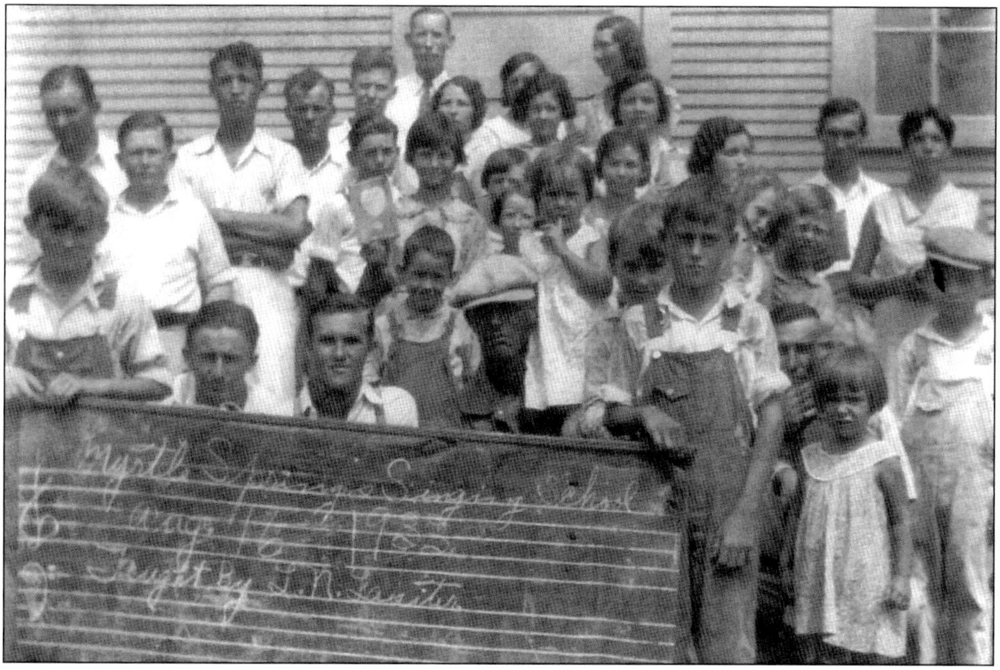

In the 1940s and early 1950s, singing schools were held during the summer at many of the rural churches in Anderson County. They lasted one or two weeks and taught how to read music and lead singing. Some of them also gave piano lessons for a fee. The Myrtle Springs Singing School was taught by L. N. Lasiter. (Courtesy of Veda DeShazo.)

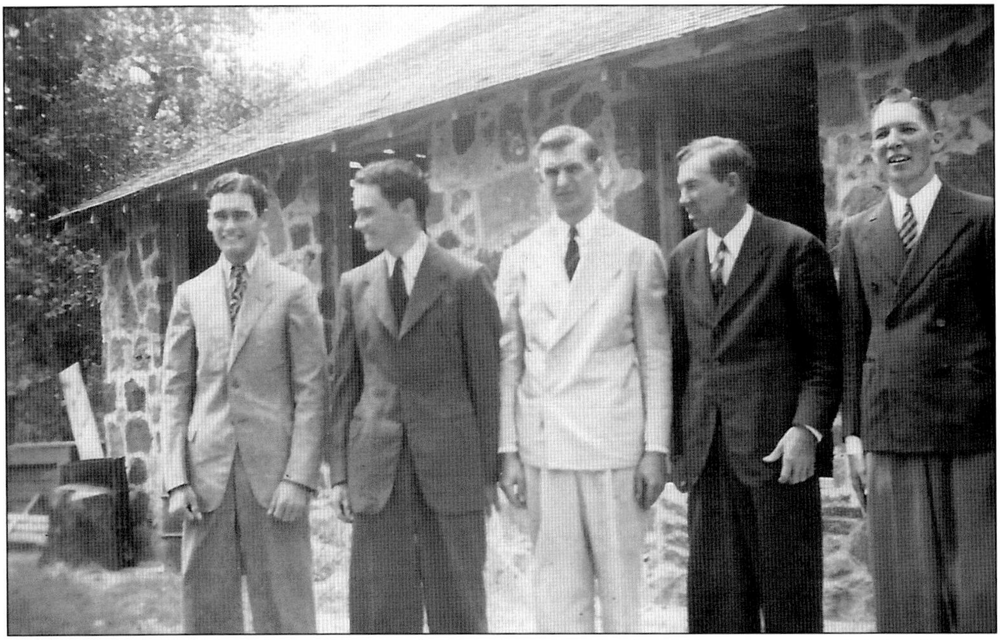

This picture was taken in front of the Rock Church. This church was located in the Sulphur Springs community on U.S. Highway 294, past Harcrow Road. Pictured from left to right are Roy Green, Joy Green, Brother Schoog, Tommy Scott, and Lonnie Callaway. (Courtesy of Rachel Bailey.)

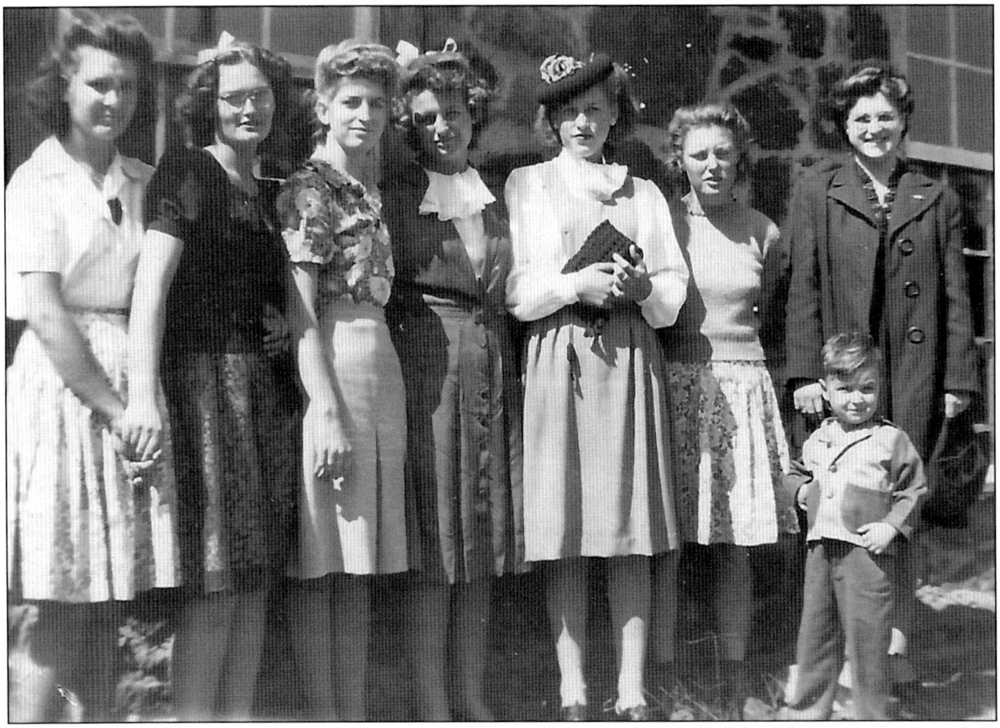

This photograph of the Sunday school was taken in front of the Rock Church. Pictured from left to right are Molly Bell Hunt, Johny Lois Milam, Willie Mae Crawford, Mary Hooper, Madeline Dunhan, Lucille Kizer, and Vivian Dunham Cummins and child. (Courtesy of Rachel Bailey.)

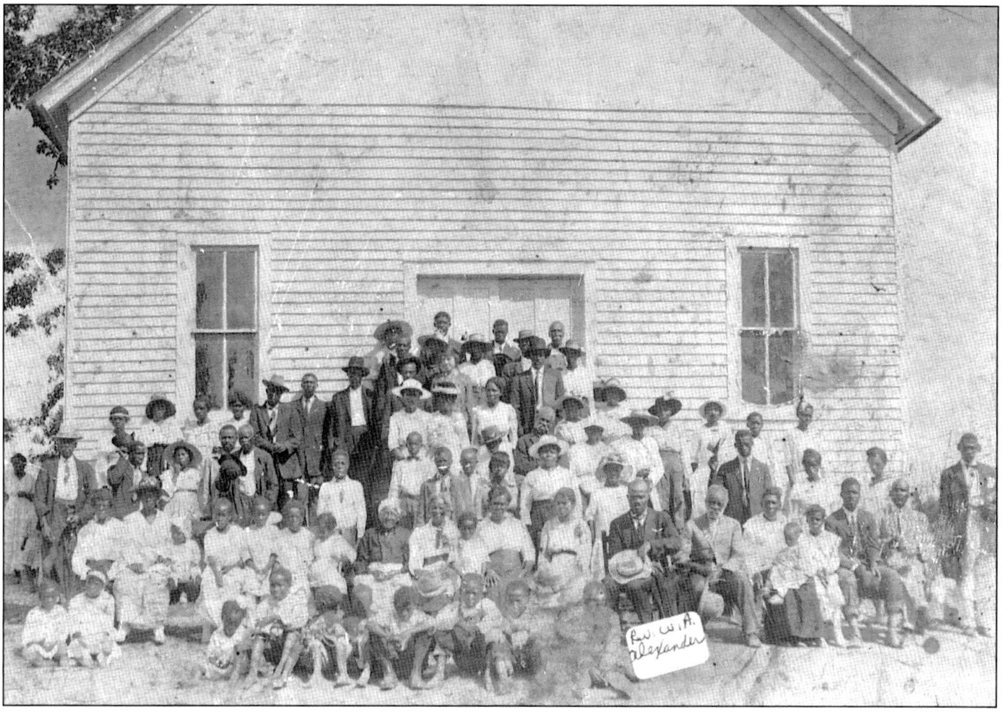

Mt. Moriah Baptist Church was built in 1882 in the Beulah community south of Palestine. The first pastor was Reverend Burgess. The building also served as Mount Moriah School from the early 1900s until 1937, when all students were sent to Henry High School in Elkhart. The church will celebrate its 128th anniversary in 2010. This information was provided by Reginald Browne. (Courtesy of Palestine Public Library)

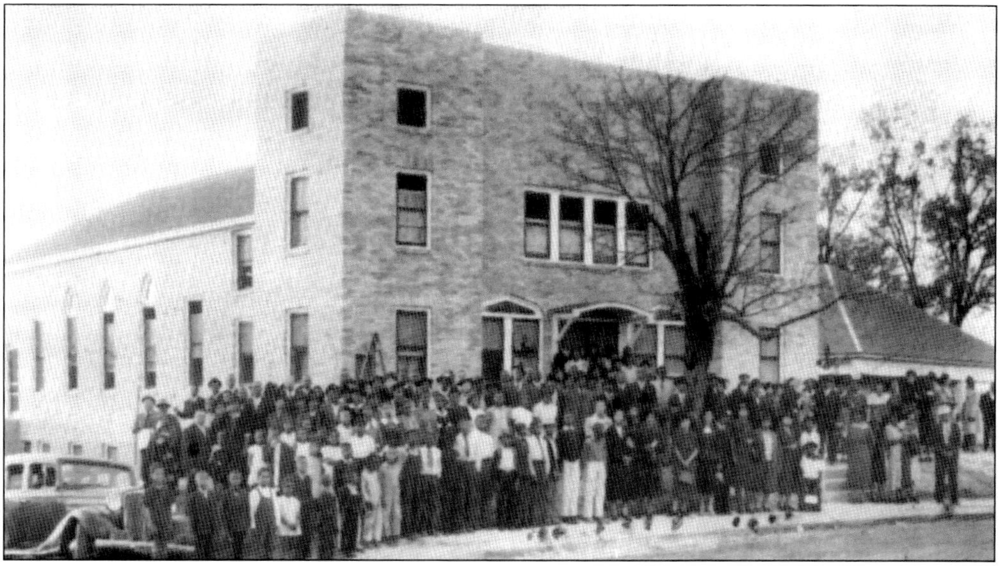

Pilgrim Rest Baptist Church was organized on October 31, 1892, in the South Union Baptist Church building on Royall Street. The first pastor was Rev. D. W. Whitting. In November 1898, their first permanent church was opened in the 1300 block of South Fulton. In 1941, the church was destroyed by fire, but it was rebuilt and rededicated in November of that year.

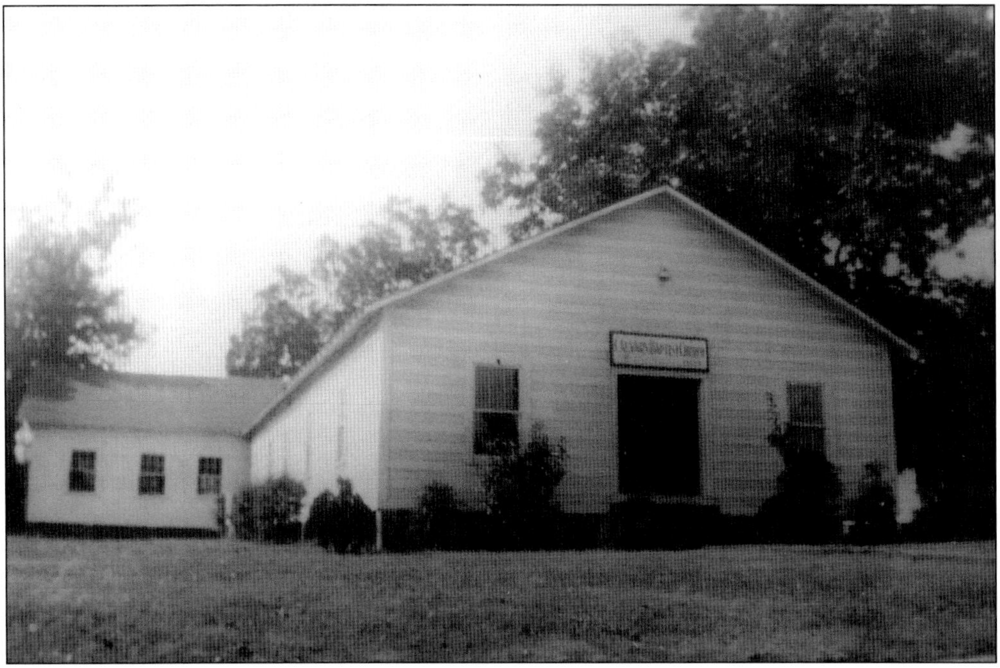

The first Calvary Baptist Church was organized sometime in the 1930s. Its initial location was on the corner of North Jackson and Louisiana Streets. About 1940, it moved to a new building at Kolstad Street and Tennessee Avenue. The present church is on Gillespie Road near Texas State Highway Loop 256.

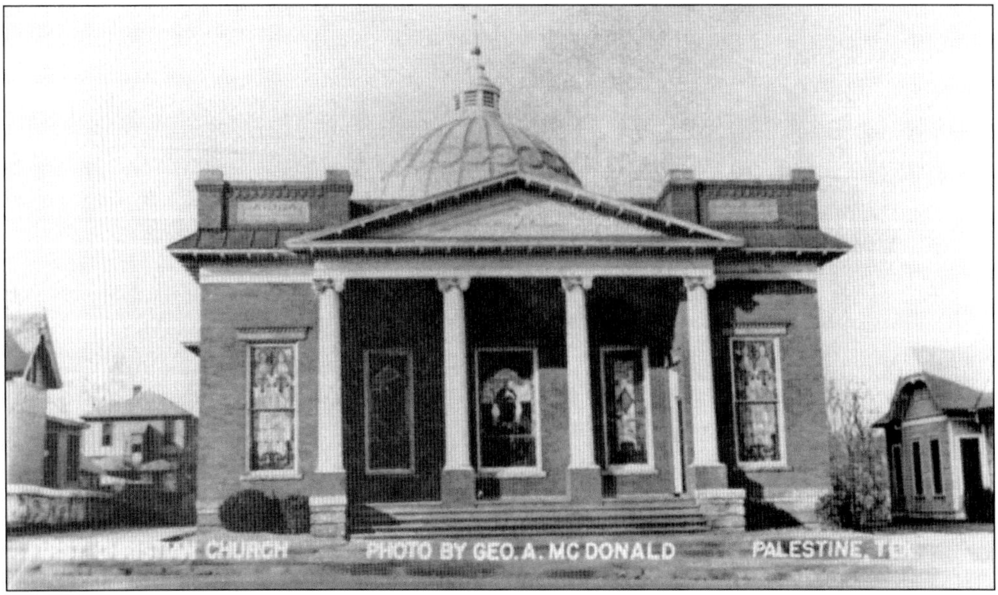

In 1847, a group met at Fort Houston and organized what later developed into the First Christian Church of Palestine. This photograph of the First Christian Church on Crawford Street was taken by George A. McDonald in 1940.

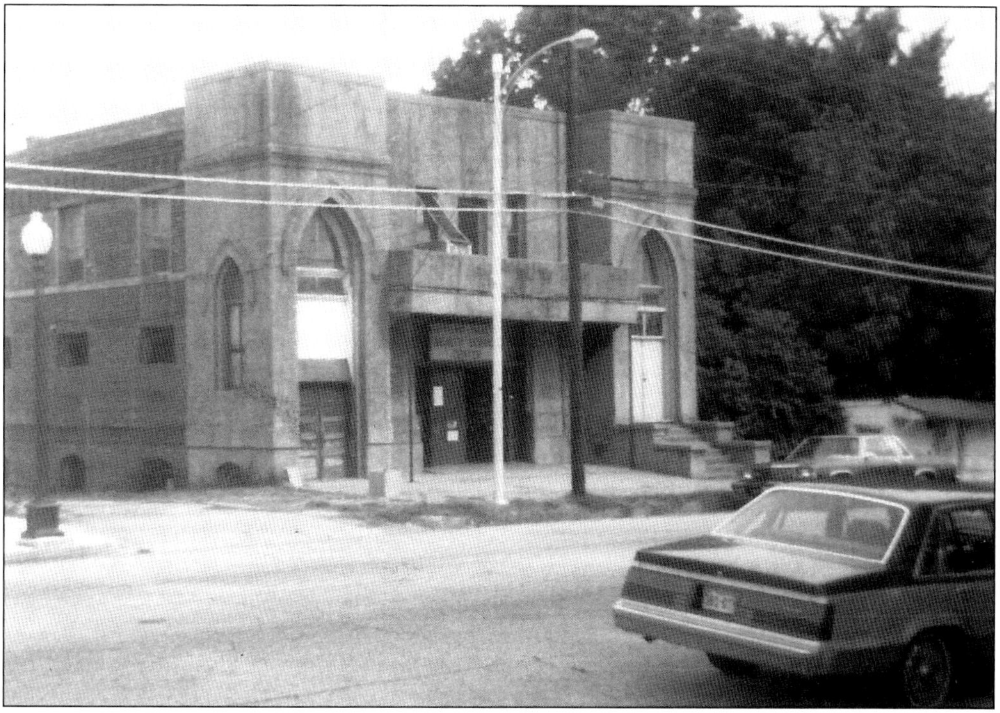

In 1881, Rev. W. E. Penn of Jefferson, Texas, conducted one of the first revivals in Palestine. From this beginning, the Avenue A Baptist Church was founded. It was better known as the Nickel Church because, at Reverend Penn's suggestion, it was built from nickel contributions. The first pastor, Rev. W. H. Wallace, was called on January 26, 1882. The free-of-debt church was completed in 1887.

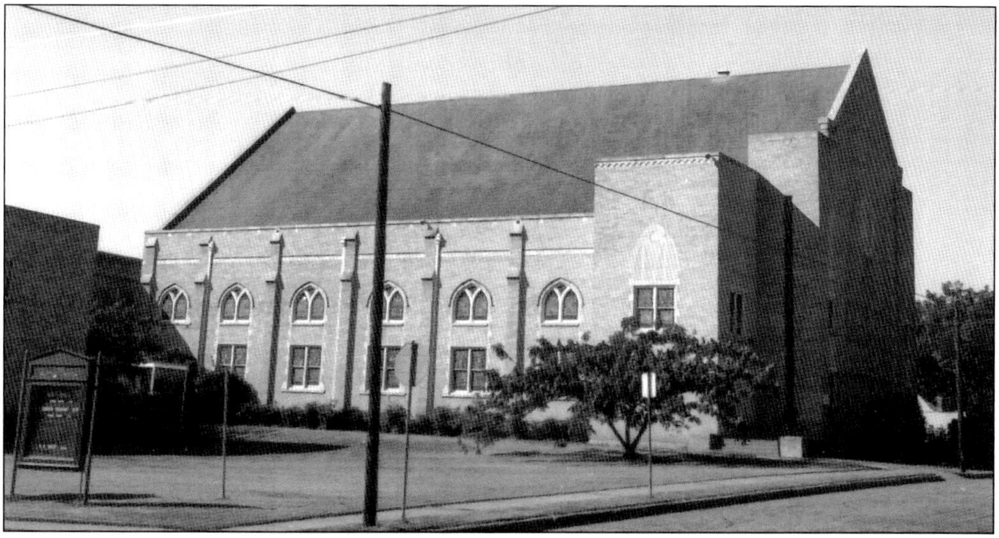

The First Baptist Church on North Sycamore Street at Kolstad Street was the second home of the church. The new church was dedicated on December 12, 1912, and replaced the Avenue A Baptist Church. In the 1950s, the second building was demolished and a new sanctuary, above, was built on the same location but facing Kolstad Street. In recent years, the church moved to a new location on Texas State Highway Loop 256.

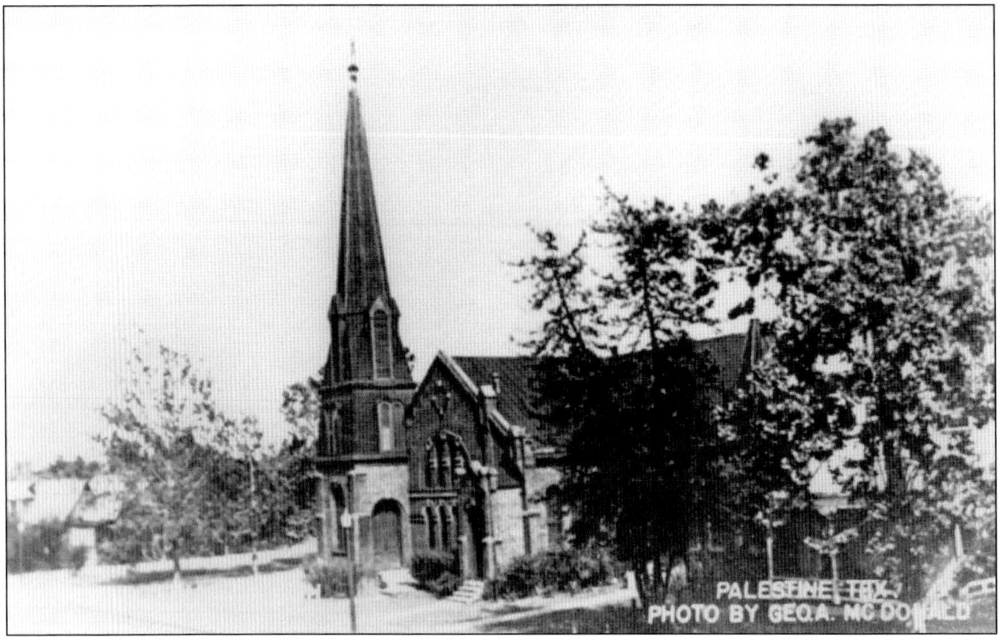

The First Presbyterian Church of Palestine was organized on November 3, 1849, by Rev. Daniel Baker and Rev. J. N. Becton, home missionaries of the Presbyterian Church of the United States. The present church, located at 410 Avenue A, was built in 1888.

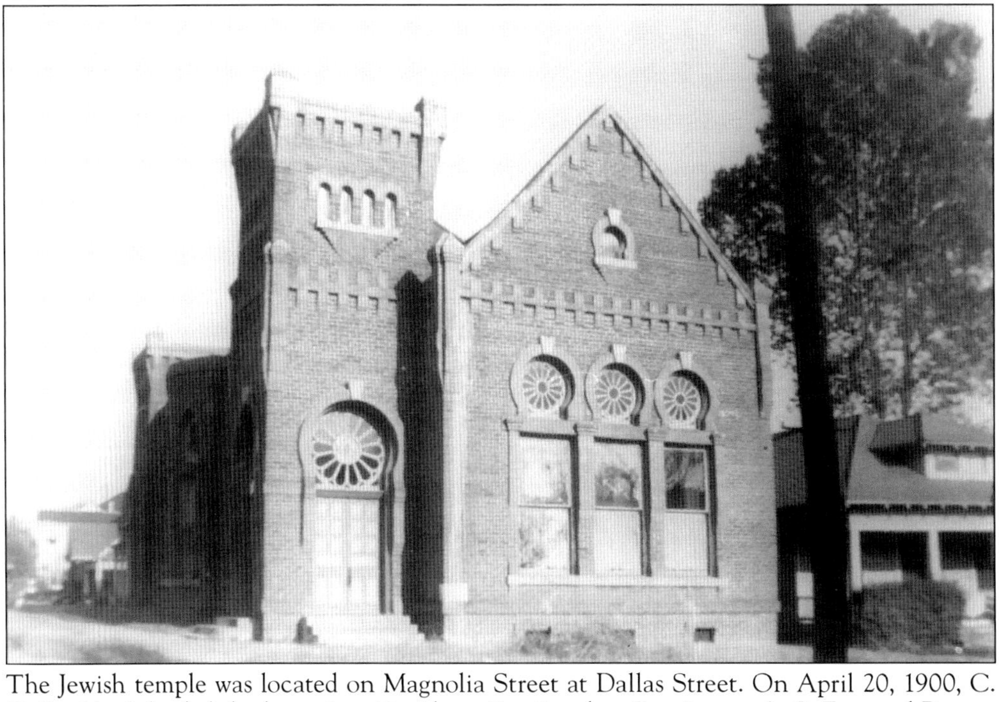

The Jewish temple was located on Magnolia Street at Dallas Street. On April 20, 1900, C. C. Stoddard deeded the lot to Leo Davidson, Ben Landau, Sam Lucas, A. S. Fox, and Barney Pearlstone. The congregation, Beth Israel, received its charter from the U.S. Department of State on June 23, 1900, and the building was begun in January 1901. In 1950, the building was leased to the Full Gospel Temple. It was demolished in 1960.

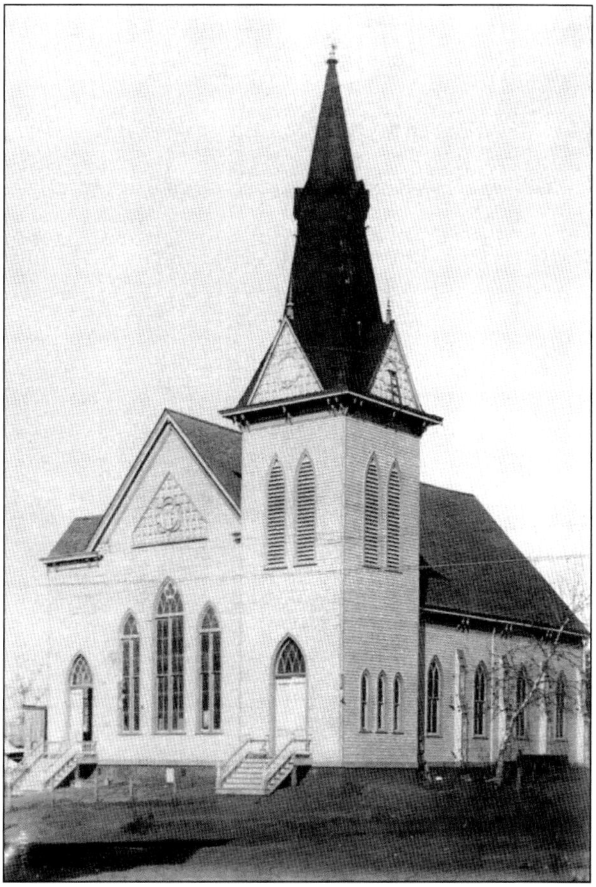

The first church built in Palestine was Bascom Chapel, located at 102 Mallard Street. It was replaced by the Centenary Methodist Church, at right, which was built in 1884 at 812 Mallard Street. It was later a residence but is now being dismantled. The church divided in 1910 when the First Methodist Church, seen below, was erected on Magnolia Street at Reagan Street. The second Methodist church became Grace Methodist Church and is located on the corner of Kolstad and Queen Streets.

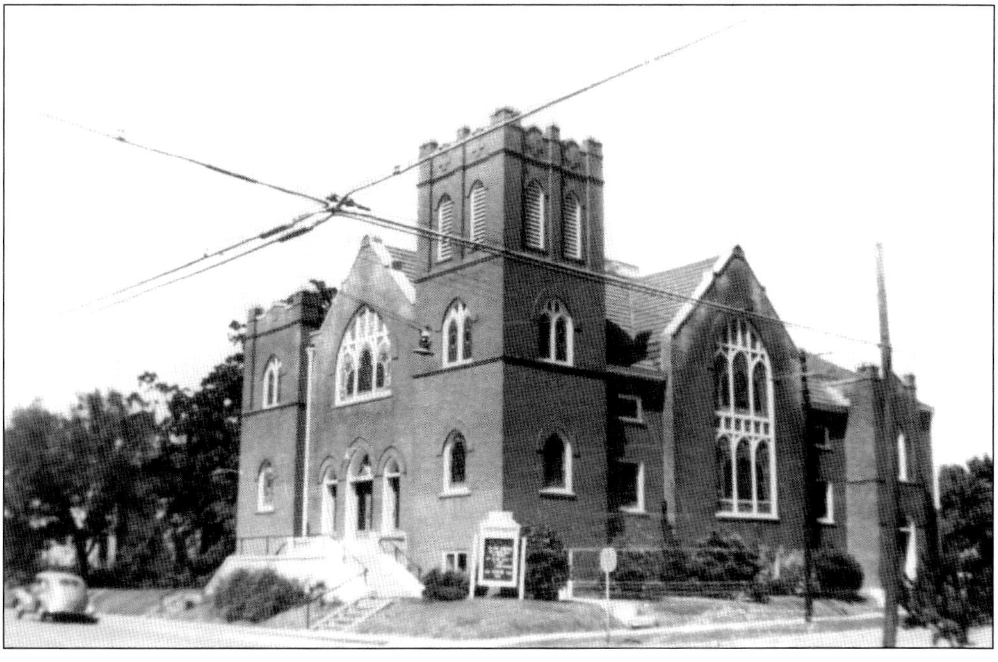

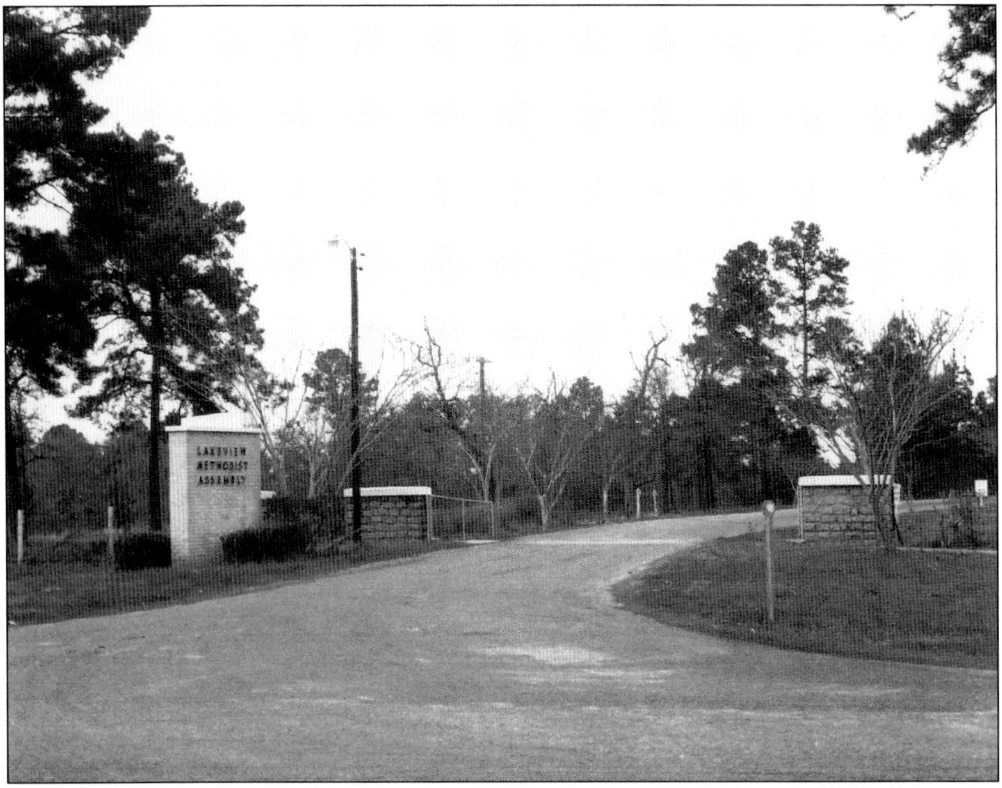

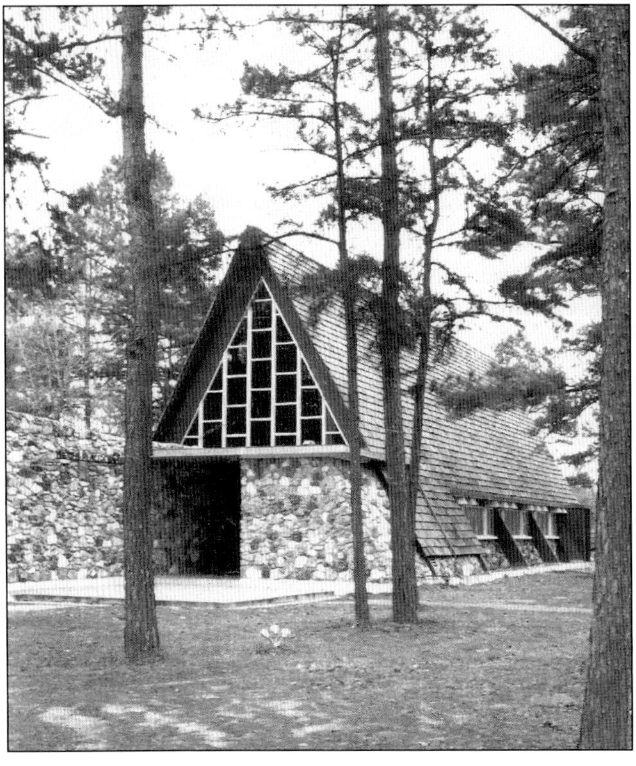

The Lakeview Methodist Conference Center is a ministry of the United Methodist Church. It is located on Texas State Highway 294 between Elkhart and Tucker in one of the most scenic areas of Texas. At left, Lakeview's Peace Chapel is a beautiful A-frame building with river rock walls on both ends and a very elegant stained glass window.

Six

SCHOOLS

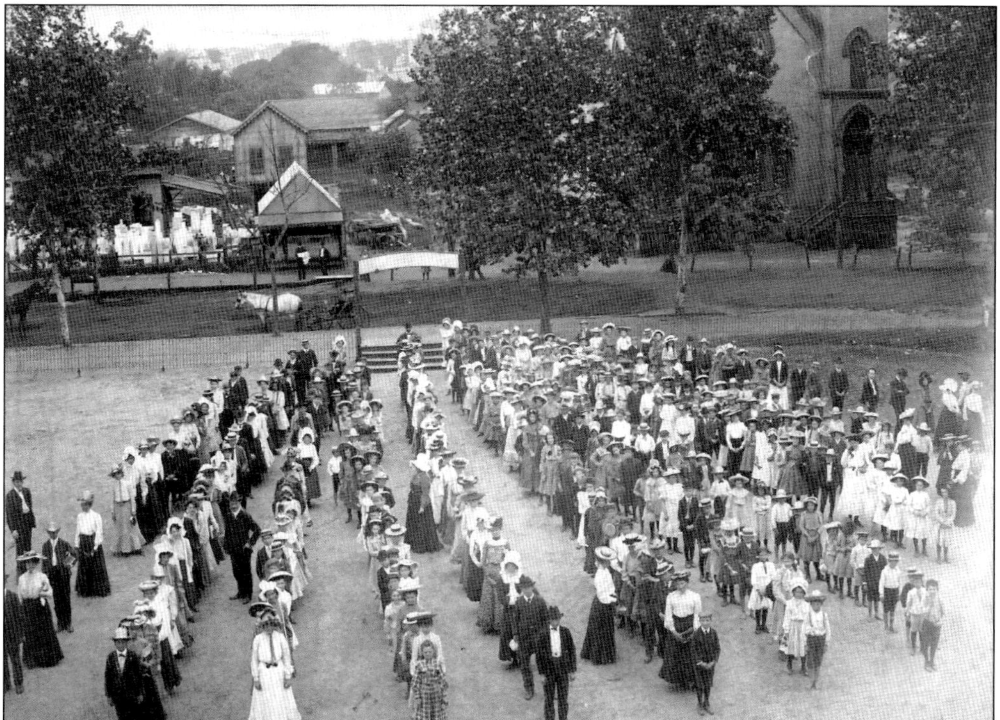

This is a gathering on the front lawn of the old Central High School on Avenue A in Palestine. The Nickel Baptist Church can be seen on the right in the background.

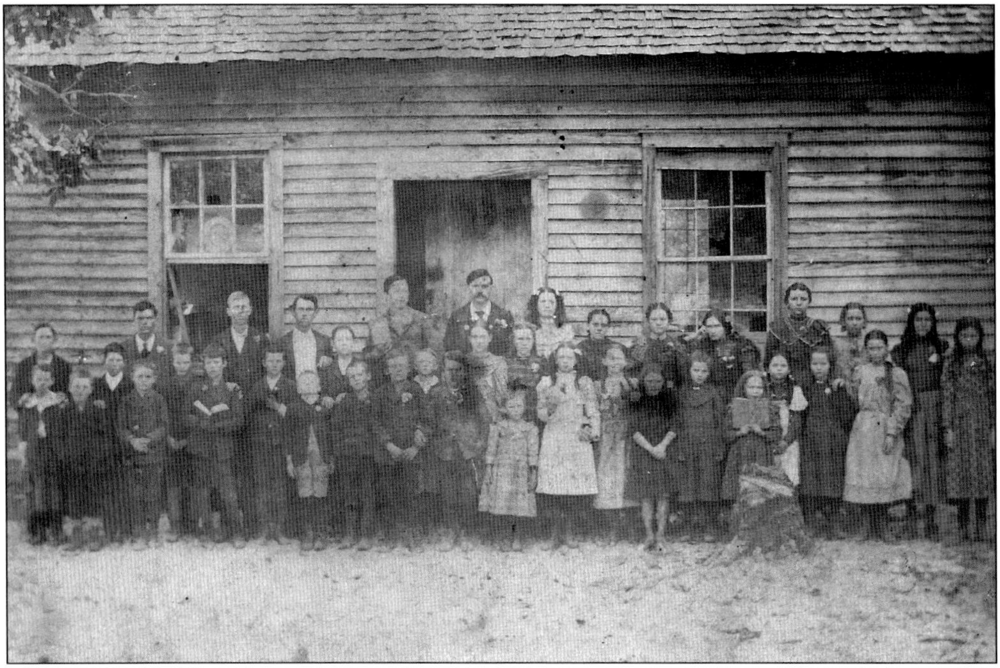

Fort Houston School was located 4 miles from Palestine. This picture was taken in fall 1898. It is thought that this school was actually closer to Chambers than to Fort Houston. (Courtesy of Floyd Barthel.)

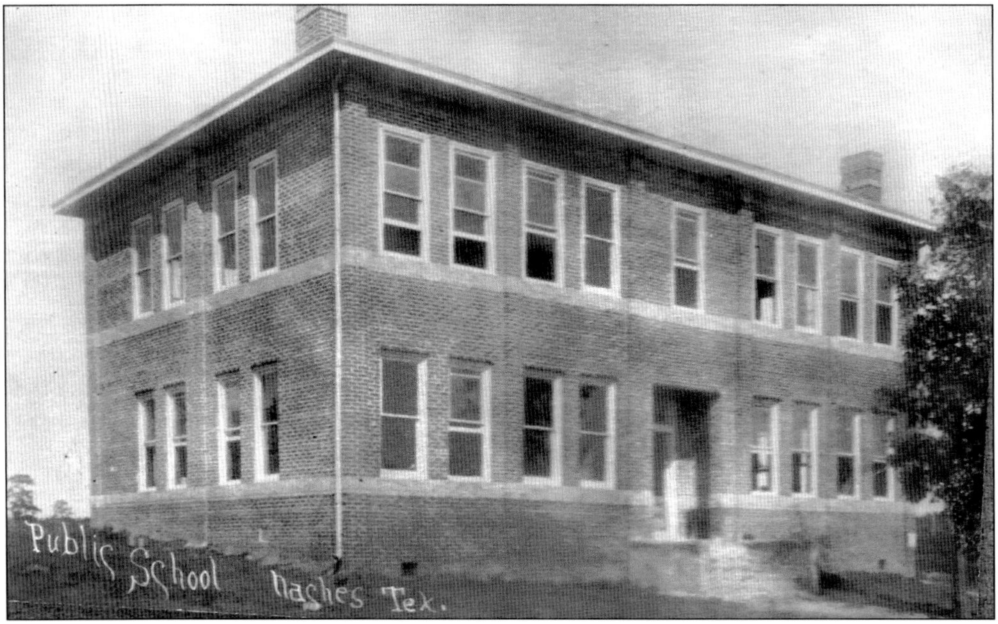

In 1866, several men chartered a school named Stovall Academy 3 miles from Neches. It was moved to Neches in 1872 and was sometimes called Neches High School but was changed to Neches Normal Institute in 1898. (Courtesy of Johnnie Belle McDonald Faucett)

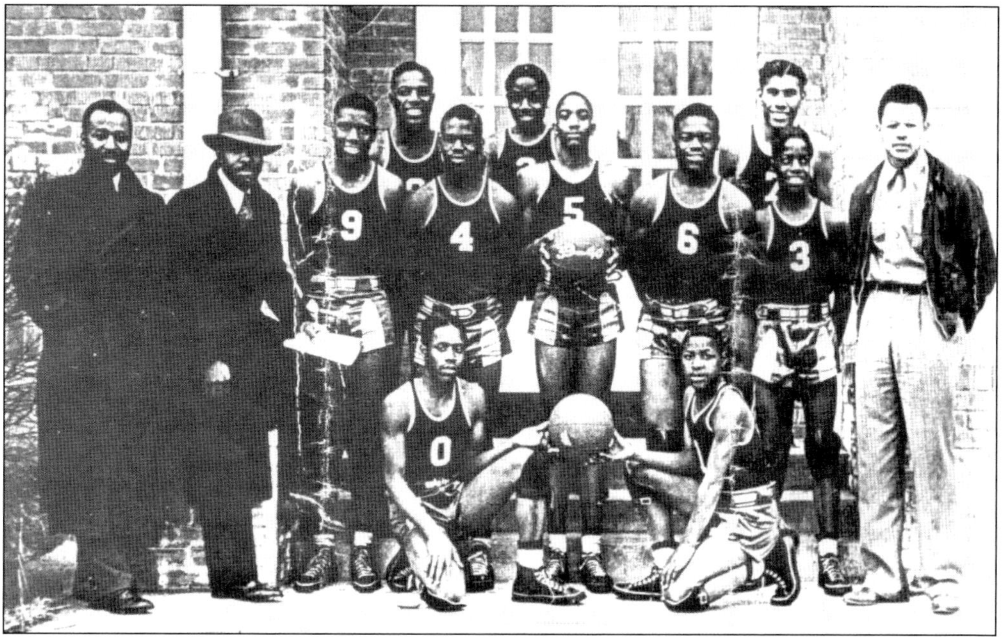

The Green Bay School grew from the Green Bay AME Church in Tucker about 3 miles from the Trinity River. About 1900, a school was built and a high school started. By 1930, a good school system had developed. Shown above is the 1939–1940 Green Bay School basketball team that was runner-up in the Class A Black Championships. From left to right are (kneeling, first row) R. Harvey Brown and Rogers Summuel; (second row) R. H. Smith, W. L. Singletary, Joshua Morrow, Felix Dorsey, Elmer Ricks, C. A. Dorsey, M. Gibson, and coach C. L. Dennard; (third row) "Buck" Hutchinson, Nathaniel "Sonny Boy" Gibson, and John Smith. Below is same team, who became Texas state champions in 1941–1942. The 1954–1955 basketball team also won the state championship. (Both, courtesy of Versalean Logan.)

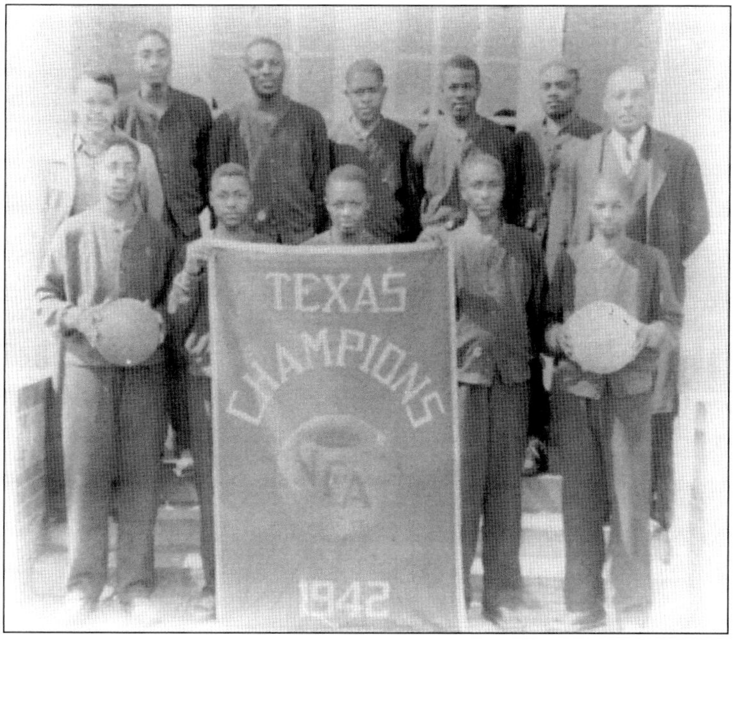

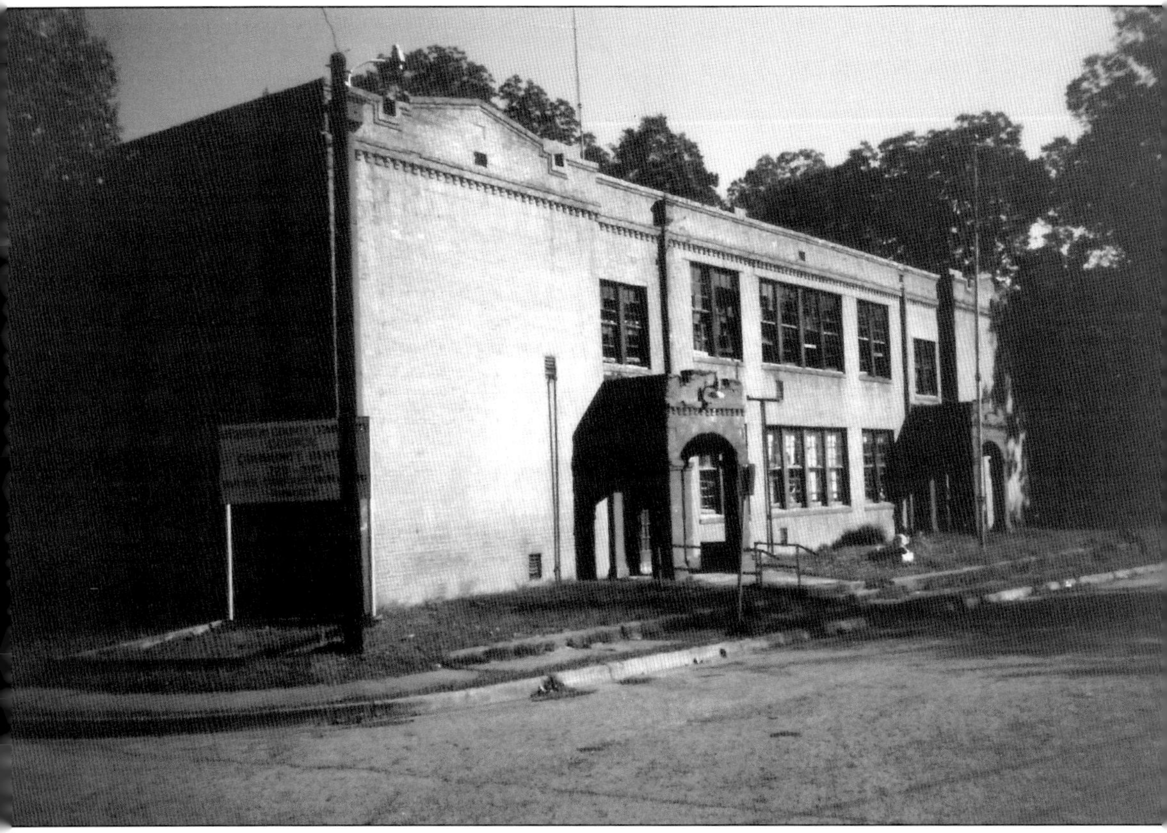

The first black high school in Palestine was opened in 1891 in Mission Church on San Jacinto Street. In 1895, the school was moved to a four-room frame building on the corner of Swantz and McClellan Streets and renamed Lincoln High School. The school burned in 1922. The first class graduated in 1896. In January 1923, the new two-story brick Lincoln High School opened in the same location. In 1965, all high school students in the Palestine Independent School District were sent to the new Palestine High School on Texas State Highway Loop 256. (Courtesy of Versalean Logan.)

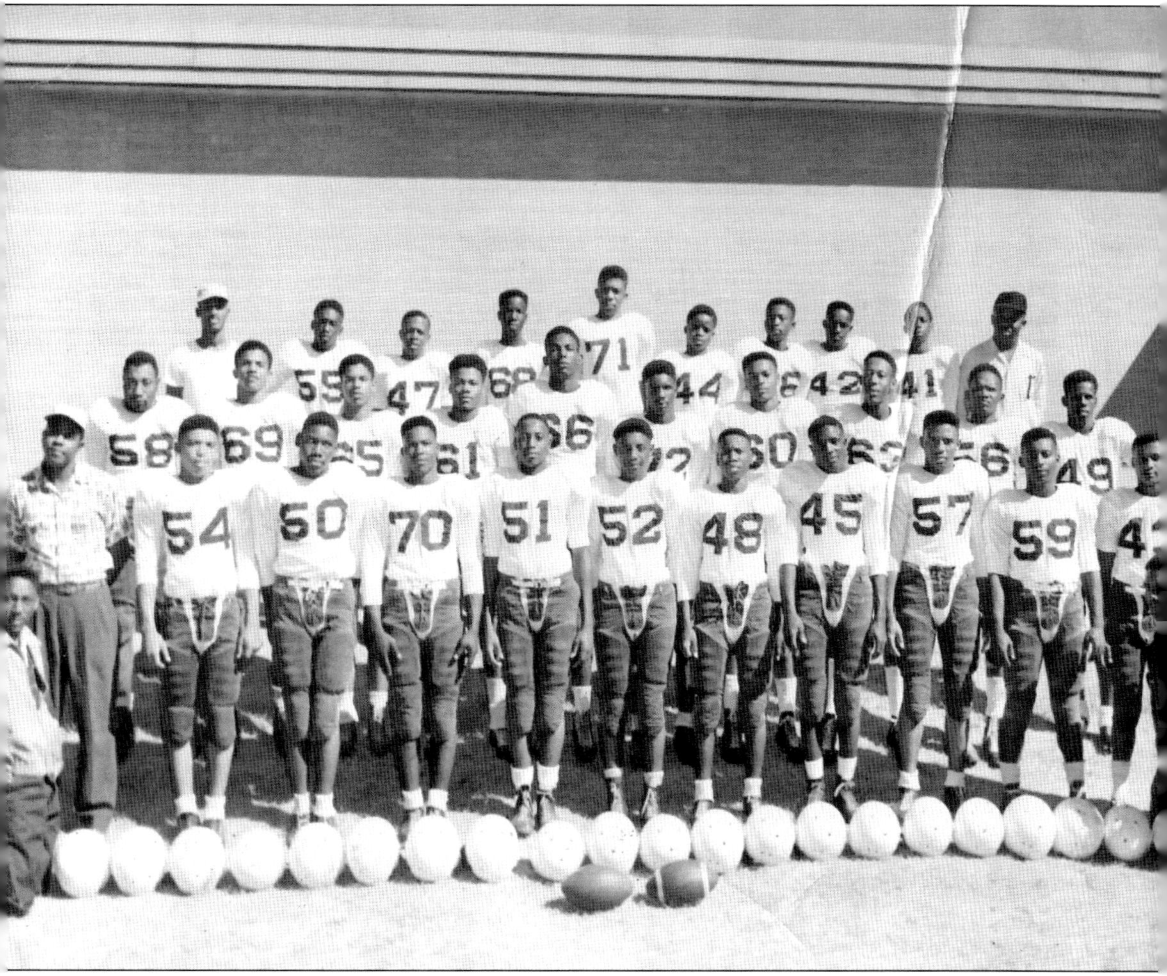

This is the A. M. Story High School football team in the 1955–1956 school year. On the left end of first row is Eddie Rogers, trainer, and an unidentified trainer on the right end. In the second row, from left to right, are coach Otis Williams, Tillie Atkins (54), Hosea Dolphus (50), Jack Coleman (70), unidentified (51), Willard Dial (52), John Ricks (48), unidentified (45), Adrian Scott (57), Bethel Lowe (59), and Paul Wagner (43); (third row) Joe Hollie (58), Roy Jamerson (69), Charles Howard (65), Robert Stubblefield (61), James Edwards (66), George Watkins (72), Silas McMorris (60), Frank Carroll (63), Ray Mitchell (56), and W. J. Spearman (49); (fourth row) unidentified trainer, Jessie Derrough (55), Verlie Taylor (47), Langrand Henderson (68), Archie Brown (71), Lencie O'Brian (44), Charlie Parks (?6), James Stephens (42), ? Barrett (41), and an unidentified trainer.

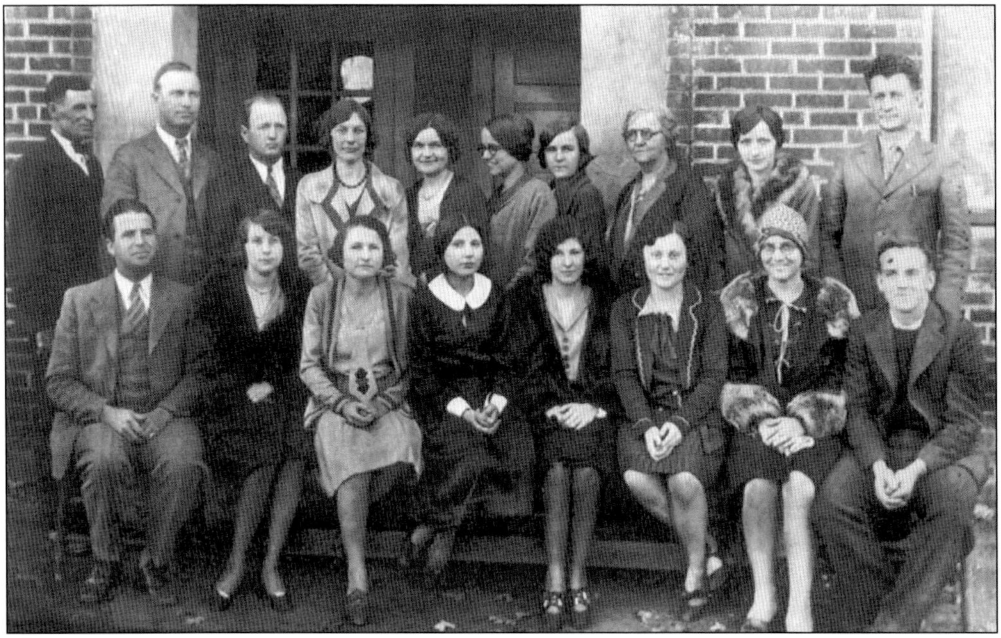

This is the Elkhart School faculty in 1929. From left to right, are (first row) Ashley Williams, Norine Williams, Ida Cupp, Louise Hathcock, Polly Pridgeon, Marie Lassiter, Johnny Lemons, and Sam Frizzel; (second row) Ben Moseley, Arthur Colvin, E. G. Garrison, Mae Kelly, Rosa Ford, Lura Wilson, Wilma Blackstone, Beulah Sheridan, Bertie Davis, and superintendent Tom Blackstone. (Courtesy of CA)

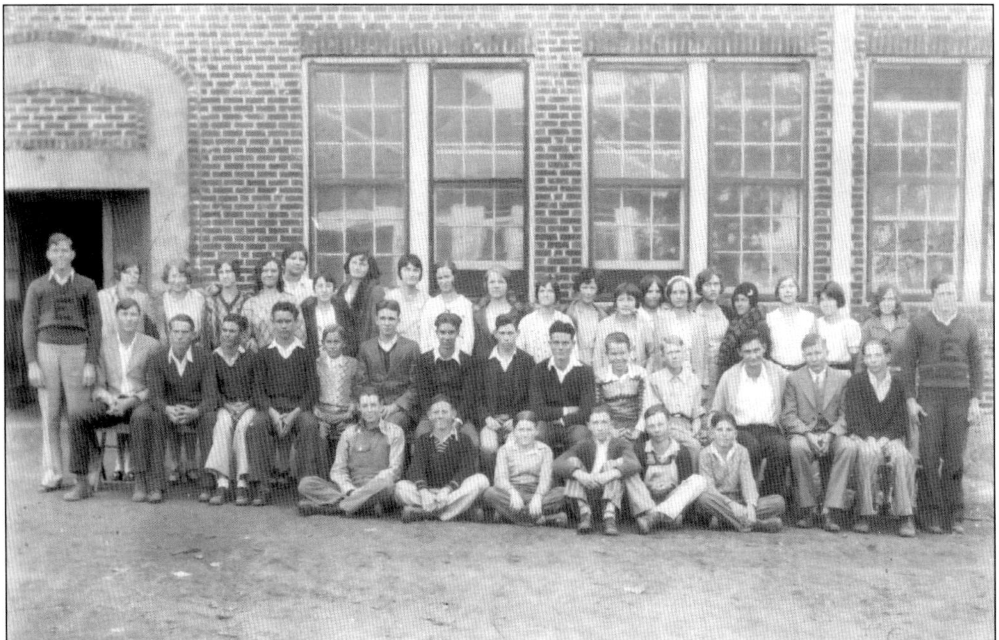

These are Elkhart school students in front of the school around 1930. The only person identified in this group is Archie Lee Trigg, seated in the second row, seventh from the left. (Courtesy of Dan Trigg.)

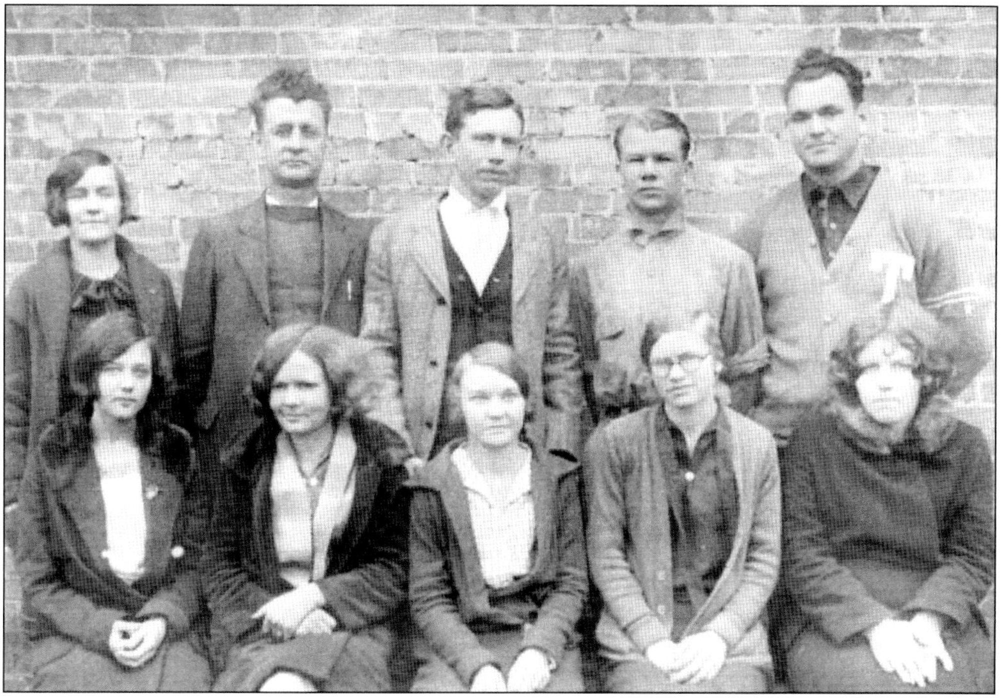

This Elkhart School photograph includes teachers and the students who graduated on May 24, 1928. From left to right are (first row) Elizabeth Oxford, Velma Kyle, Vergie Peterson, Flora Mae Starr, and Alda Lively; (second row) Wilma Blackstone (teacher), Tom Blackstone (teacher), Isaac Davis, Dennis Frazier, and Luther Star (teacher). At that time, O. L. Lively was president, T. D. Oxford was secretary, Tom Blackstone was superintendent, and Luther Starr was principal. (Courtesy of Karren Jones.)

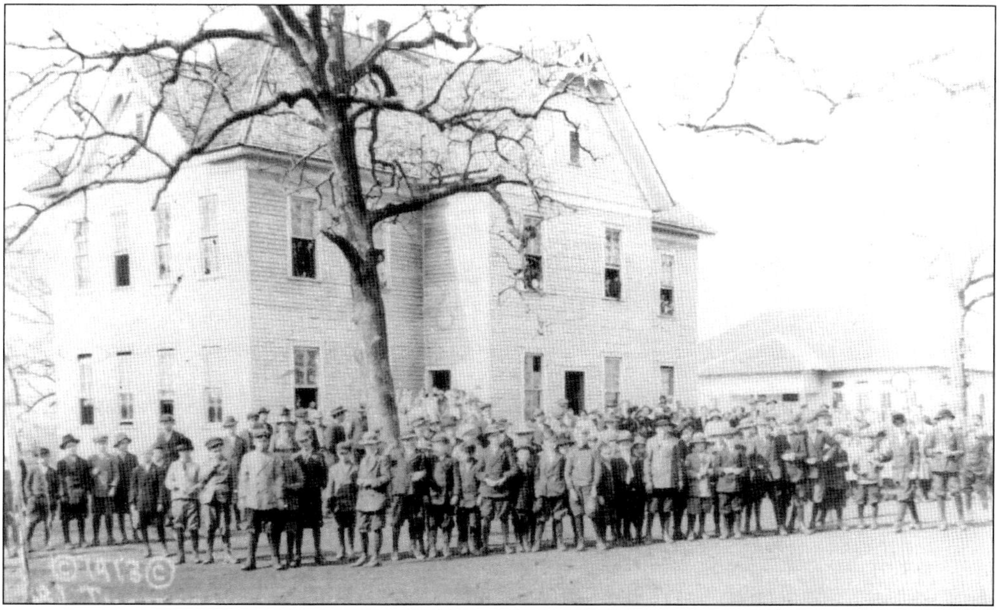

These students are standing in front of the old Elkhart School in 1913.

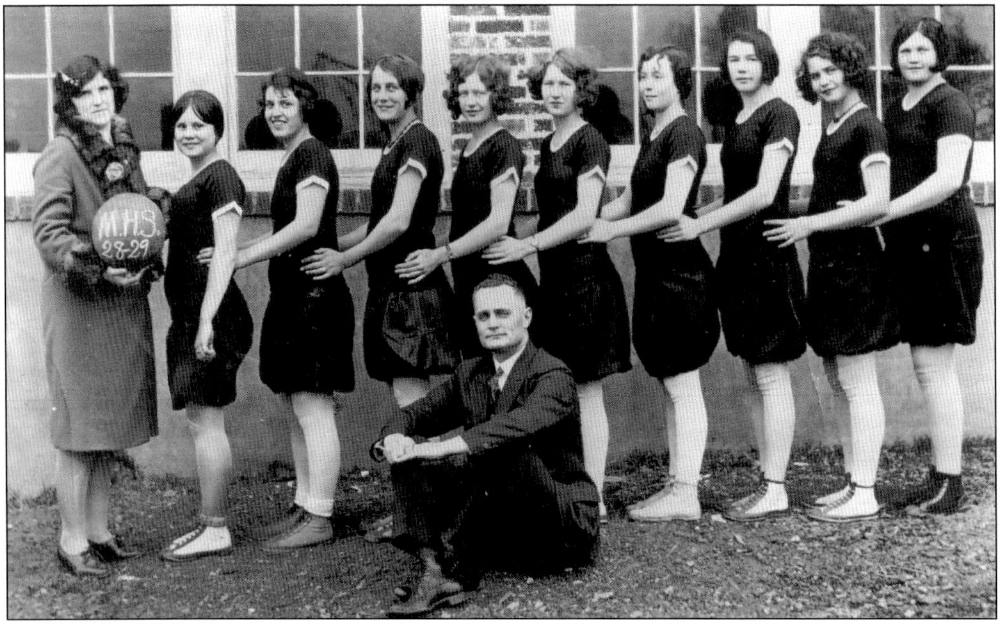

This is the Montalba High School 1928–1929 basketball team. Seated in the first row is Ben L. Keene, principal and coach. In the second row, from left to right, are Pearl Keene, Agnes Johnson, Norma Sutherlin, Ola Vee Ward, Odell Taylor, Jewel Taylor, Oma Lee Ward, Laura May Thompson, Ruth Williams, and Willie Mae Ritchey. (Courtesy of Elsie McGee.)

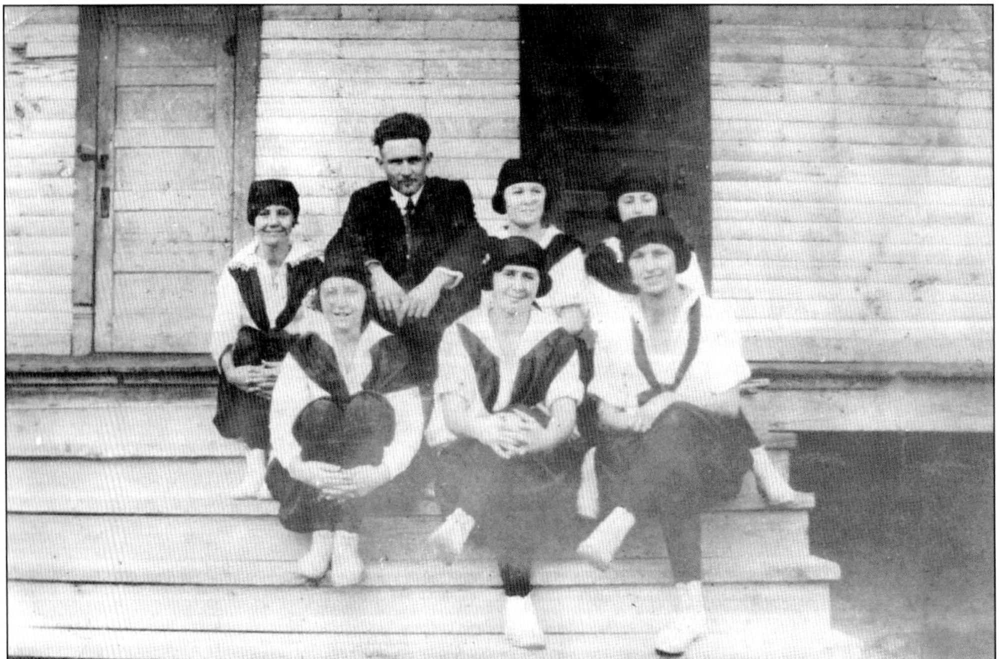

This photograph was taken in front of the two-story wooden school in Montalba about 1920. From left to right are (first row) Savanna Link, Audrey Hanks (Bassett), and Hester Johnson (Brooks); (second row) Maudie Ferguson (Simmons), George H. Brooks, Jessie Mae Auld (Bullock), and Freddie Auld (Brooks). (Courtesy of Elsie McGee.)

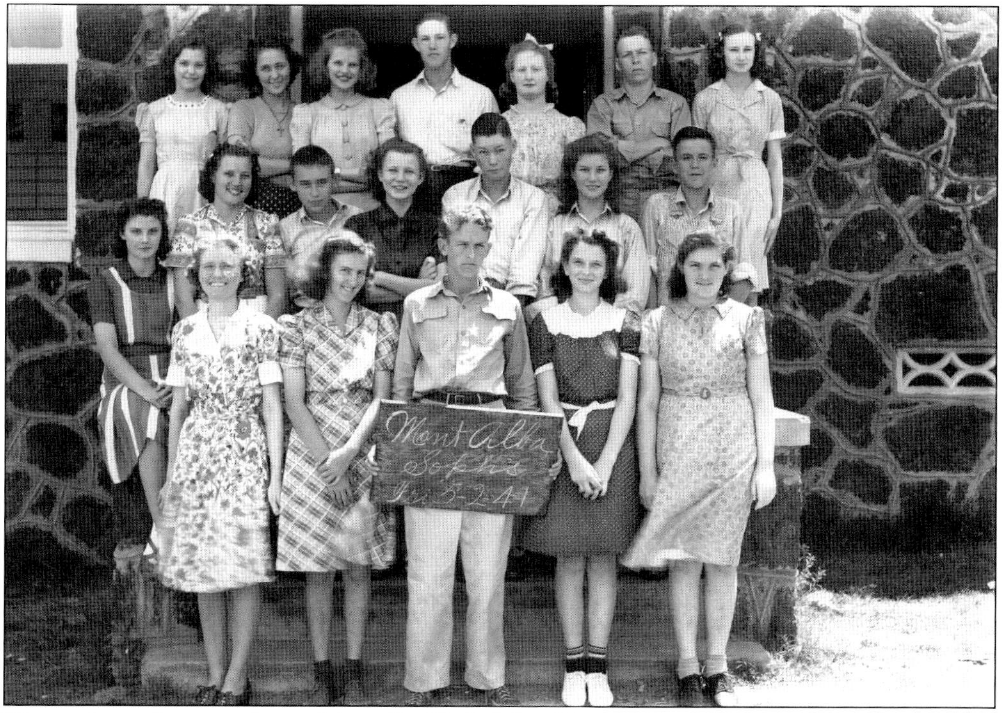

This is the sophomore class at Montalba High School for 1940–1941. From left to right are (first row) Mary Collins (teacher), Roena Sutherlin, Edward Sutherlin, Katherine Mize, and Lucille Thornton; (second row) Pauline Vannoy, Erma Lee Thornton, H. L. Chandler, Phylis MacKersh, Jack Coleman, Ruth Pate, and Kenneth Wilbanks; (third row) Elsie Beasley, Jane Knighton, Mary Wingate, Melvalee Davis, Betty Jane Pickle, Milo Taylor, and Evelyn Holcomb. (Courtesy of Elsie McGee.)

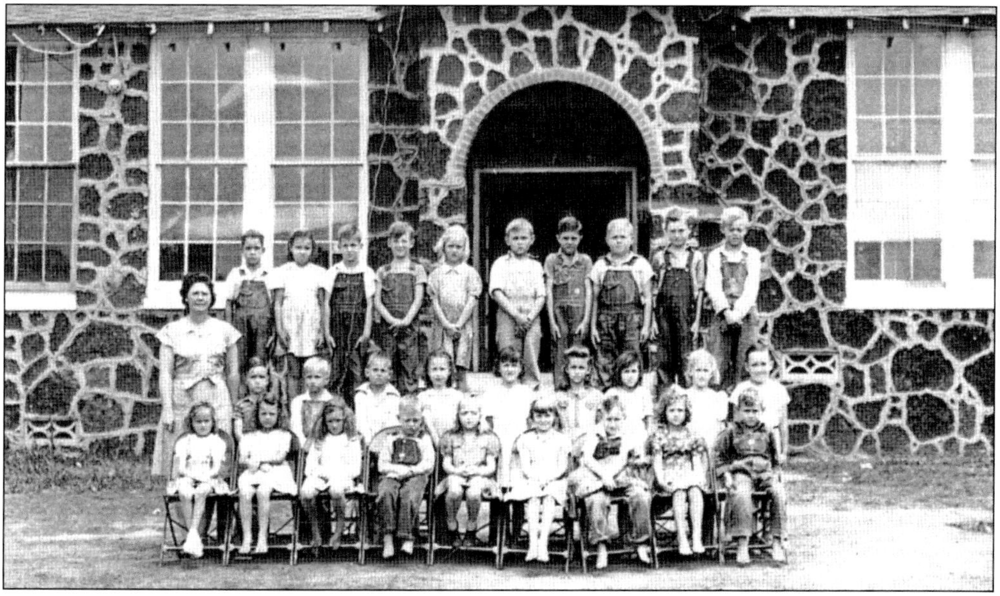

This is the first and second grade at Montalba School for 1945–1946. The teacher, Gladys Johnson, is standing on the left end of the second row. (Courtesy of Marita Denson Stovall.)

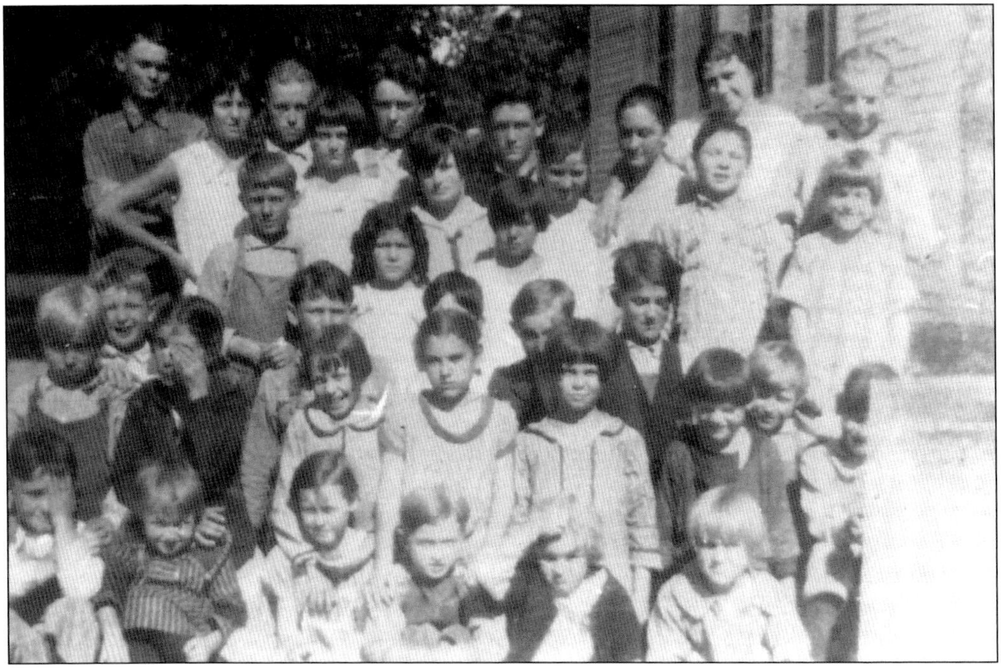

The Sulphur Springs School was located on Dipping Vat Road. Some of the following students are in the school group: Velma Bailey, Agnes Mack, Adele Parker, Doug Kizer, Rachel Jones, Mildred Evans, Griffy Ray, Gert Milam, Ben Swann, Mage Axum, Virgil Parker, Carl Swann, Maude Axum, Annie Milam, Arnold Mack, Bessie Milam, Emmy Jenkins, Boots Axum, Tucker Axum, Fronie Swann, Elma Coker, Estelle Axum, and Johnny Mack.(Courtesy of Rachel Bailey.)

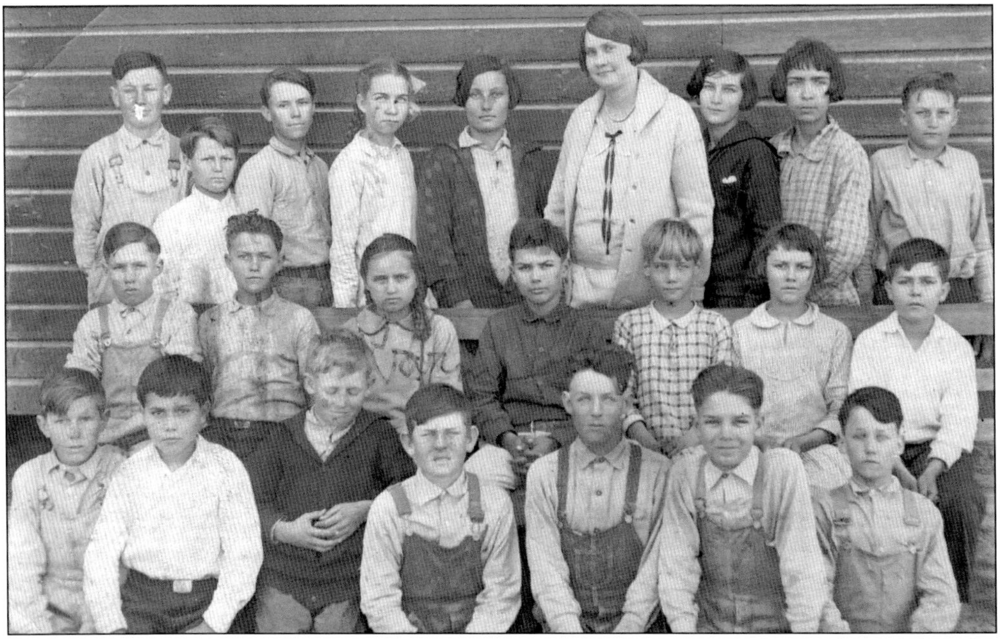

This is Salmon School around 1924. Archie Lee Trigg (first row, second from the right) is the only student identified in this school photograph. After the Salmon School closed around 1928, the students attended Elkhart schools. (Courtesy of Dan Trigg.)

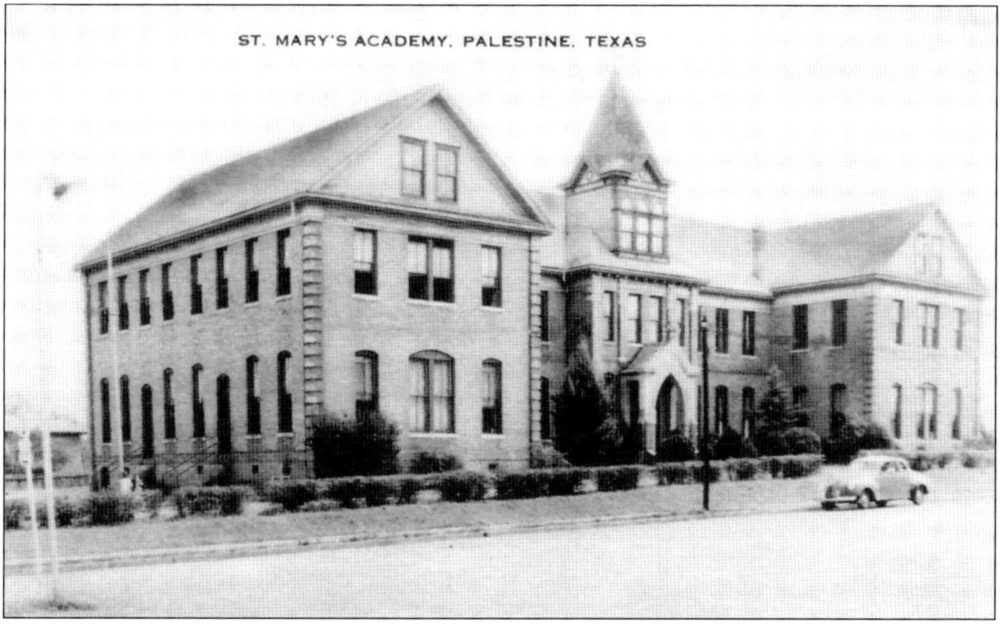

The Catholic school St Mary's Academy was located at 503 North Queen Street behind the Sacred Heart Catholic Church. The academy was a two-story brick building with gables, a central entry bay, and spire and was built in 1901.

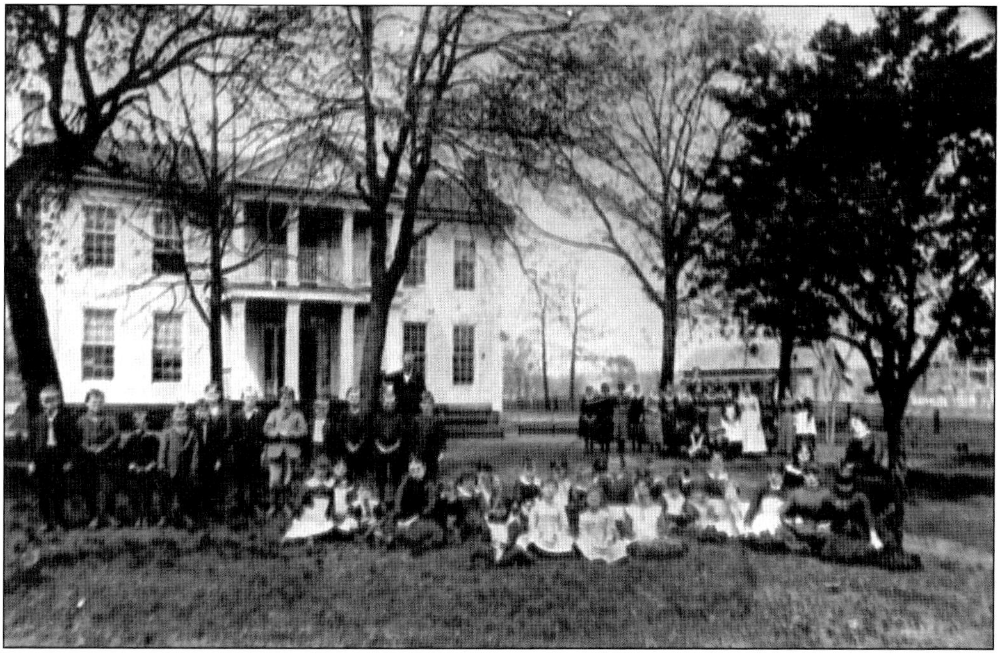

Amende School was a private school in Palestine around 1884. It was located on the corner of Spring and Line (now Queen) Streets.

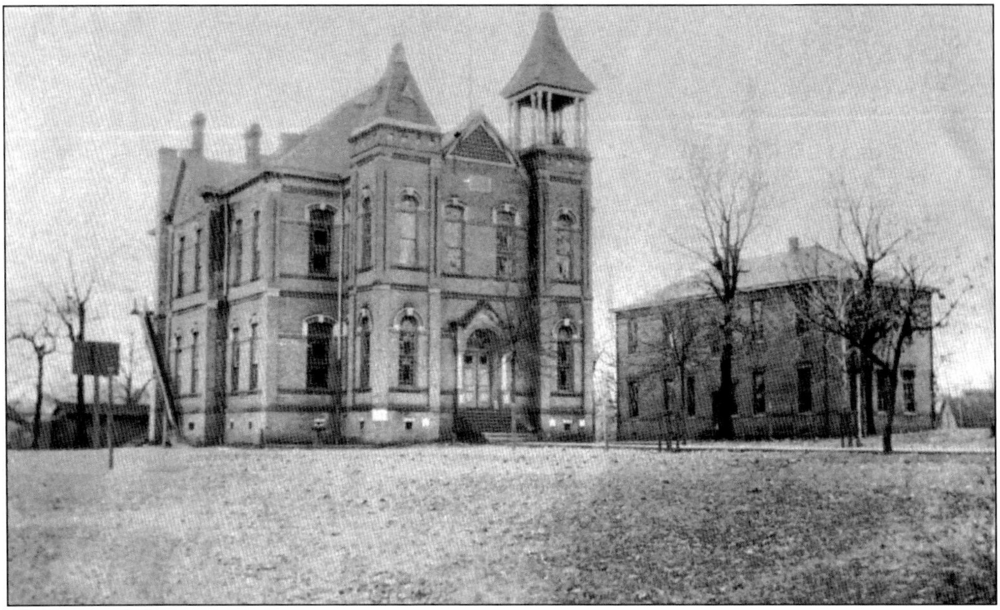

Central High School was built in 1888. It was located on Avenue A just east of the Presbyterian church. Davy Crockett Junior High School (later Palestine High School) was later built on this site. On the right is the Palestine Female Institute. In 1856, the citizens of Palestine voted to build the school for women.

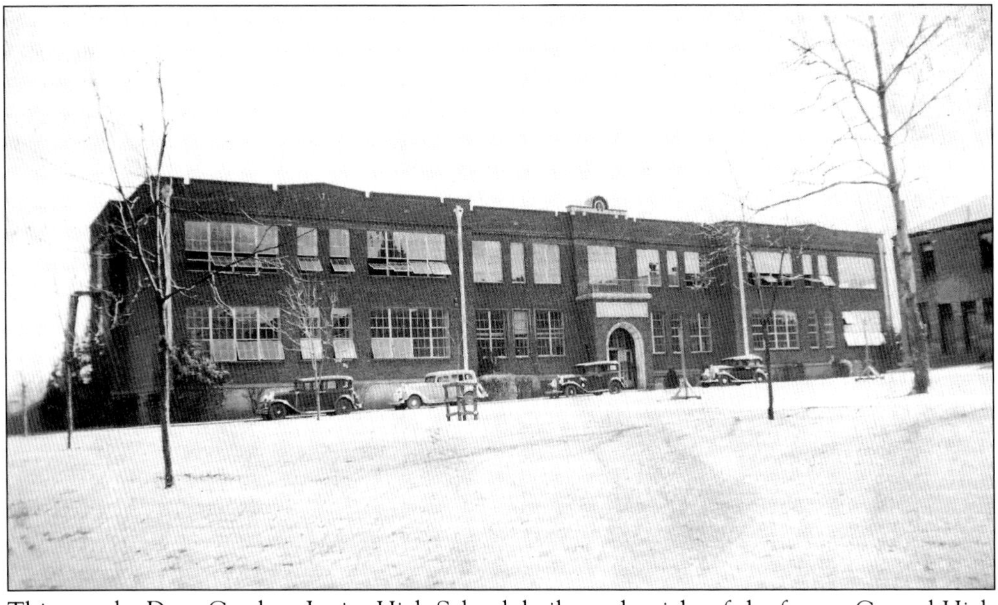

This was the Davy Crockett Junior High School, built on the sight of the former Central High School and Palestine Female Institute. In 1939, the school became Palestine High School when the junior high was moved to the Reagan school building. It served as the high school until the new high school on Texas State Highway Loop 256 was completed in the mid-1970s.

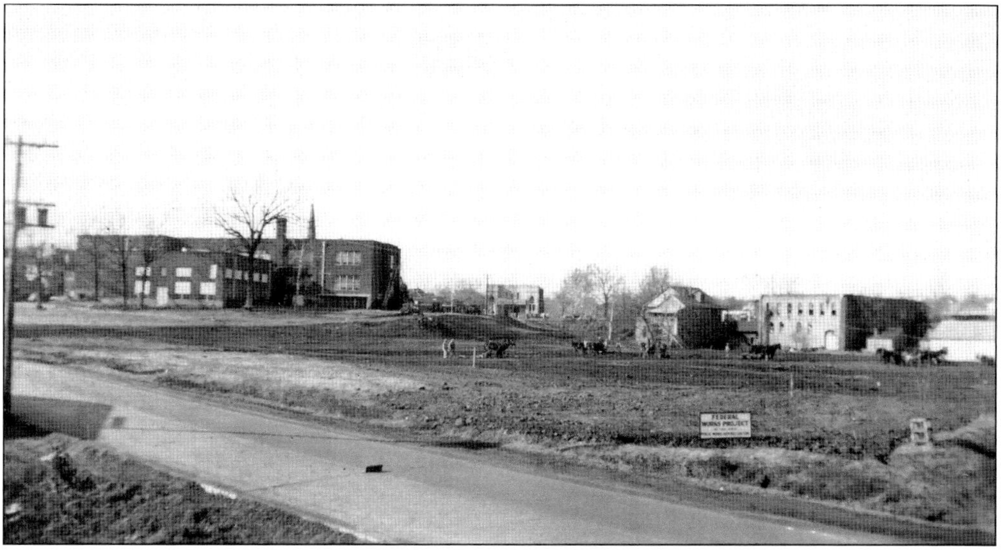

This photograph shows the construction of Luckett Kolstad Field, the football stadium for the Palestine High School Wildcats when the school was on Avenue A. The field, which opened on September 18, 1936, was named for Luckett Kolstad, who was president of the school board. The high school and gymnasium are on the left. Notice the sign on the lower right indicating that the project is a Federal Works Project.

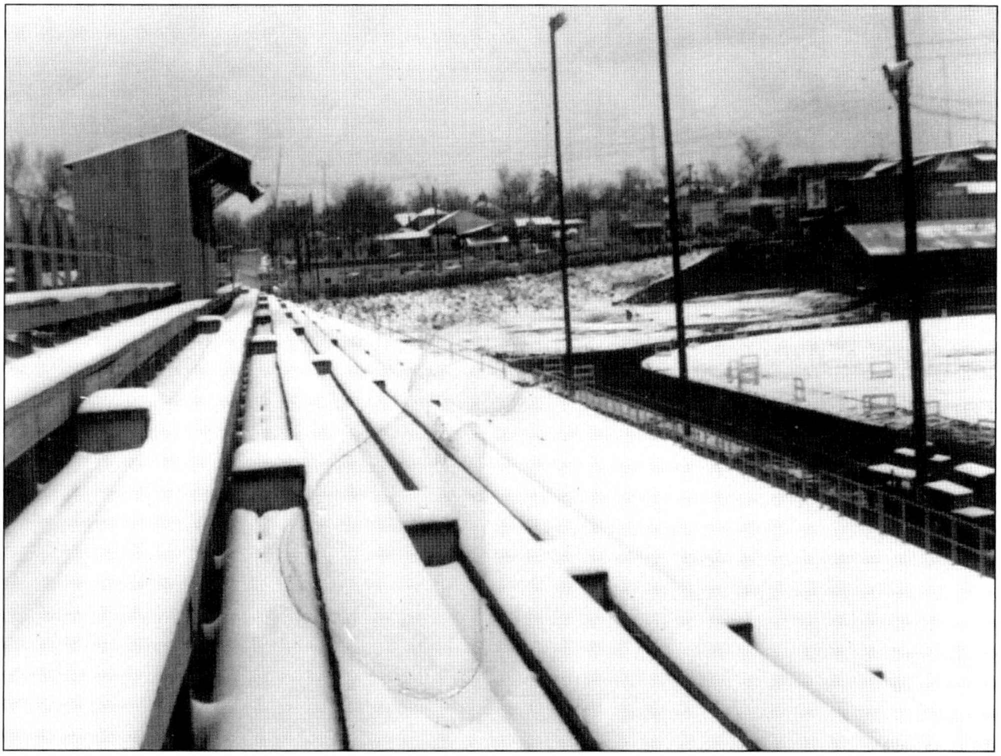

Wallace Odom snapped this shot of the snow on Luckett Kolstad field in 1954 or 1955. The Kroger shopping center now stands on the site where the stadium was located. (Courtesy of Wallace Odom.)

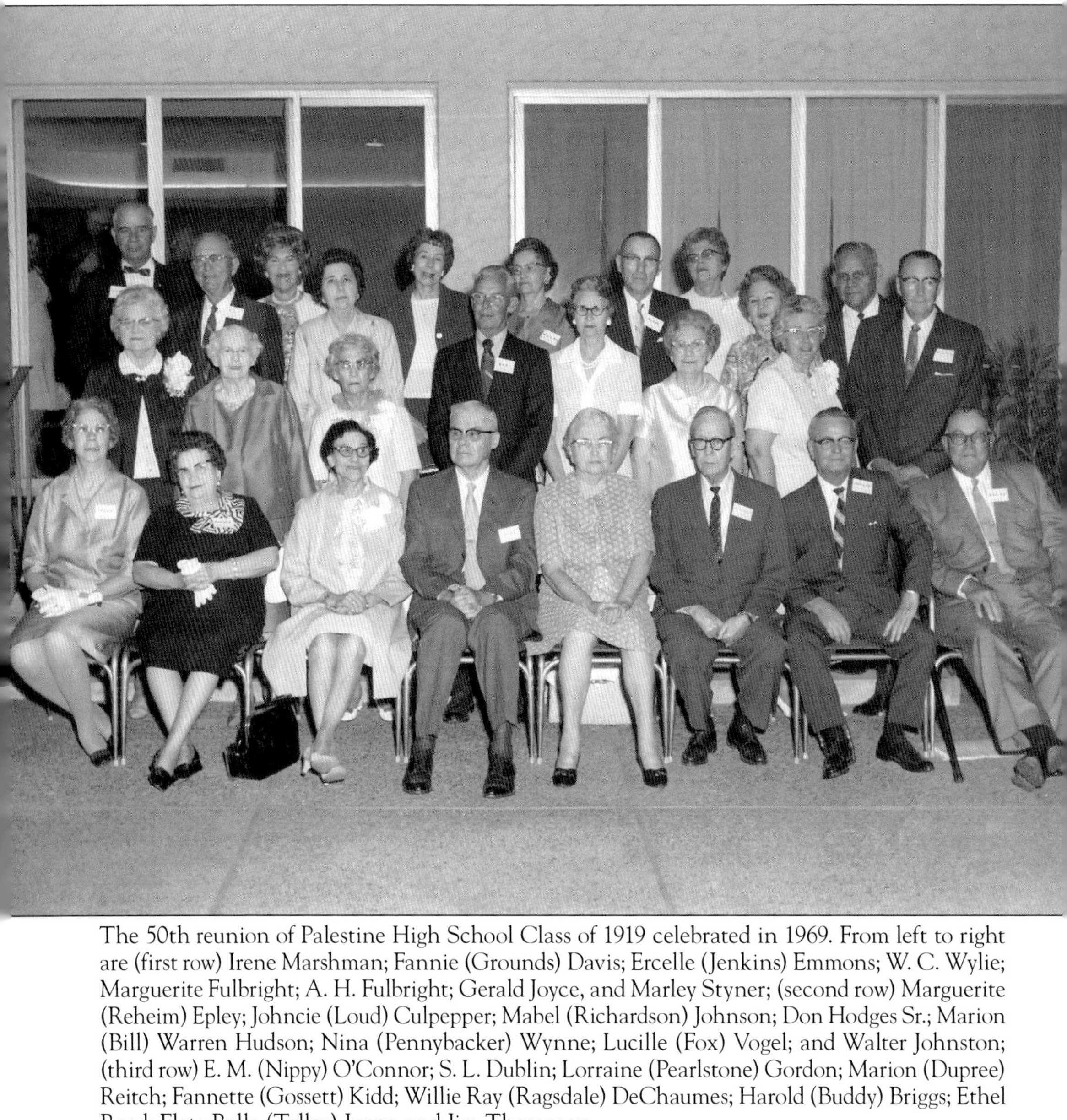

The 50th reunion of Palestine High School Class of 1919 celebrated in 1969. From left to right are (first row) Irene Marshman; Fannie (Grounds) Davis; Ercelle (Jenkins) Emmons; W. C. Wylie; Marguerite Fulbright; A. H. Fulbright; Gerald Joyce, and Marley Styner; (second row) Marguerite (Reheim) Epley; Johncie (Loud) Culpepper; Mabel (Richardson) Johnson; Don Hodges Sr.; Marion (Bill) Warren Hudson; Nina (Pennybacker) Wynne; Lucille (Fox) Vogel; and Walter Johnston; (third row) E. M. (Nippy) O'Connor; S. L. Dublin; Lorraine (Pearlstone) Gordon; Marion (Dupree) Reitch; Fannette (Gossett) Kidd; Willie Ray (Ragsdale) DeChaumes; Harold (Buddy) Briggs; Ethel Reed; Fleta Belle (Talley) Jones; and Jim Thompson.

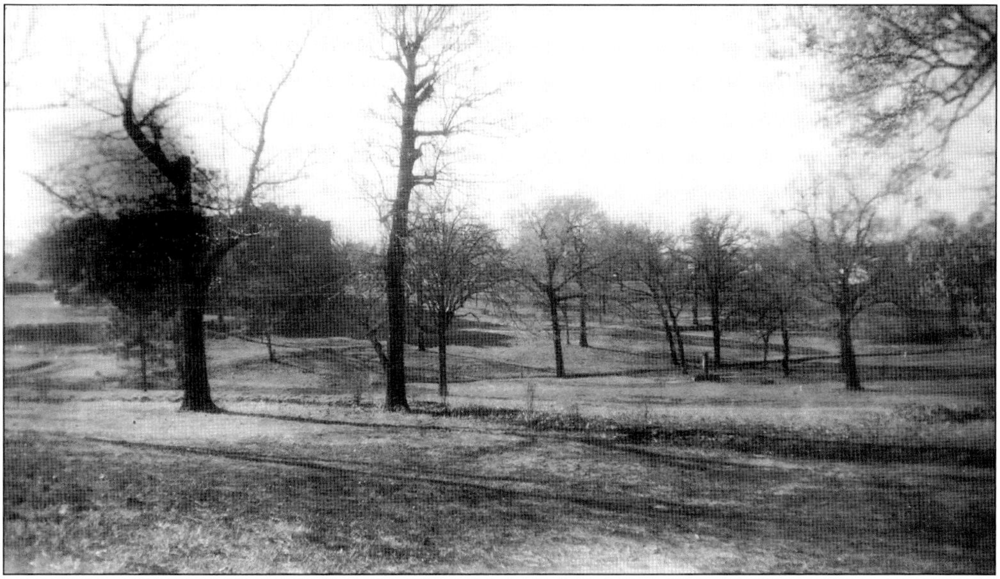

Photographed here is the new Reagan Park with the John H. Reagan school in the background.

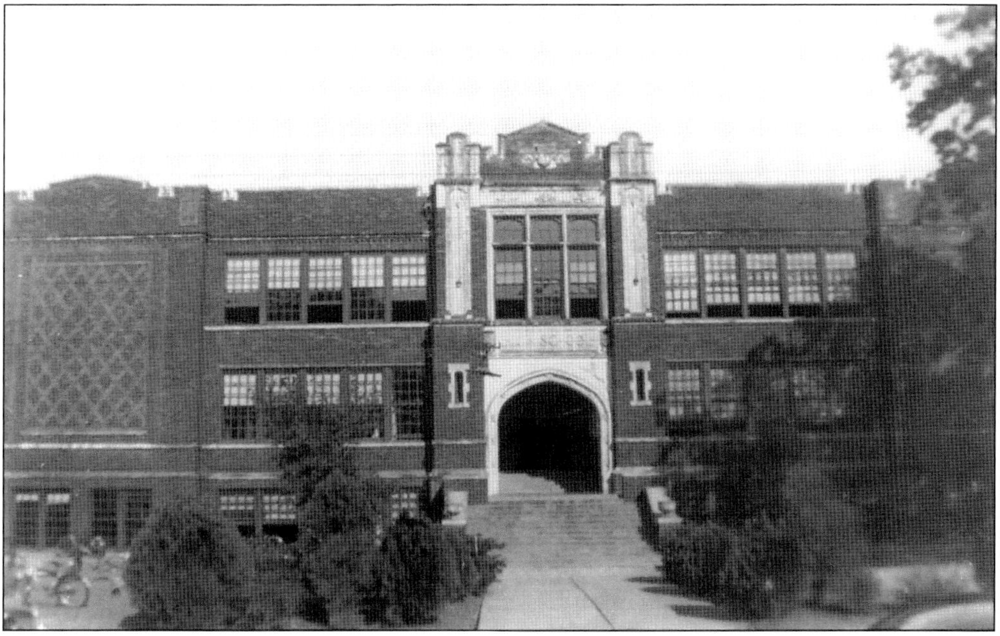

The John H. Reagan High School building on Micheaux Street stands majestically on the hill overlooking Reagan Park. It was built in 1915 and 1916. It was the high school until 1939 when the high school was moved to the Davy Crockett building on Avenue A. It then served as the junior high school until it became an elementary school from 1966 to 1976. It presently houses the Museum for East Texas Culture.

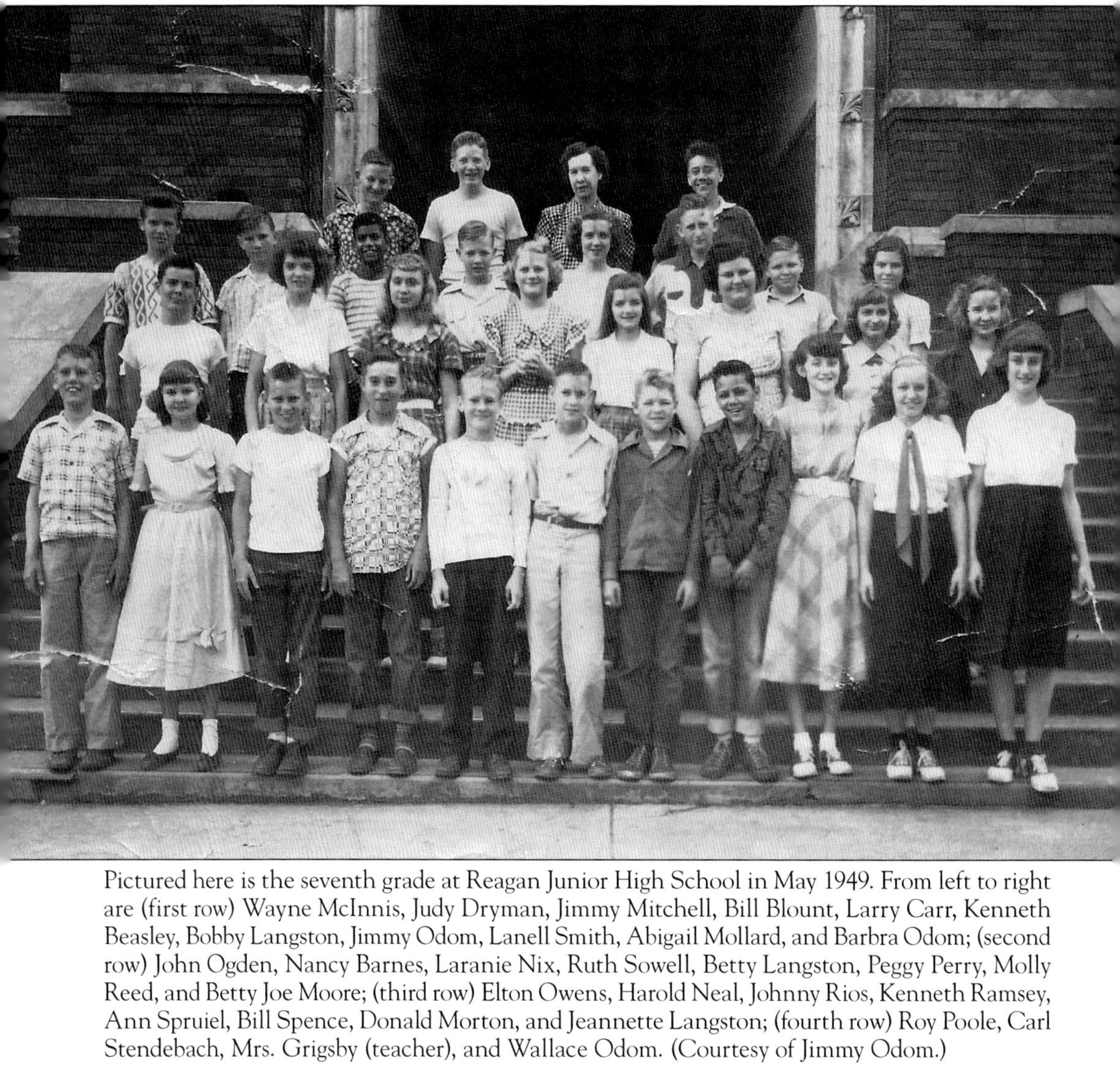

Pictured here is the seventh grade at Reagan Junior High School in May 1949. From left to right are (first row) Wayne McInnis, Judy Dryman, Jimmy Mitchell, Bill Blount, Larry Carr, Kenneth Beasley, Bobby Langston, Jimmy Odom, Lanell Smith, Abigail Mollard, and Barbra Odom; (second row) John Ogden, Nancy Barnes, Laranie Nix, Ruth Sowell, Betty Langston, Peggy Perry, Molly Reed, and Betty Joe Moore; (third row) Elton Owens, Harold Neal, Johnny Rios, Kenneth Ramsey, Ann Spruiel, Bill Spence, Donald Morton, and Jeannette Langston; (fourth row) Roy Poole, Carl Stendebach, Mrs. Grigsby (teacher), and Wallace Odom. (Courtesy of Jimmy Odom.)

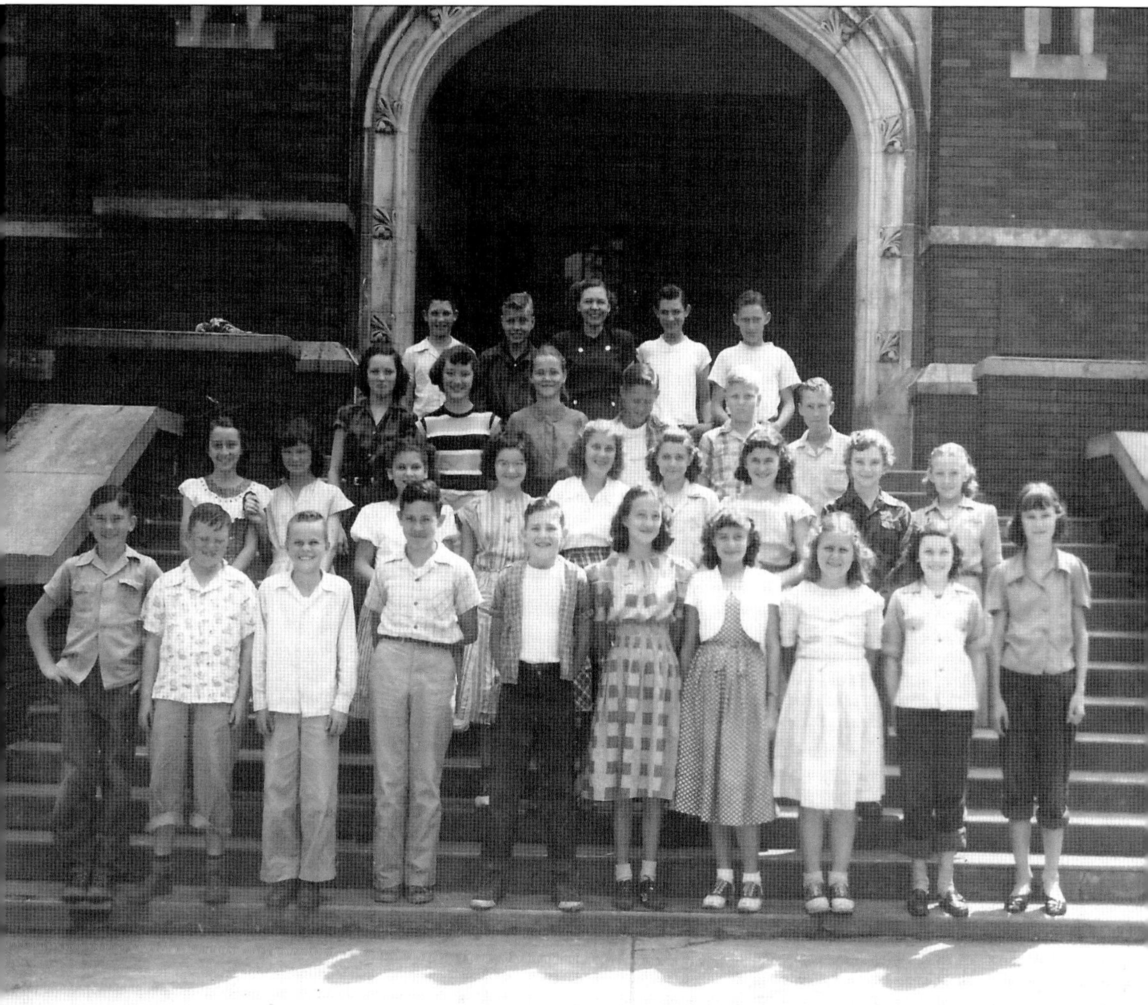

Pictured here is the sixth grade at Reagan Junior High School in 1949. From left to right are (first row) Charlie Rogers, Joe Ross, Lloyd Linthicum, C. E. Owen, Cecil Tumlin, Mary Helen Westmoreland, Marcilee Wilkinson, Billie Vineyard, Frances Bailey, and Marion Thomas; (second row) Greta Walston, Patsy Powell, Vanoy Langston, Mary Walker, Myrtis Sharbutt, Frances Myers, Kathryn Moore, Shirley Harris, and unidentified; (third row) Jane Ann Rogers, Barbara Lafitte, Annie Laura Cross, Alfred Weir, Rodney Wall, and J. D. Crum; (fourth row) Thomas Reed, Bill Keeling, Pauline Bunton (teacher), Ray Smith, and Glen Woods. (Courtesy of Kathy Moore Odom.)

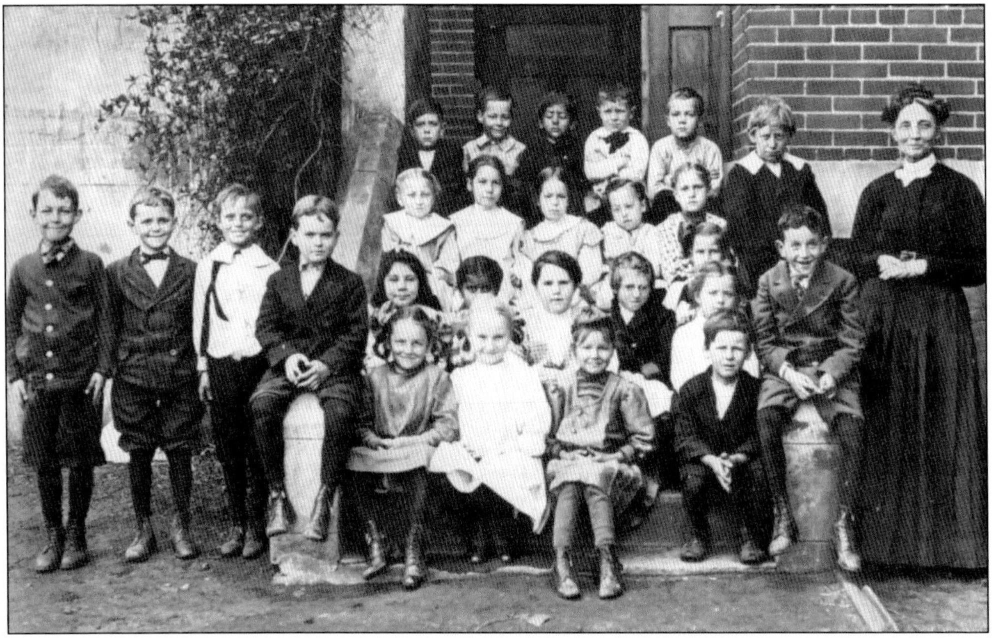

These are the first-grade students of the Third Ward School and their teacher, Sue DeVaney, in 1909. The Third Ward School was later replaced by Lamar Elementary School.

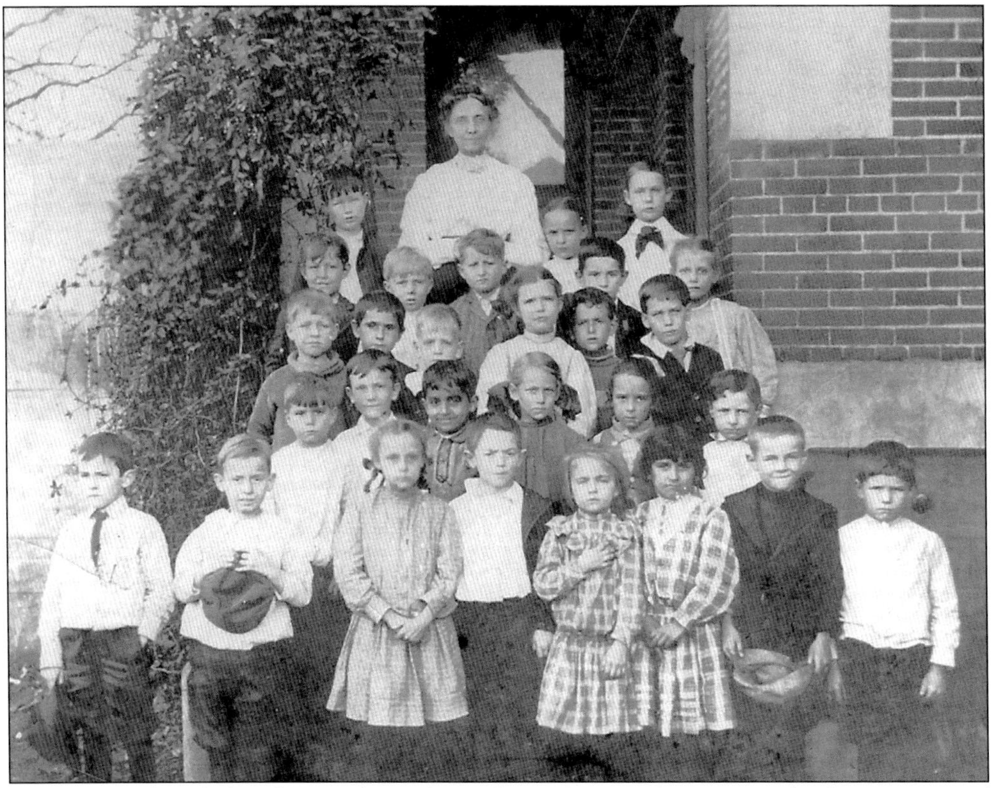

These are unidentified students and a teacher in front of Lamar Elementary School. Lamar opened in 1912 on Brazos Street.

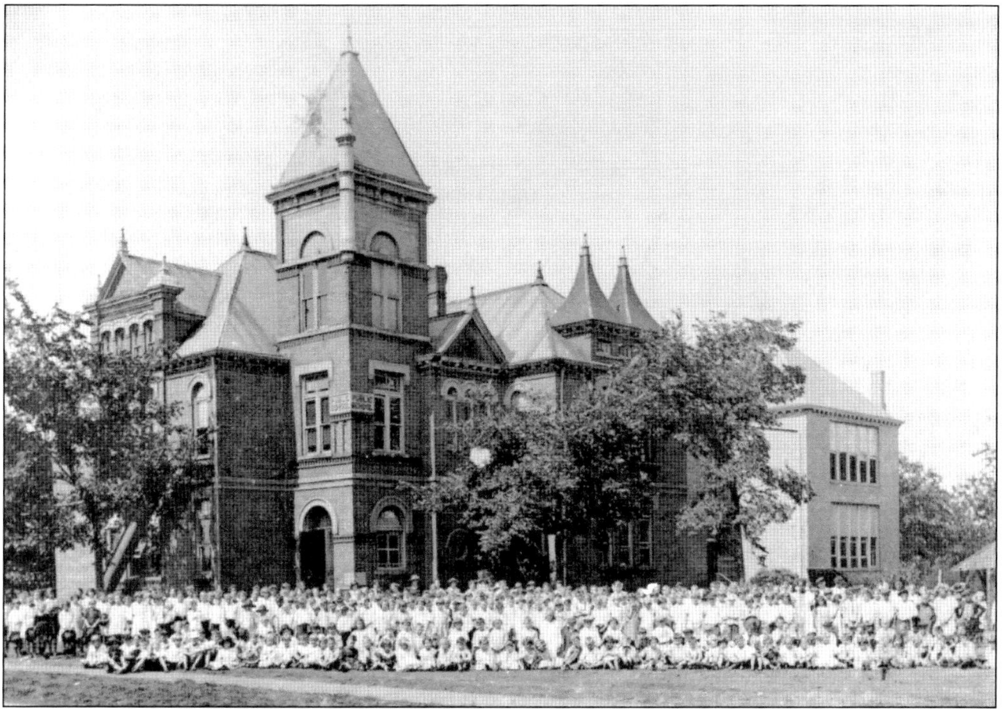

The Second Ward School was built in 1897 on what is now Palestine Avenue. The photograph with the student body posed in front of the school was taken between 1921 and 1923. Pauline Hunter was principal of the school. These are believed to be most of the students in Palestine Public Schools at that time. In 1938, the new building, renamed Thomas J. Rusk Elementary School, replaced the former Second Ward School. The new school is still there, but it is no longer used for classes. The photograph below is of the Rusk School rhythm band.

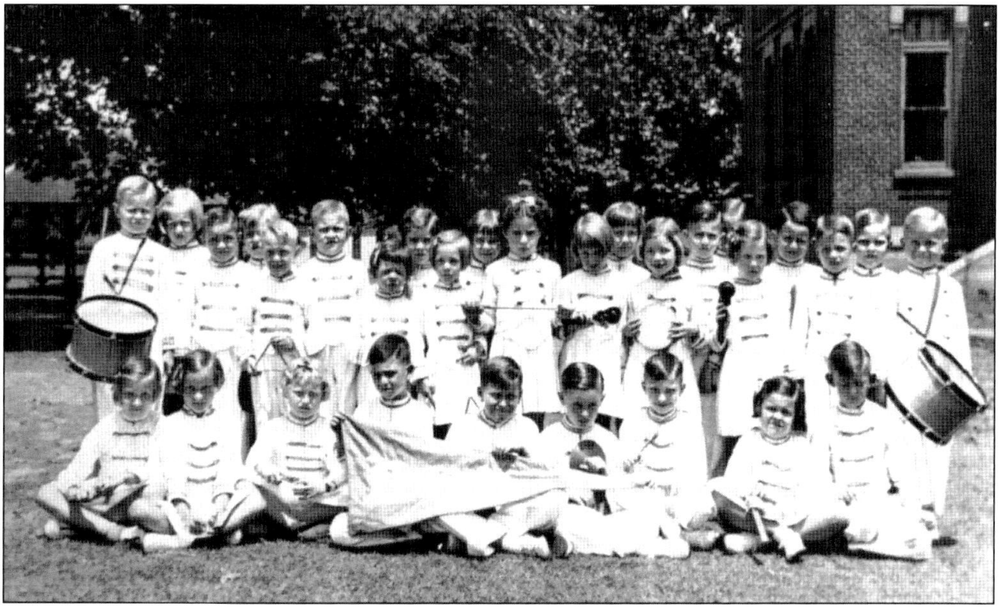

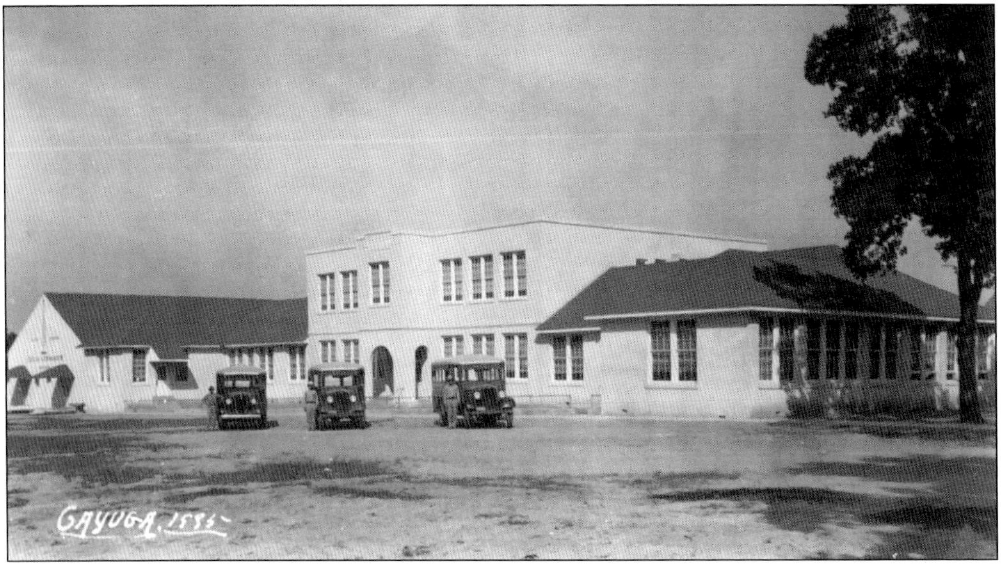

In 1923, Cayuga School was built on the site of the present-day Judson Church. The one-story brick building was enlarged to two stories in 1925. A gymnasium was added in 1935. The new gymnasium is on the left in this photograph taken in 1935. This school burned and was rebuilt in 1936. In 1970, that school was demolished after the construction of current school. (Courtesy of CA.)

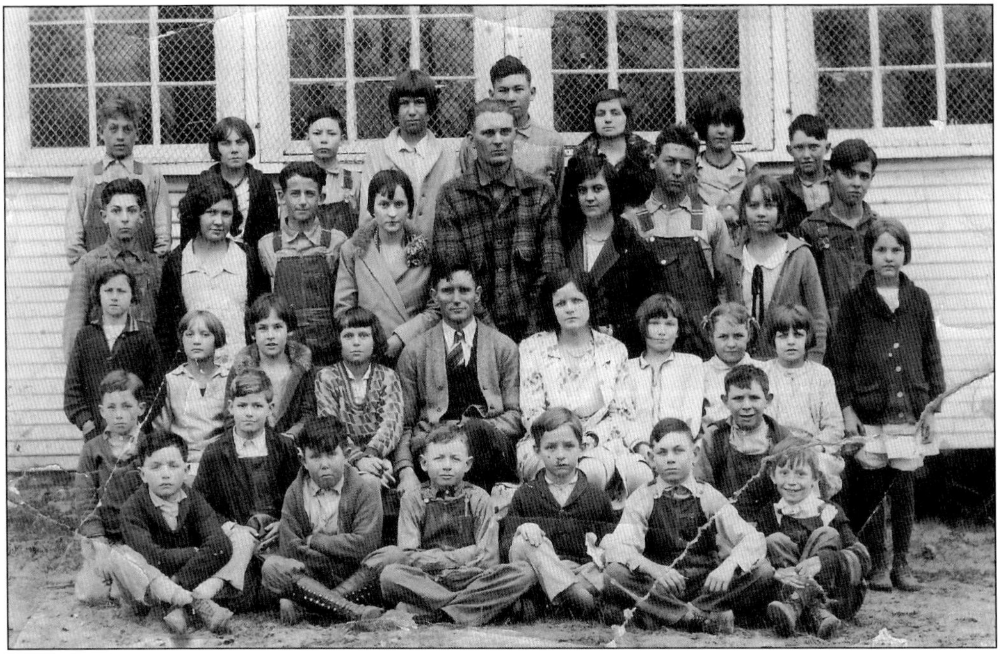

The Ward School was located south of Farm Road No. 2330 on County Road No. 2419. It eventually consolidated with Blackfoot and Springfield and became known as WBS (Ward Blackfoot Springfield). A later consolidation with Tennessee Colony became known as Stafford Springs. This photograph was taken 1927–1928 and includes the following students: Frankie Henry, Ed Hogg, Charlie Gilbert, Mary Gilbert, Albert Shitosky, Georgia Shitosky, Fay Gage, Audrey Ward, L.E. Mannis, Ray Gage, and Chester Brown. Teacher Alton Price is also pictured.

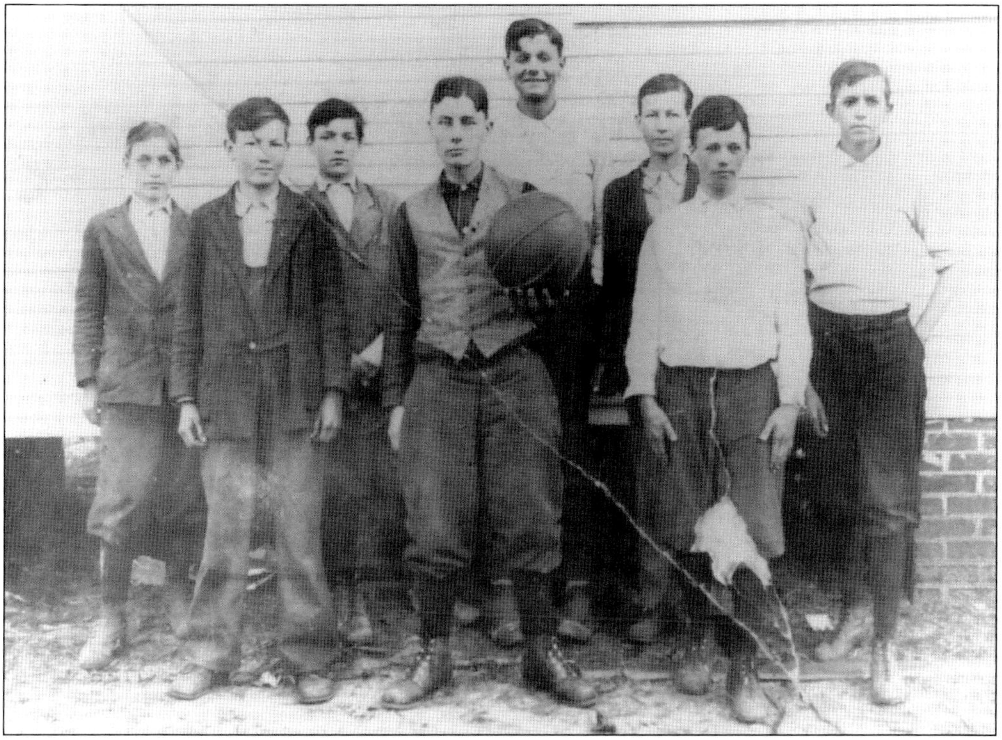

These photographs were taken about 1917 at Watts School on what is now Anderson County Road No. 397 off of U.S. Highway 84 east near Fields Chapel. The basketball team includes, from left to right, Chub Hassell, Calvis Killion, Frank Denning, Seals Odom (holding ball), Adam Killion, unidentified, Arvie Odom, and Floyd Hassell. Not all of the students in the second picture are identified. Some of the students are Susie Langston, Irene Main, Edith Main, Lottie Main, Cora Mae Main, Odie (O. B.) Langston, William Seals Odom, Arvie J. Odom, Douglas Odom, Nora Odom, Floyd Hassell, Adam Killon, Allen Lasiter, Julius (Dude) Odom, Elsie Worley Young, Lude Lasiter, Seldon Lasiter, Alvin Main, and Floyd Hassell. (Both, courtesy of Jimmy Odom.)

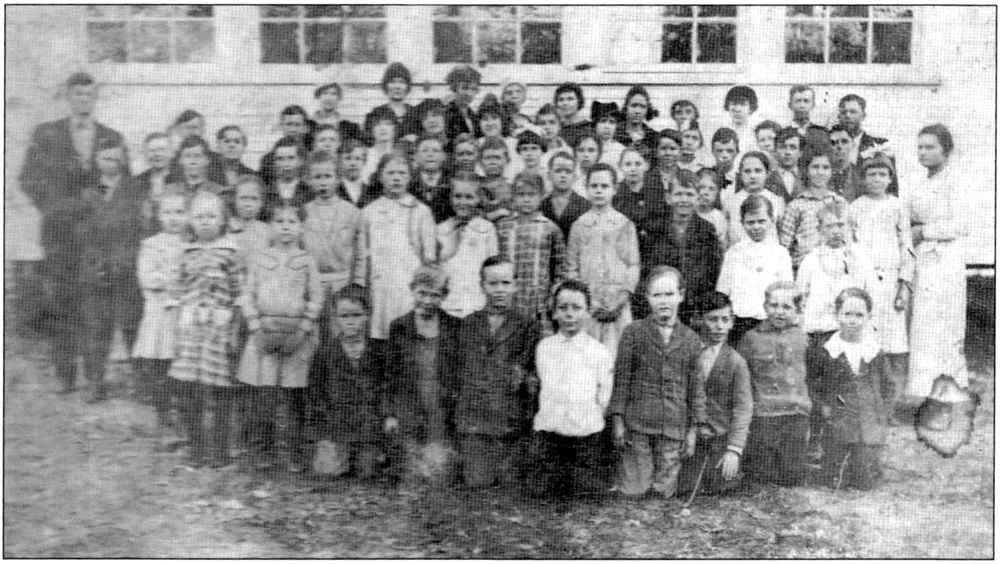

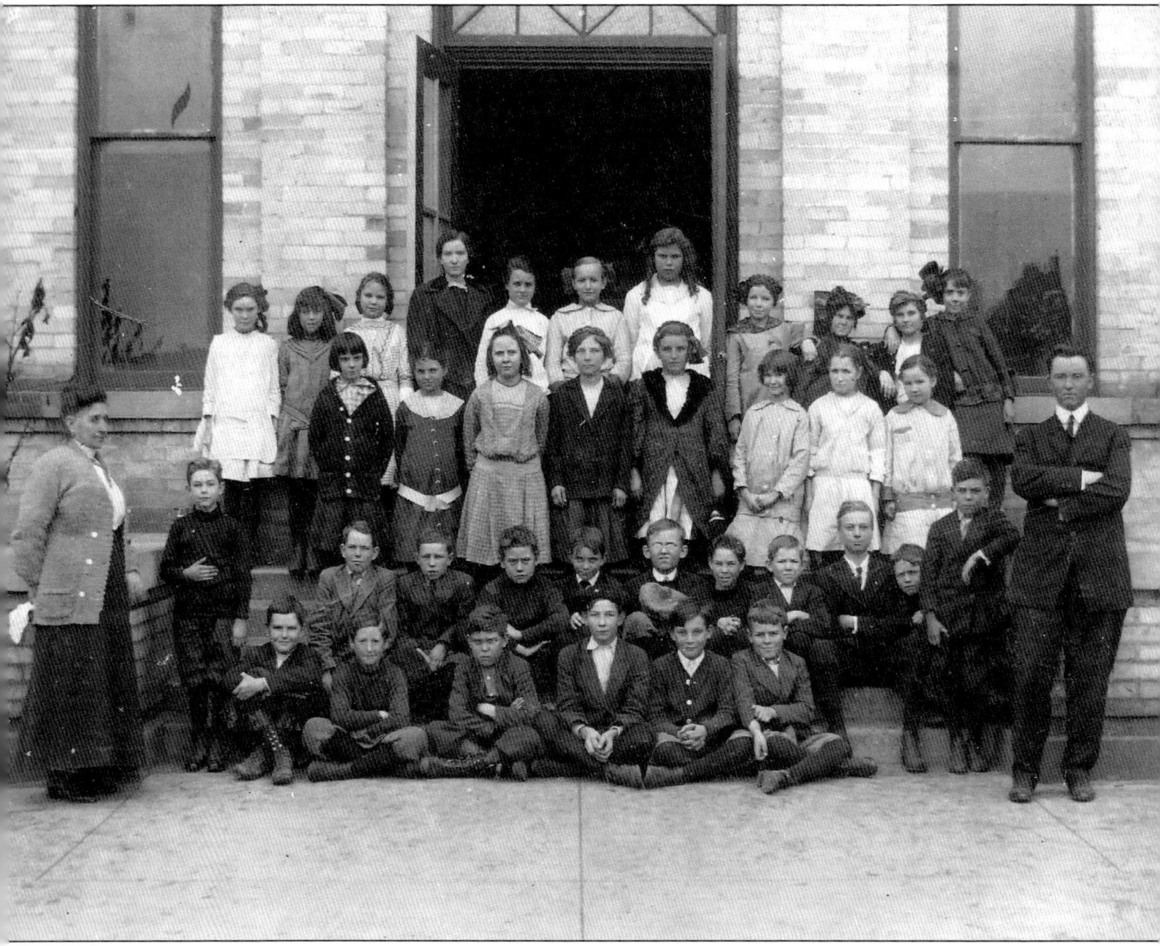

These are students and teachers in front of Alamo School shortly after it opened in 1912 on Cedar Street.

Seven

Life in Anderson County

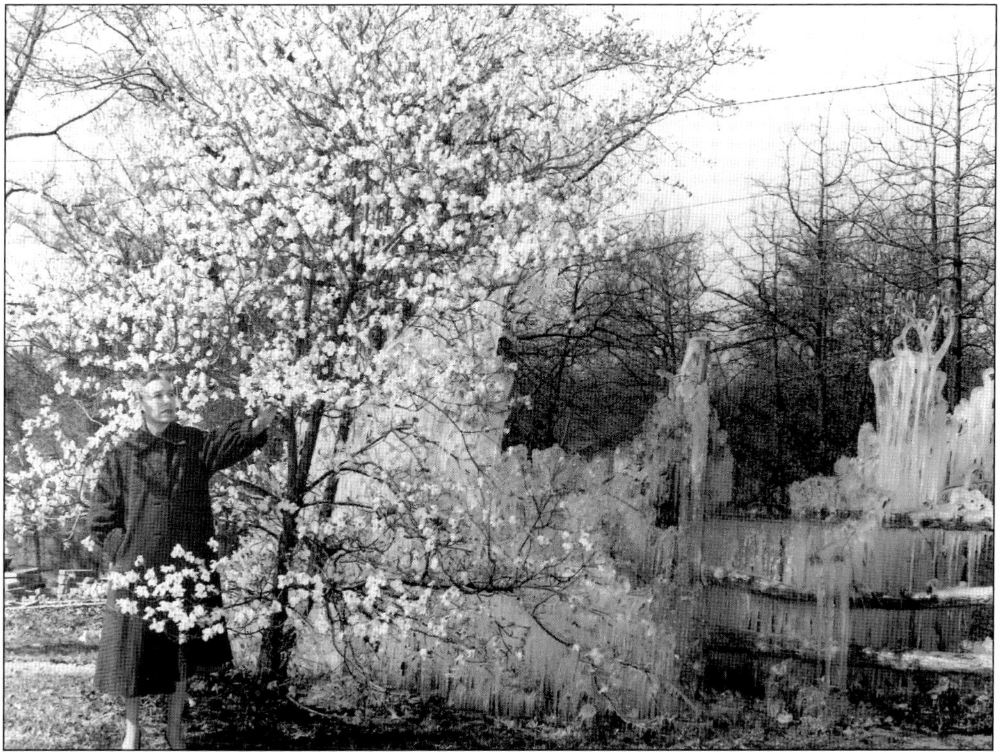

There is an old saying, "Nothing is normal about the weather in Texas." This photograph proves that statement is definitely true in Anderson County, where spring weather is very unpredictable. The year this picture was taken, the dogwoods were in their full glory when a late freeze produced a wonderland of ice and blooms.

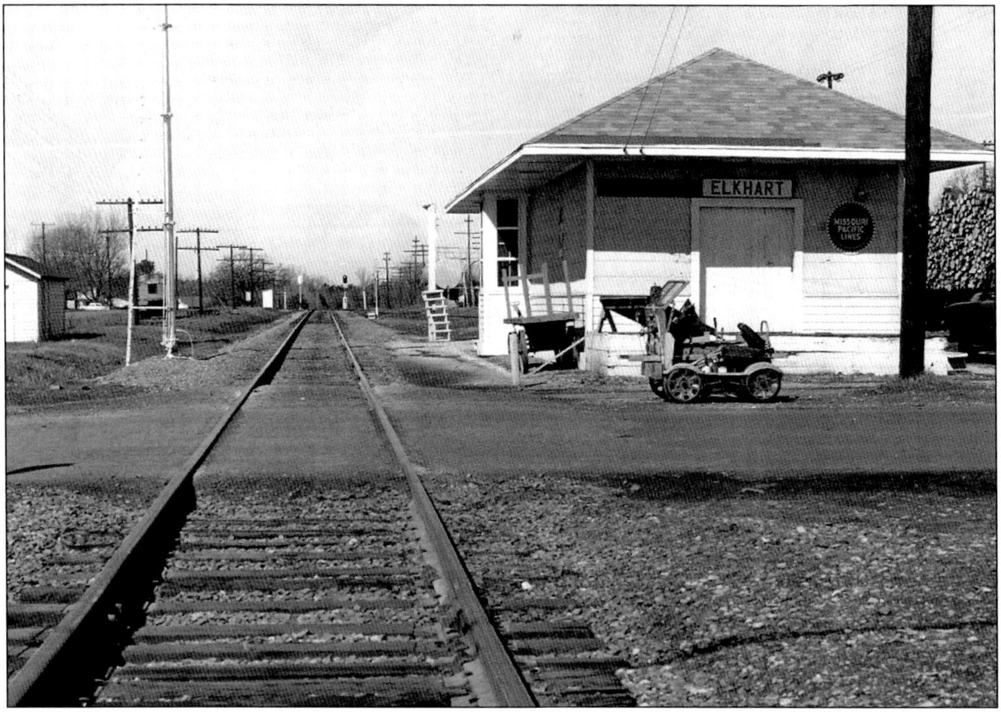

This photograph shows the Elkhart depot as seen in 1955 when the Missouri-Pacific Railroad was in operation. (Courtesy of Karren Jones.)

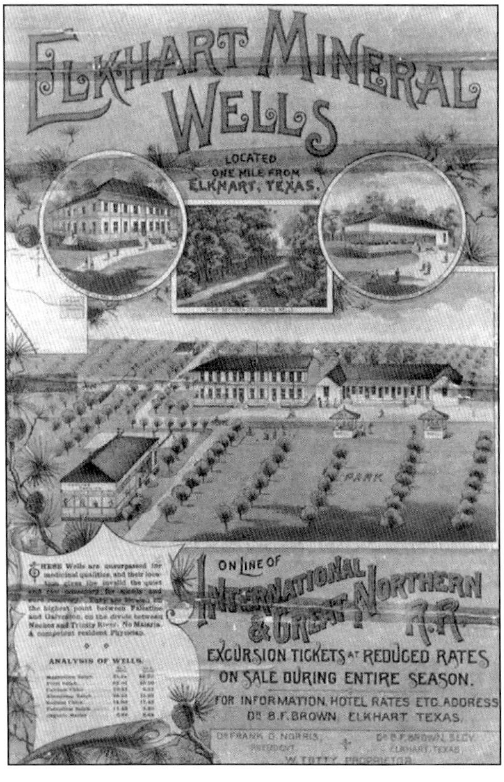

According to this poster published by the I&GN Railroad for the Elkhart Mineral Wells, the resort was located 1 mile east of Elkhart. "These wells are unsurpassed for their medicinal qualities, and their location gives the invalid the quiet and rest necessary for speedy and sure recovery. They are located on the highest point between Palestine and Galveston, on the divide between Neches and Trinity Rivers. No Malaria. A competent resident physician." The resort included a hotel, a dance pavilion, a billiard hall, a bathhouse, several wells, a croquet court, and a park. Another source says one of the wells was 8 feet square and 100 feet deep. In the 1880s, the resort attracted visitors from throughout Texas, as well as other states. However, an article published in the *Palestine Daily Visitor* on August 5, 1902, asked what had become of the Elkhart Mineral Wells. The article suggested the resort would attract visitors from abroad if it were well equipped and properly managed. Apparently it was never revived, and one source says the hotel was torn down around 1910. (Courtesy of CA.)

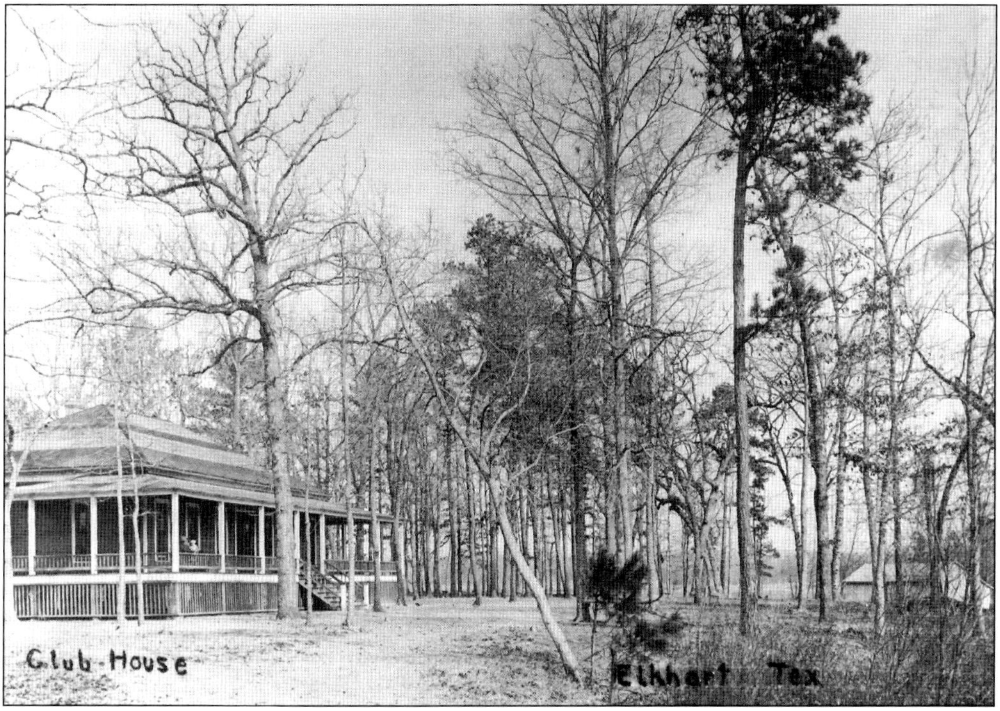

The Pine Lodge Club House, located 1.6 miles east of Elkhart, was built in 1907 by a group of Palestine business leaders after the wells at the nearby Elkhart Mineral Wells resort failed. The building committee consisted of Dr. J. H. Grant, Judge Ned Morris, and W. B. Flanagan. The old Elkhart depot that had previously been moved to Palestine was moved again to the Pine Lodge Club as a residence. Today Pine Lodge Club is more commonly called Elkhart Lake. Pictured below, two ladies and a gentleman are seen boating on the lake at the Pine Lodge. (Both, courtesy of METC.)

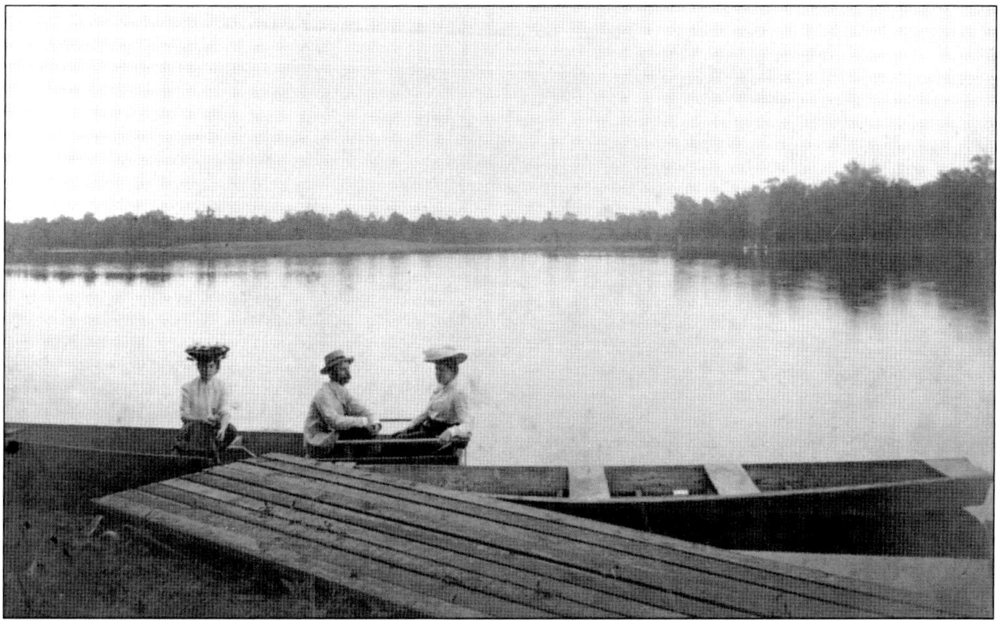

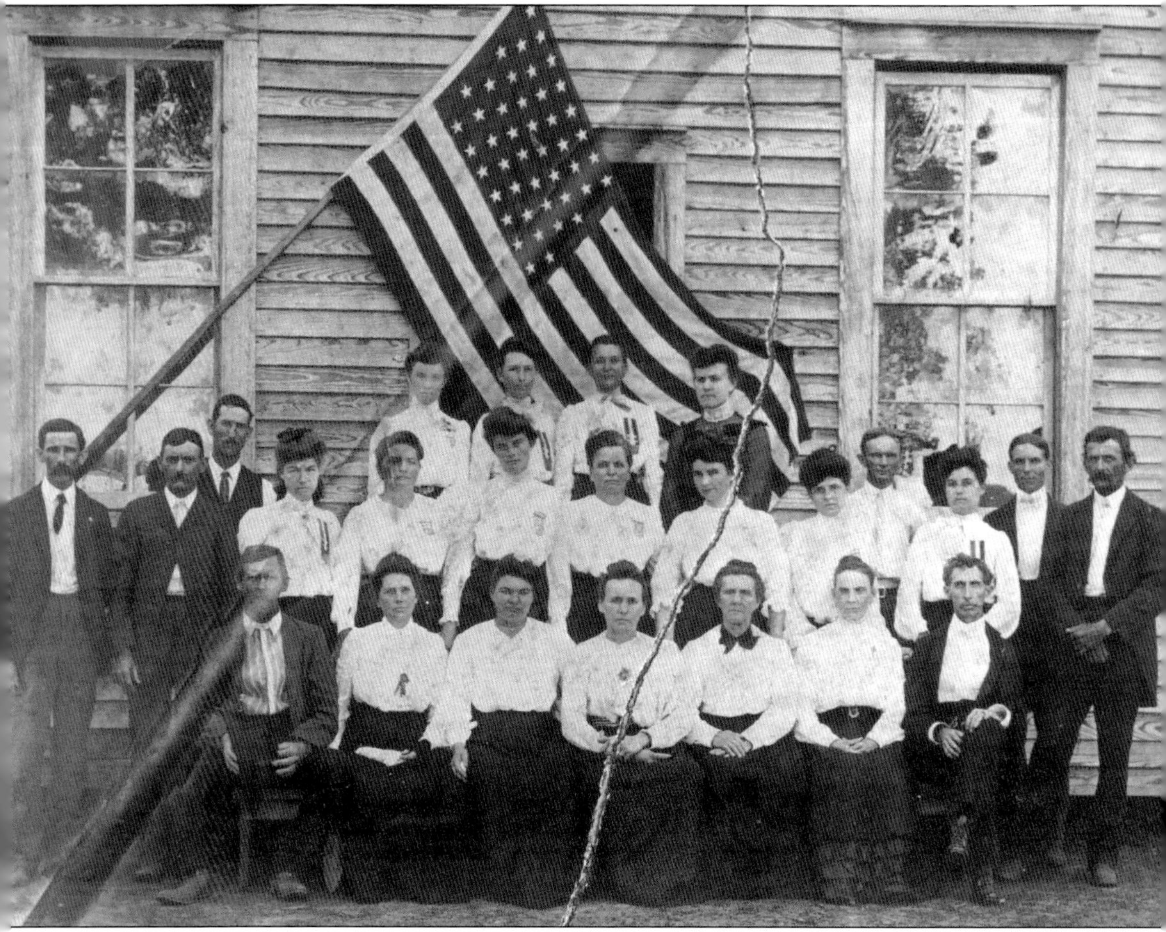

This photograph shows the Woodmen Circle in Elkhart, taken around 1906. Among those pictured are Charlie Sheridan, Lula May Sheridan, Emma Daile Hawthorne, Mrs. Quarles, Mrs. Will Neel, Will Neel, Albert Douthit, Will Hawthorne, Eddie Bernice Watkins, Josephine Horn, Nancy Jane Douthit, Cora Wright, Pharibee Stubblefield, Gene Kennedy, ? Driskell, Betty Douthit, Mrs. Stevens, Leo Docia Watkins, and Hope Cromwell. (Courtesy of CA.)

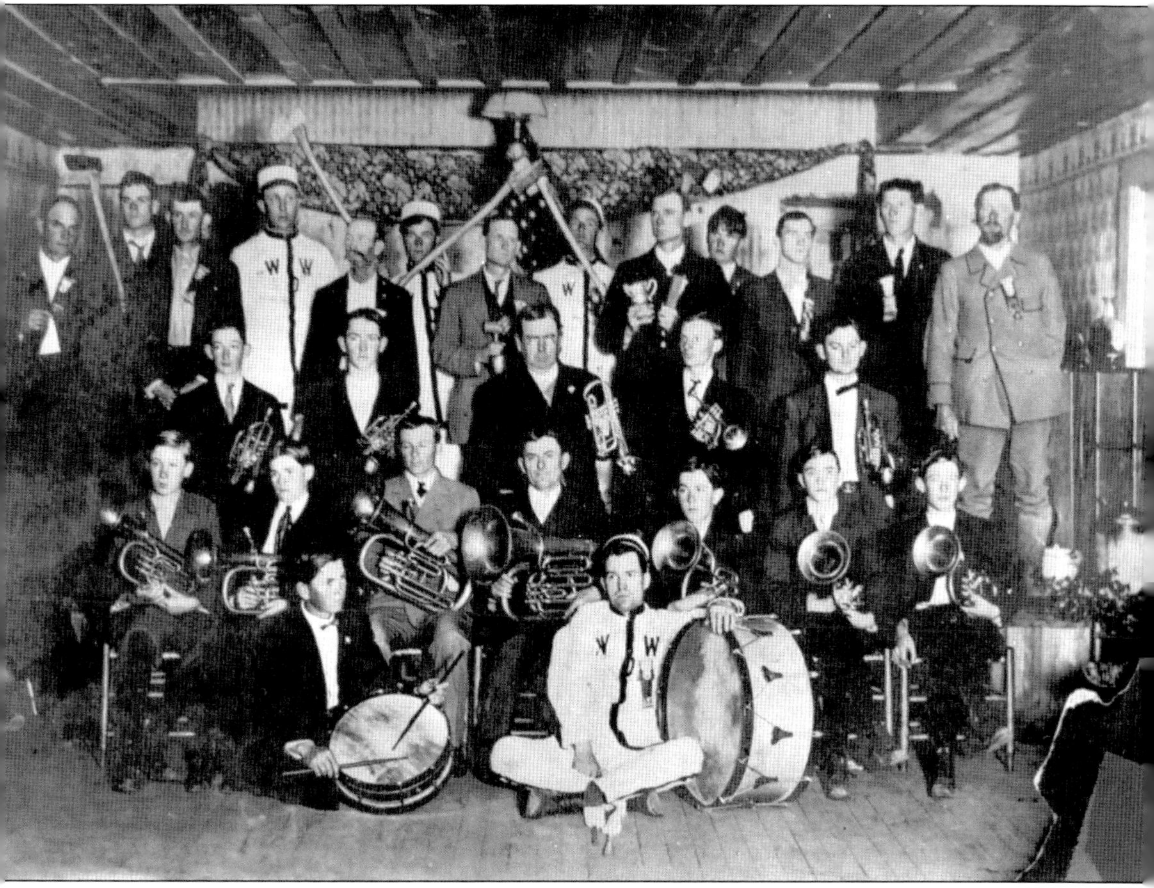

This photograph shows the Elkhart Woodmen of the World band, taken around 1906. Pictured are, from left to right, (first row) Elmo Whitley and an unidentified drummer; (second row) Milton Weatherford, unidentified, Webb Tyler, Albert Douthit, Joe Stokes Paxton, Roy Hawthorne, and unidentified; (third row) Charlie Neel, Edwin Paxton, band director Mr. Lorraine, Albert Tyler, and Allie Douthit; (fourth row) Bacon Hemby, Frank Shelton, unidentified, Node Corley, two unidentified, Ben Parker, three unidentified, Charlie Watkins, Will A. Montgomery, and Charlie Sheridan. (Courtesy of CA.)

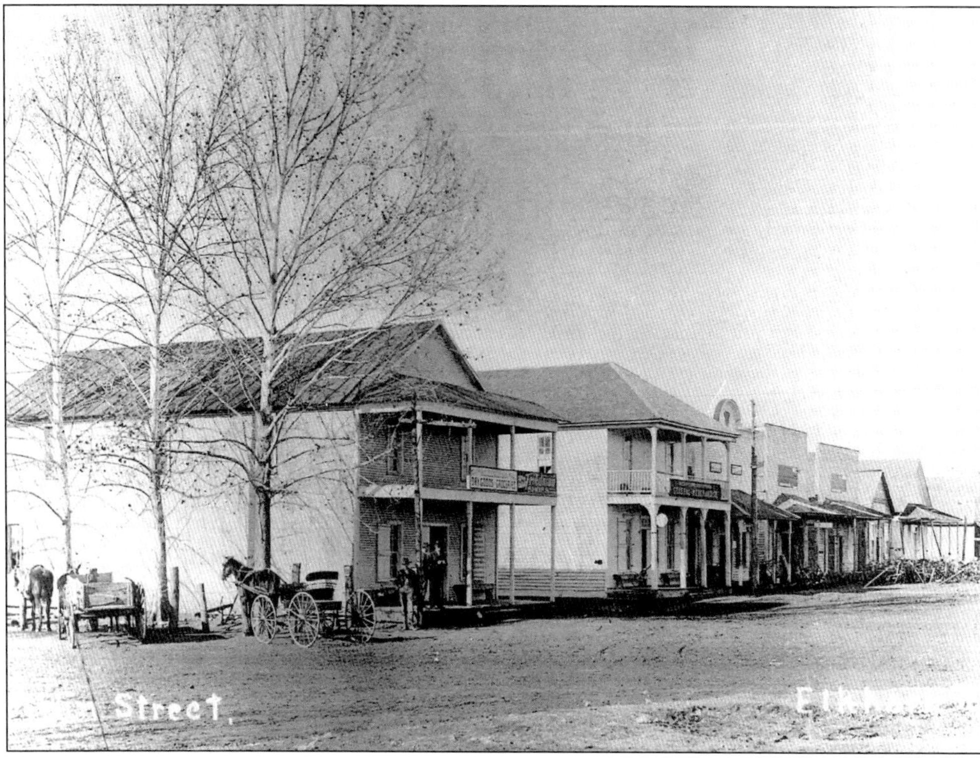

This photograph shows Main Street businesses in Elkhart; seen here are, from left to right, Gad Watkin's Store, which was later occupied by the Guaranty Bank; Dupuy and Weatherford; Neel Drug Store; the post office; vacant; the Burris family's home on the corner; Driskill Grocery; Driskill Barbershop; Allie Douthit, the Woodard House; and another barbershop. (Courtesy of Karren Jones.)

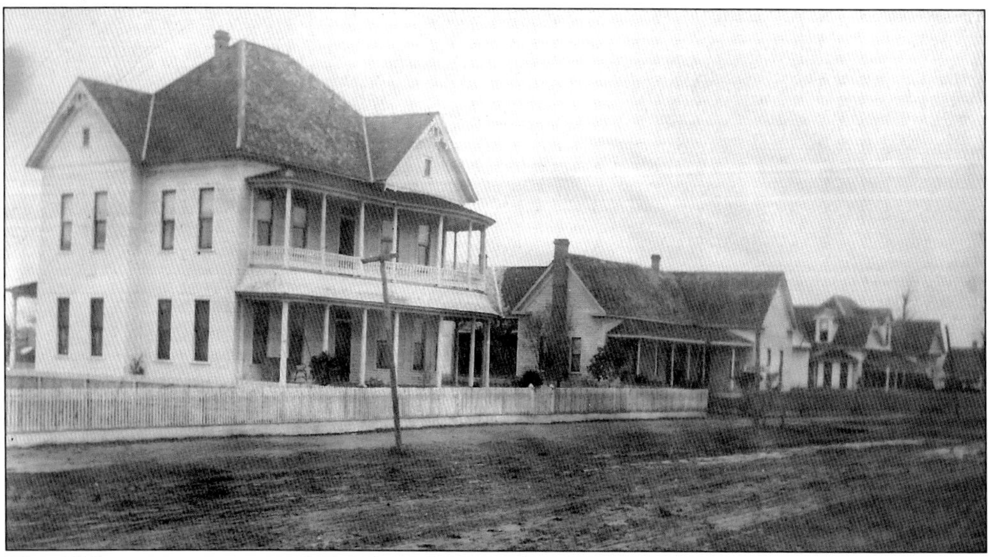

This Elkhart street scene includes three homes. The first is unidentified, the middle house has a sign identifying it as a hotel, and the third is the home of the Will Neel family. (Courtesy of Wilda Page Collection.)

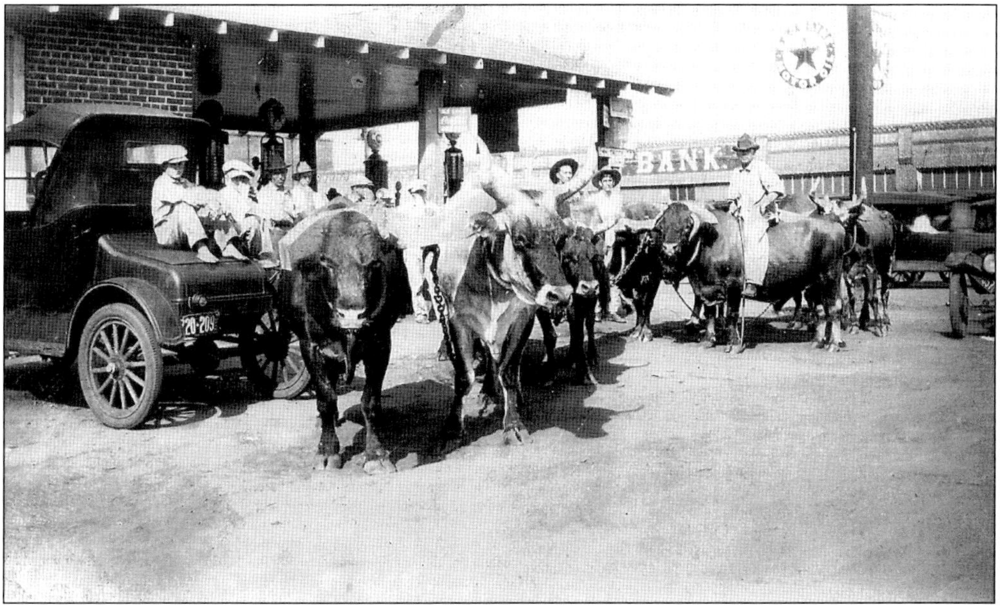

These photographs of cattle being driven through the streets of downtown Elkhart are not dated. In the above picture, Moran's Service Station can be seen in the background. C. J. Moran Sr. operated the station until sometime after 1940. (Both, courtesy of Karren Jones.)

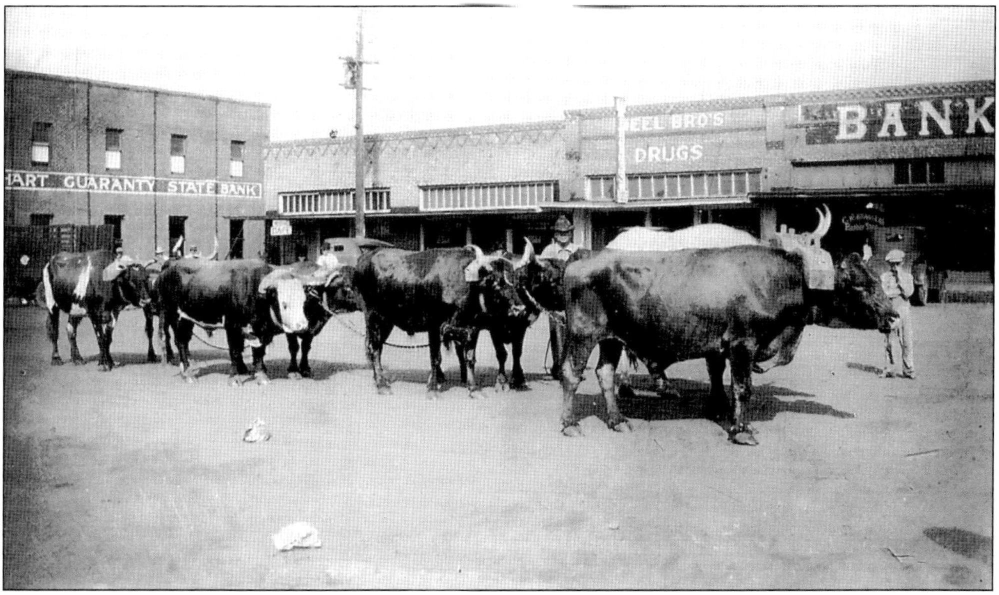

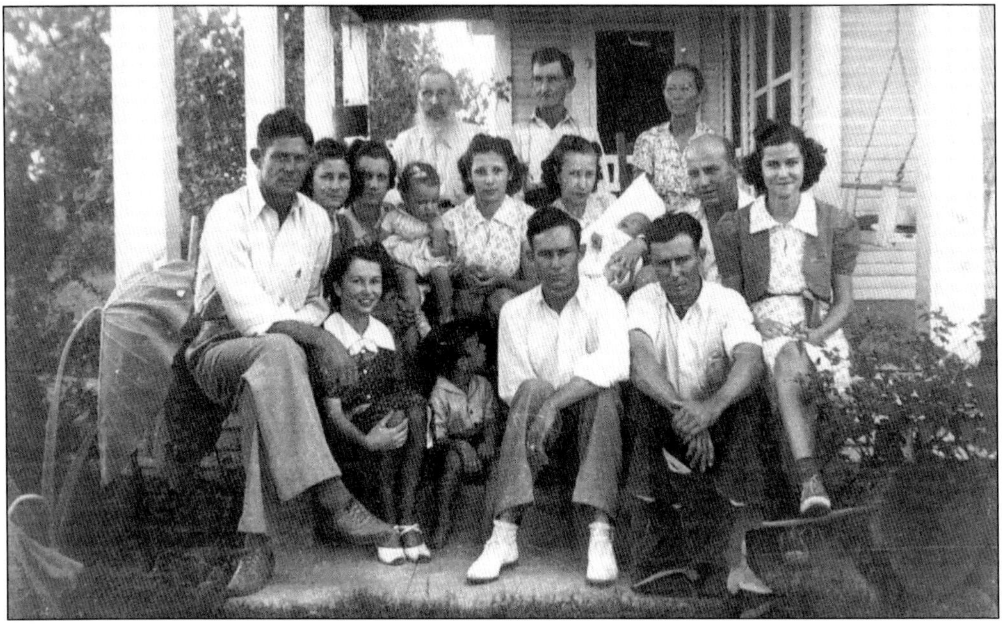

Miles Bennett was a soldier in the Texas Army of Independence. In this picture taken in 1938 in Elkhart are, from left to right, (first row) Elwin, Adelle, Gary, Odell, Eldridge, and Dorris; (second row) Lula, Corene Chapman Bennett and Norma, Doris, Junie Bennett Rosson and Bobby, and Darwin Rosson; (third row) Bennett's son Richard, his grandson William Robert, and William Robert's wife, Iciphenia Kennedy Bennett. (Courtesy of Dan Trigg.)

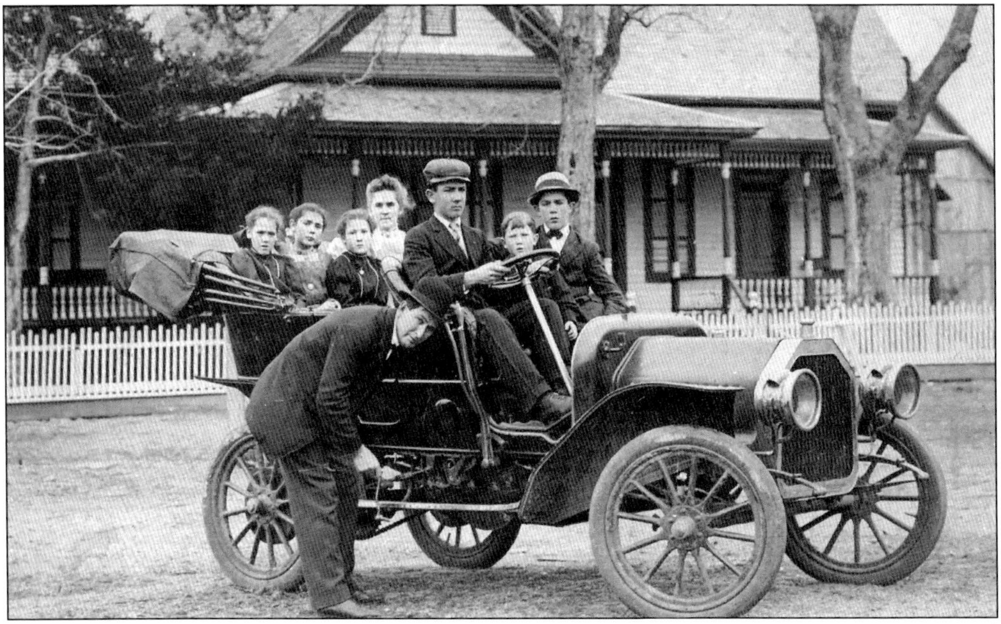

This is the Dr. Joseph Harper Paxton and family in 1910. Dr. Paxton was a pioneer physician and surgeon who moved to Anderson County in 1899 and practiced medicine here for more than 50 years. Pictured in Elkhart's first automobile are, from left to right, his family: Eleanor, Lurlene, Florence, Jennie Keen Paxton, Dr. Paxton at the crank, Edwin, Tom Keen, and Joseph Stokes Paxton. (Courtesy of CA.)

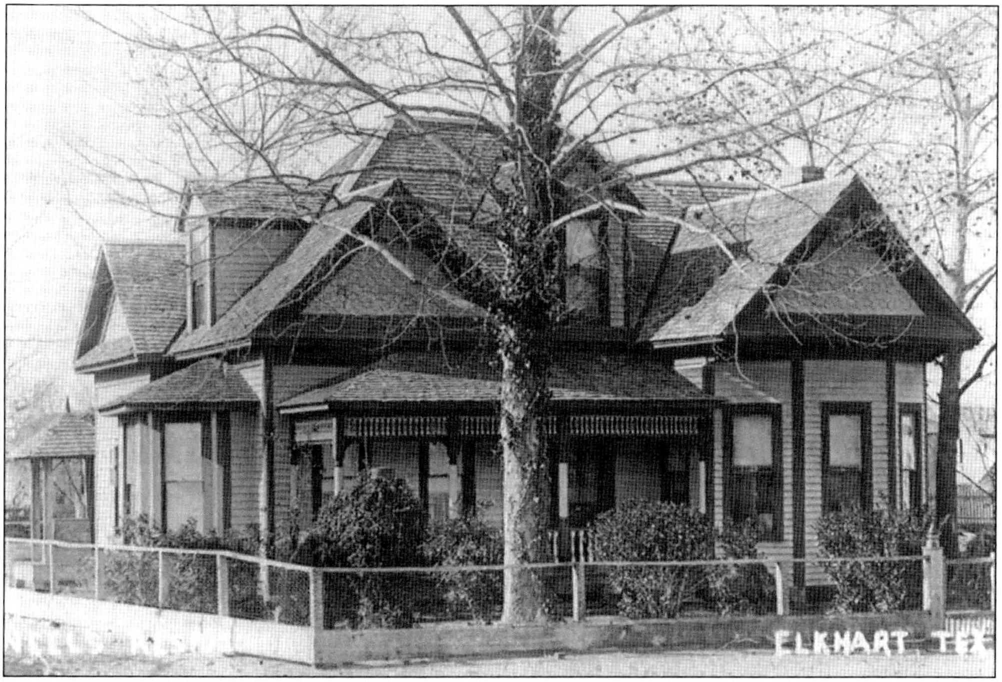

This is a postcard photograph of Will Neel's home in 1908. Neel owned and operated a drugstore in Elkhart for many years. (Courtesy of CA.)

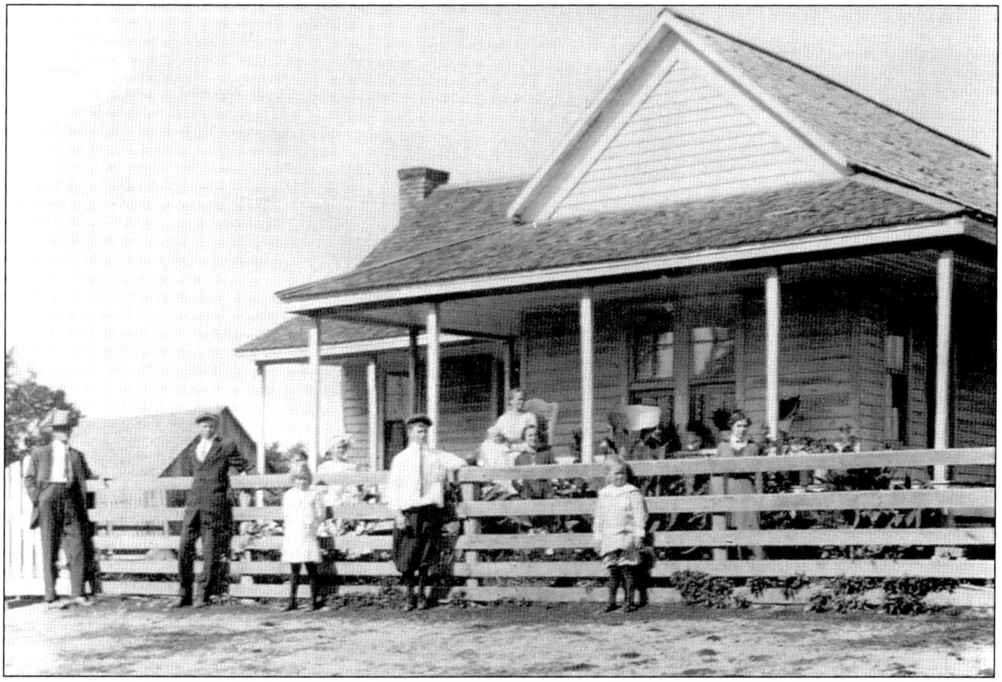

This picture includes the family and home of Ben J. and Docia Permelia Kennedy Parker. From left to right are (first row) Ben J. Parker, Ross Parker, Lorene Parker, Joe Bailey Parker, and Jack Parker; (second row) Charm Parker, Docia Parker (seated, holding Dale Parker), Estelle Parker, and Lucinda Ellen "Lula" Parker. (Courtesy of CA.)

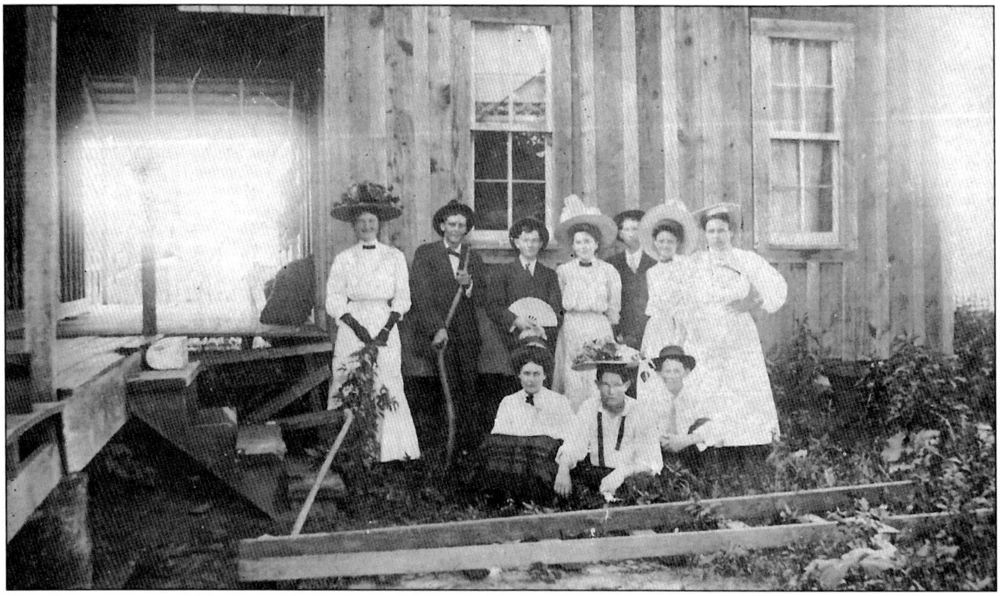

This was taken in 1906 in Elkhart. From left to right are (first row) Laura Franks McCracken with husband Cody McCracken and Boy Kennedy; (second row) Dora McCracken Irby, Check Wilson, Wesley McCracken, Hazel Quarles Gammage, Austin McCracken, Emma Bennett Taylor, and Ula Quarles Whitley. (Courtesy of Wilda Page Collection.)

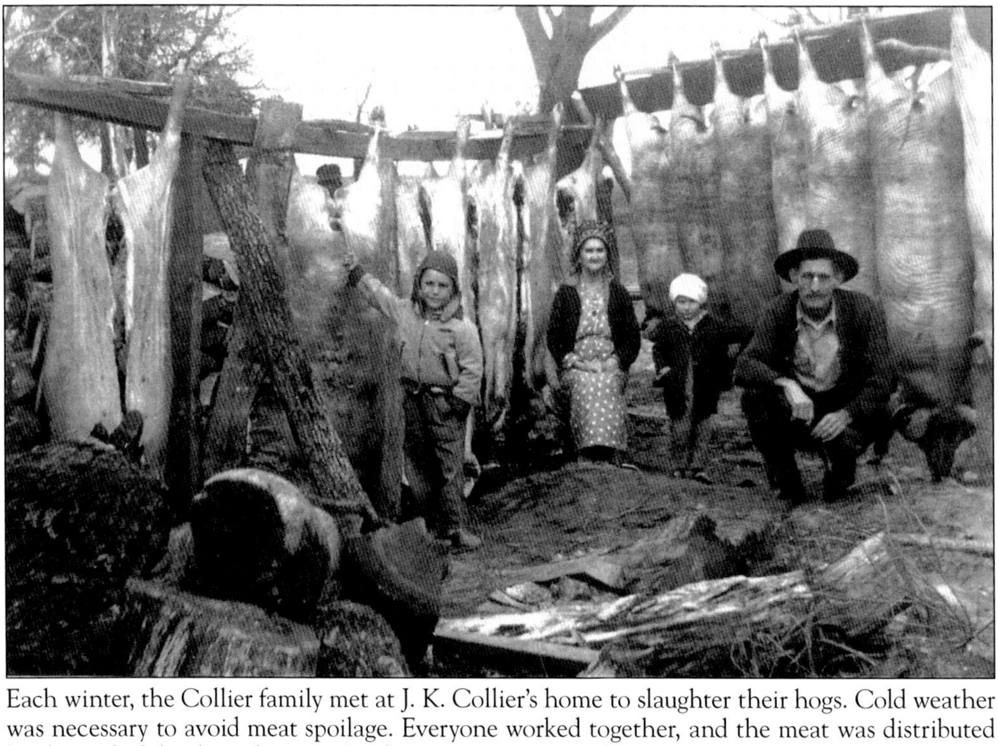

Each winter, the Collier family met at J. K. Collier's home to slaughter their hogs. Cold weather was necessary to avoid meat spoilage. Everyone worked together, and the meat was distributed by the end of the day. This was 5 miles out on Farm Road No. 1990. From left to right are Ben Graves, Mittie Collier, Mary Ann Collier, and J. K. Collier. The photograph was taken in the winter of 1938–1939. (Courtesy of Louise Spaith)

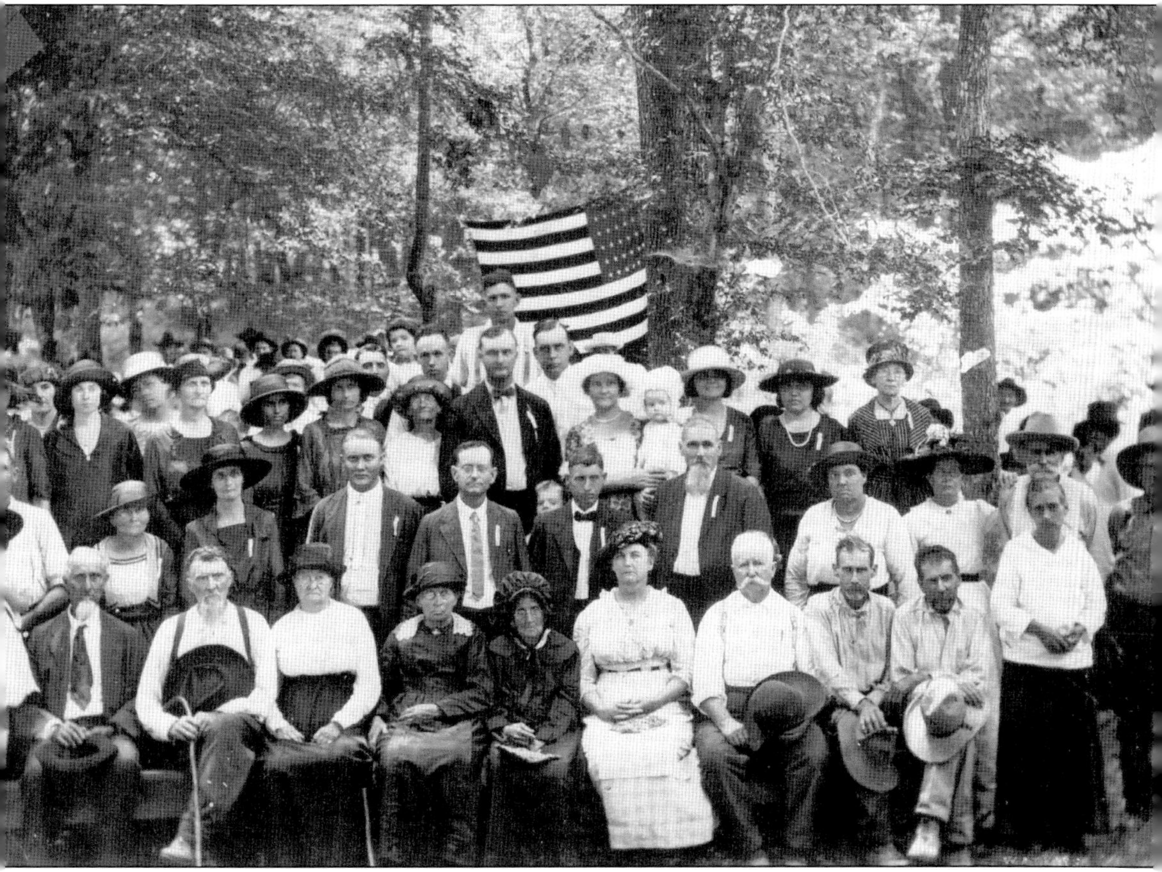

This is the Parker family reunion at Pilgrim Cemetery in 1923. Among those pictured are J. J. Brooks, Daniel Parker, Becky Brooks, Cynthia Parker, Laura Bennett, Mrs. Sanders, George Parker, Jessie Parker, Dan "Humphy" Parker, and Jessie Parker; (second row) Irene Bennett, S. J. Bennett, Docia Parker, Mary Parker, Leodis Brooks, Ben Parker, Kelly Woodard, Miles Parker, John H. Starr, Mrs. George Parker, Susie Hendricks, Ben Hendricks, and J. L. "Bud" Kennedy; (third row) Ona Parker, Hattie Parker Gilmore, Nannie Walling, Patsy Parker, Thelma Jane Parker, Rene Bennett, Fagan Parker, Laura Woodard, Martha Parker, Edwina Parker, and Mrs. Tom "Sissy" Davis; (fourth row) Emma Woodard, Lilly Glenn, and Lee Parks. (Courtesy of CA.)

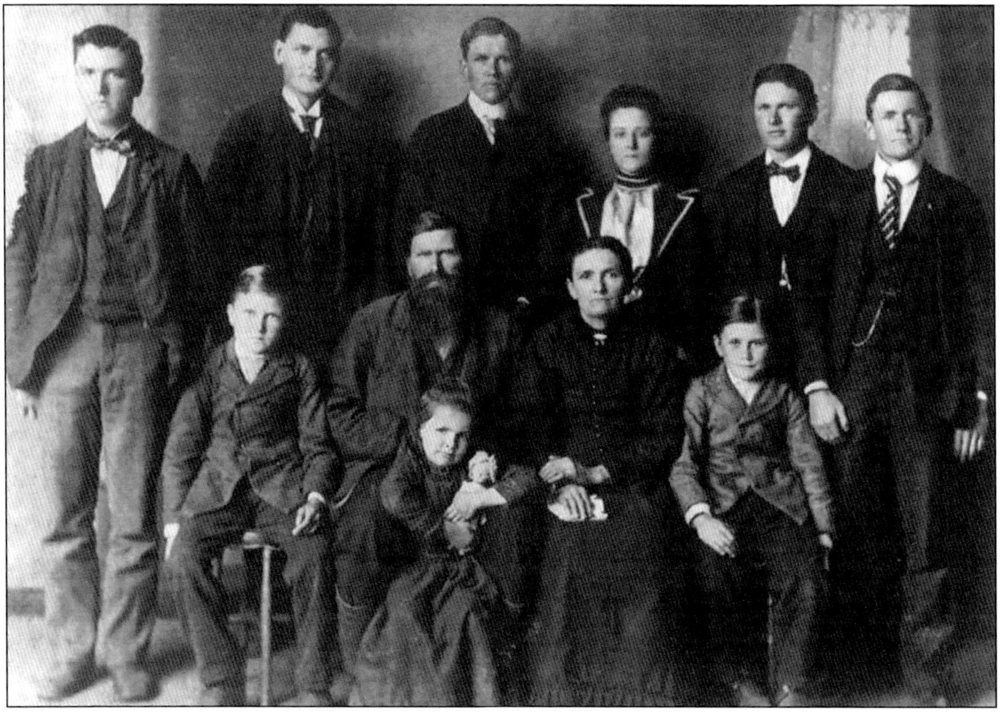

This portrait of the Thomas Jefferson Starr family is dated 1900. From left to right are (seated) Alonzo, Alice, Thomas Jefferson, Sophronia (Mrs. T. J. Starr), and Arthur; (standing) Allen, Alvin, Asa and wife Belle, Ara, and Albert Starr. (Courtesy of METC.)

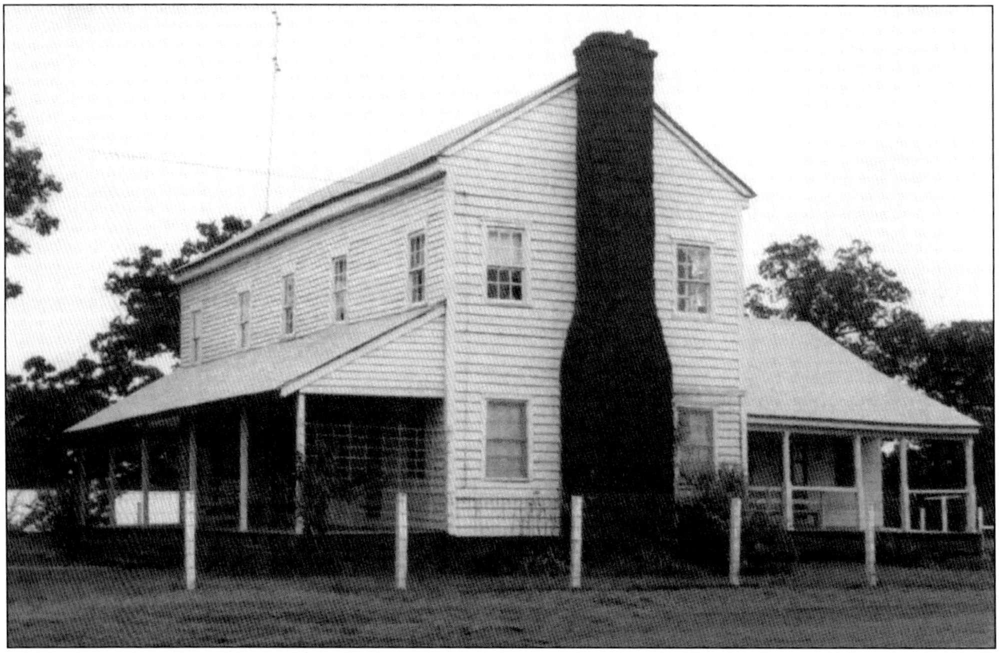

John Starr came to Starr Hill in 1848 on a snowy Christmas Eve. He married Susannah Parker, daughter of John Parker and sister of Elder Daniel Parker. The house of late Greek revival style was built in 1856 and is still owned by Starr descendants. (Courtesy of CA.)

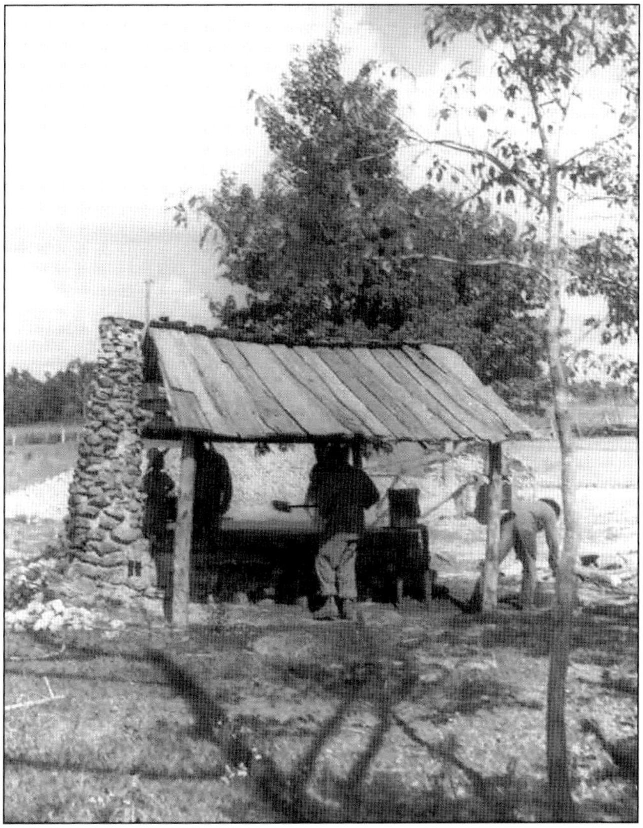

It once was a common practice for each family to make their own syrup. The photograph at right is of a syrup mill that was on the Frankston Highway. The photograph below shows Lester Starr making sorghum syrup in the ancient black kettle at Starr Hill north of Elkhart. (Right, courtesy of CA; below, courtesy of PPL.)

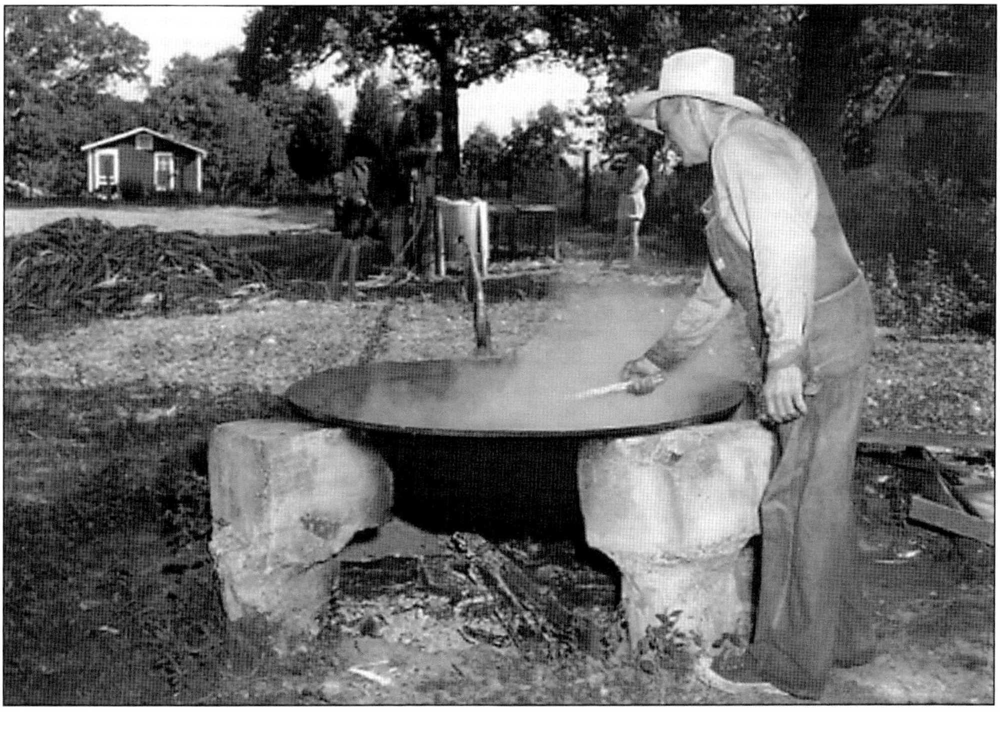

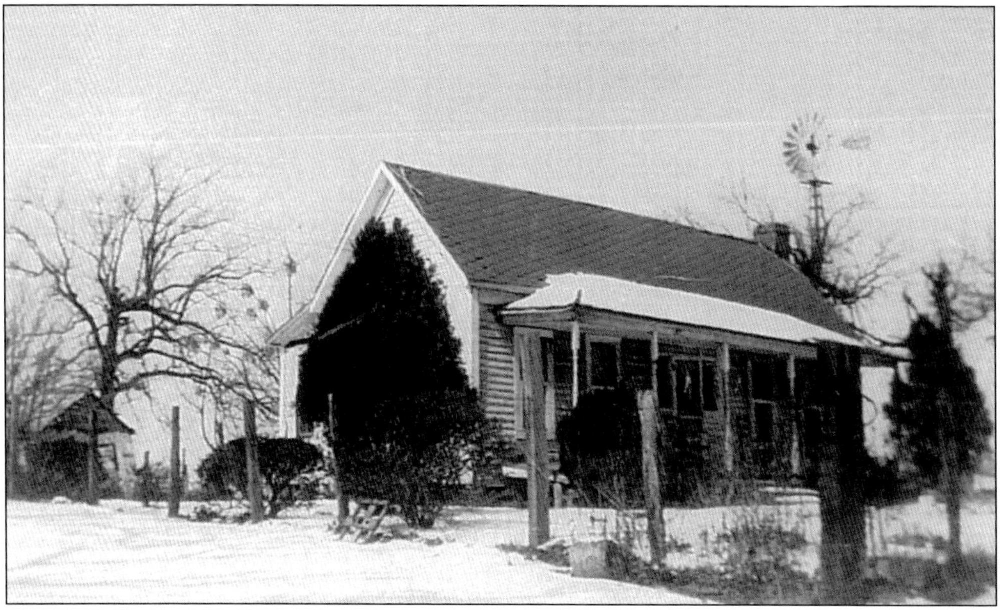

This is the home of S. F. and Cornelia Coleman. It was built in 1910 and located about 13 miles south of the loop off Farm Market Road No. 322 on Anderson County Road No. 127. It was demolished in the 1960s when S. F. Coleman died. The Colemans raised five children who in adulthood all lived within 1.5 miles of this home. It was a working farm of 900 acres. They raised cotton and their water was supplied by a windmill. They received electricity in 1947, but the only thing it electrified was a wind charger to power a radio.

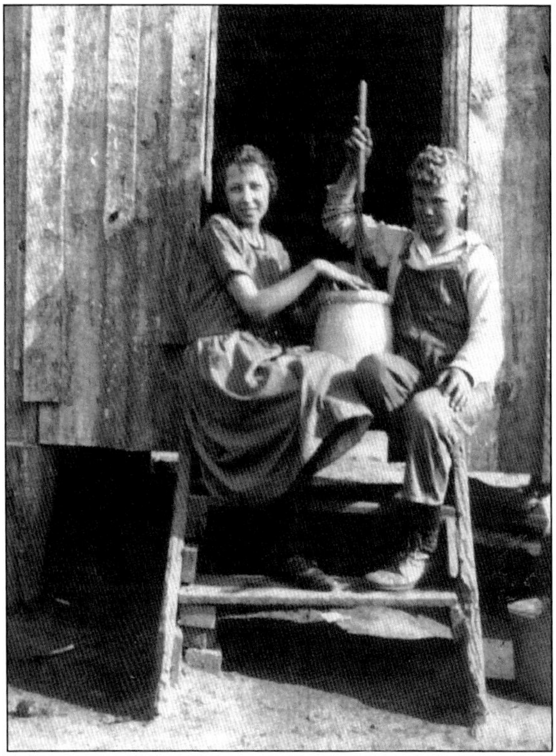

The woman pictured is Etta Coleman Burke. The boy is unidentified but is thought to be a nephew. Burke is doing what most women had to do in that time period: churn butter.

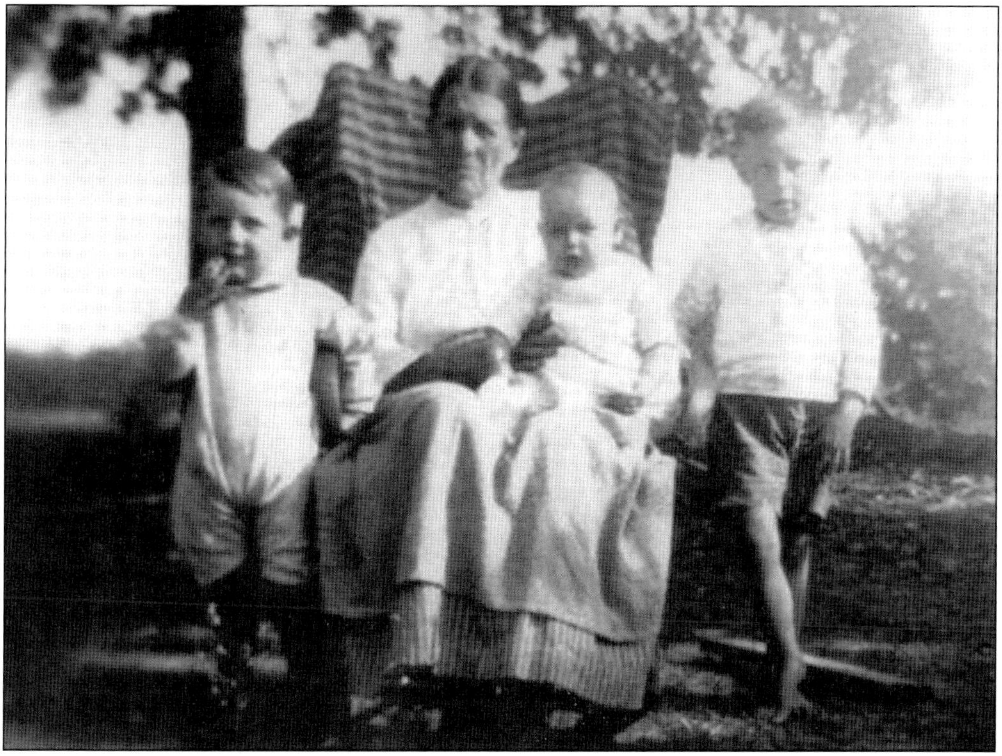

This is Mary Lovenia Pilcher Marsh with her Marsh grandchildren. From left to right are Frank, Mary Lou, and Herman. (Courtesy of Rachel Bailey.)

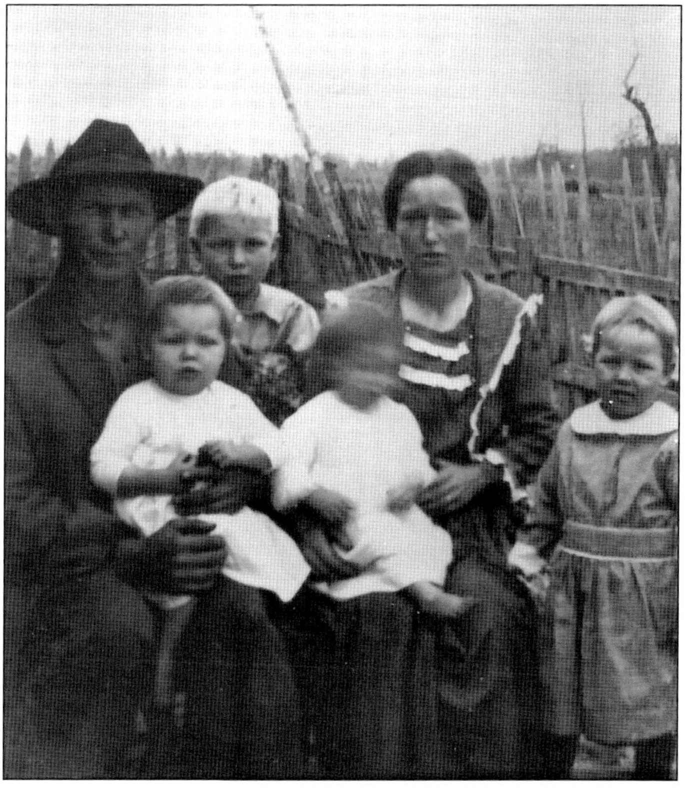

This is the family of Monroe and Livie Kizer, who lived in the Sulphur Springs (also known as Scroughout) area near Elkhart. Monroe is holding Ola and Livie is holding Oda. Their son, Doug, is standing between his parents, and their daughter Velma is standing on the right beside her mother. (Courtesy of Rachel Bailey.)

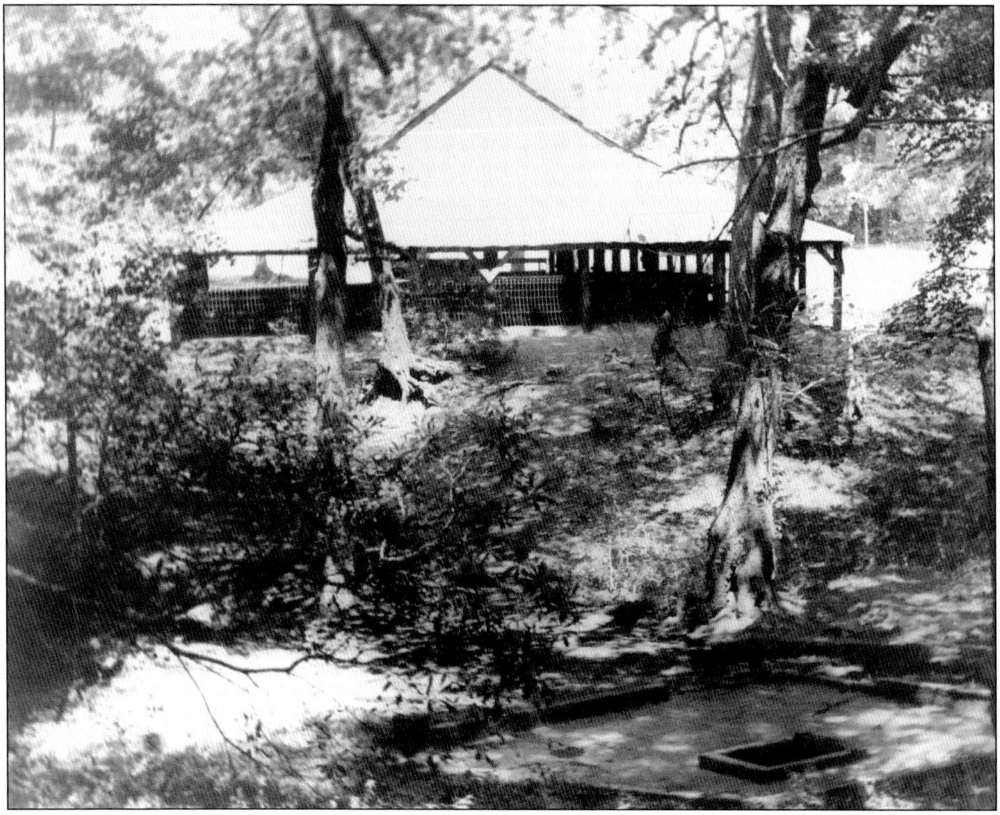

On July 9 and 10, 1859, the first recorded revival was held at what today is known as Brushy Creek. The camp was located adjacent to a natural artesian spring and near Brushy Creek. At that time, it was called Paines Chapel. On September 8, 1871, the records show the name had changed to Camp Ground. It was also called Anderson County Camp Ground. The original arbor was built in 1874. In 1893, the name was changed to Brushy Creek. (Both, courtesy of CA.)

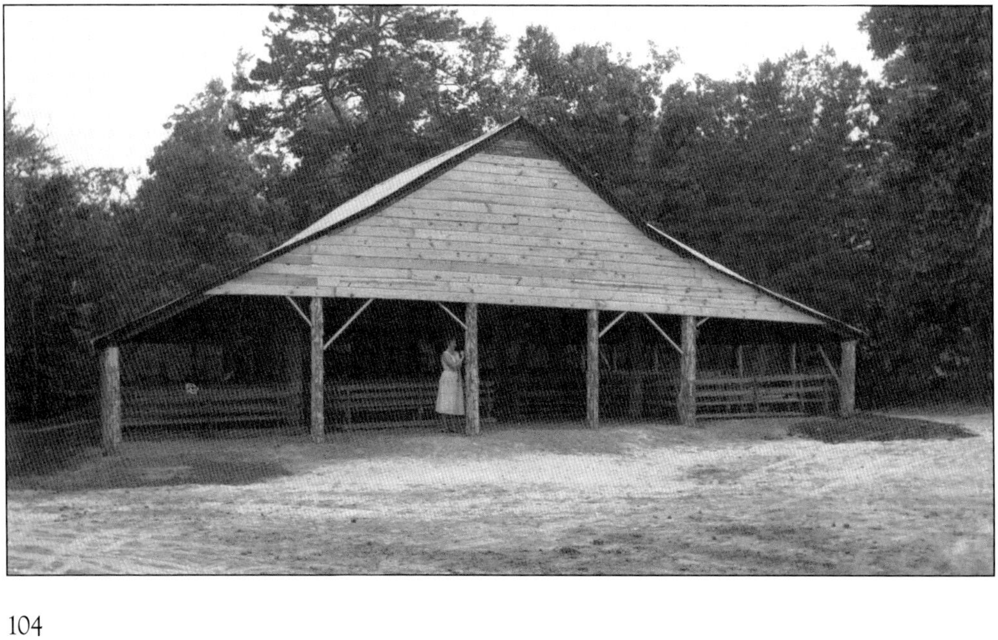

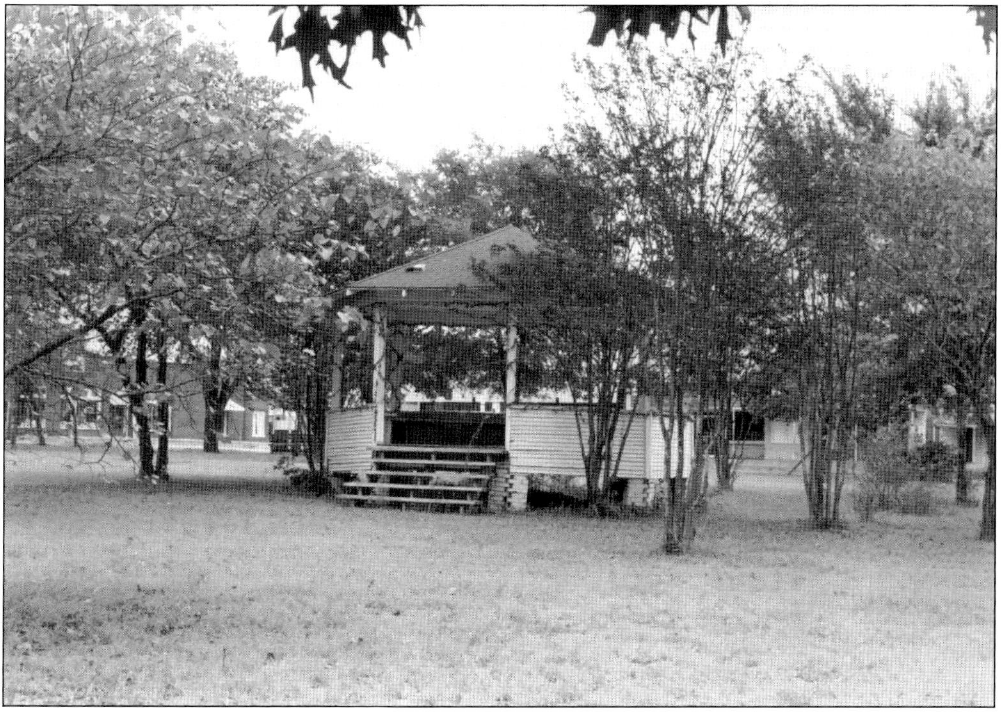

May 17, 1903, was the date of the first train in Frankston. The discovery of oil became a factor in Frankston's economy. Founded around 1902 with the arrival of the Texas and New Orleans Railroad, the first citizens relocated from the village of Kickapoo, Texas, 2 miles southeast of present Frankston. The first post office was named Ayers (as was the town), but the name was changed when a Miss Frankie Miller donated land for a city park. Above is the bandstand in Frankston. Below is a Texas and New Orleans Railroad depot. (Both, courtesy of CA.)

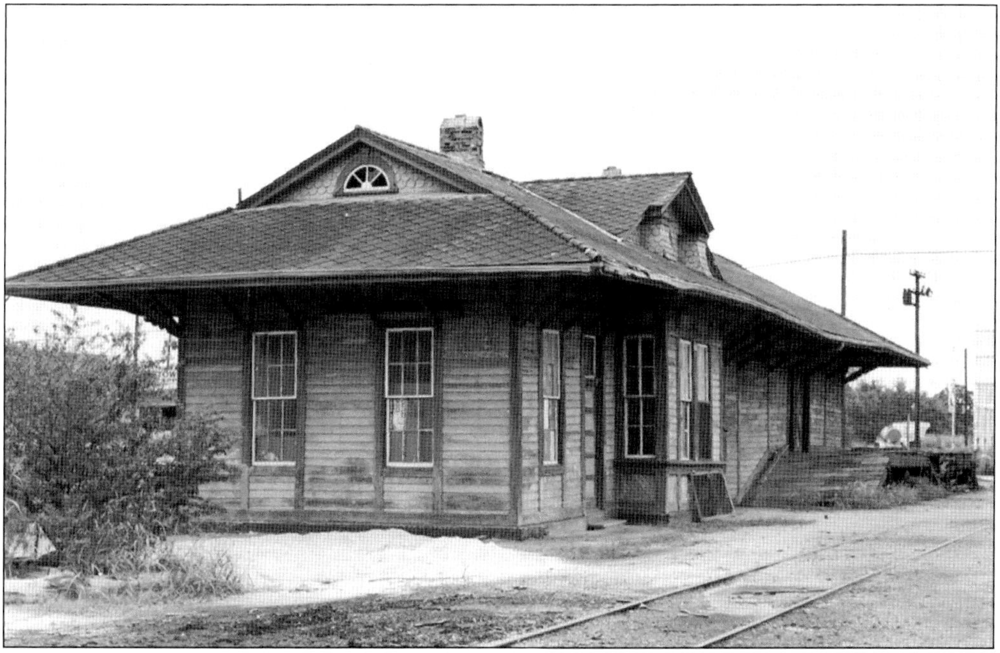

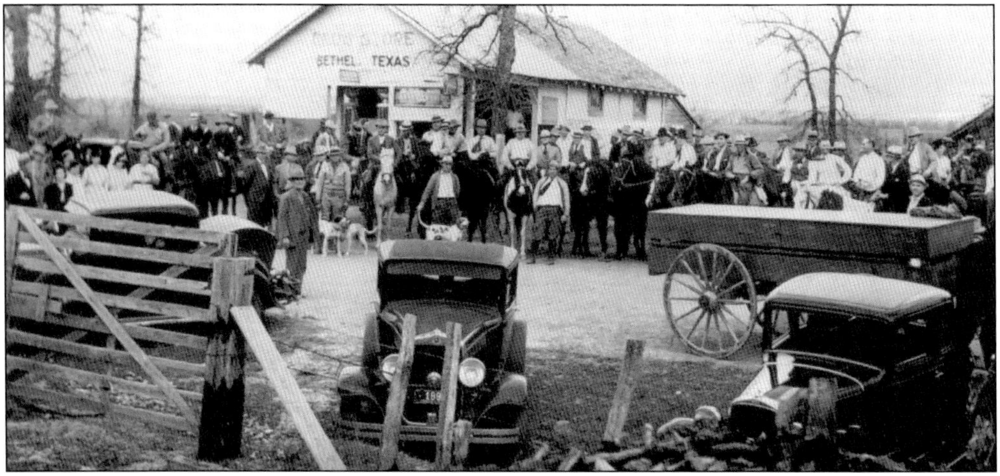

This is the Texas open championship coon hound field trials held at Bethel during the 1920s. (Courtesy of CA.)

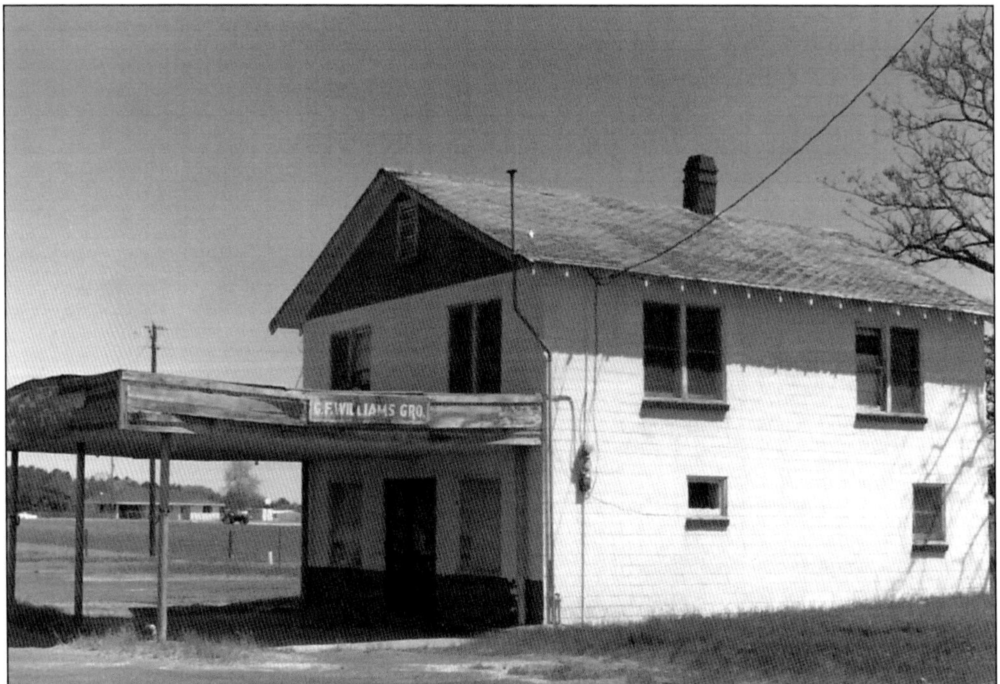

The original name for Pert was Mount Vernon. But because there was already a Mount Vernon, Texas, the name was changed. The original Pert store and post office was owned by W. J. Dennis. Dennis served as postmaster until the post office was closed in 1905. The community retained the name of Mount Vernon after the closing of the post office. (Courtesy of Edwin Dabbs.)

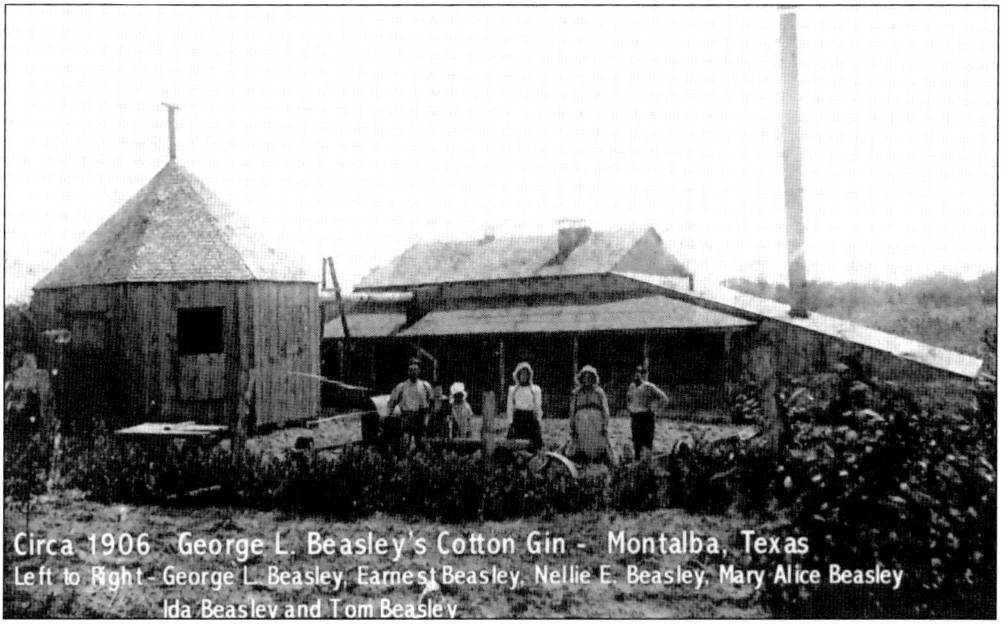

This photograph of George L. Beasley's Cotton Gin in Montalba, Texas, was taken around 1906. From left to right are George L. Beasley, Ernest Beasley, Nellie E. Beasley, Mary Alice Kilpatrick Beasley, Ida Beasley, and Tom Beasley. (Courtesy of Elsie McGee.)

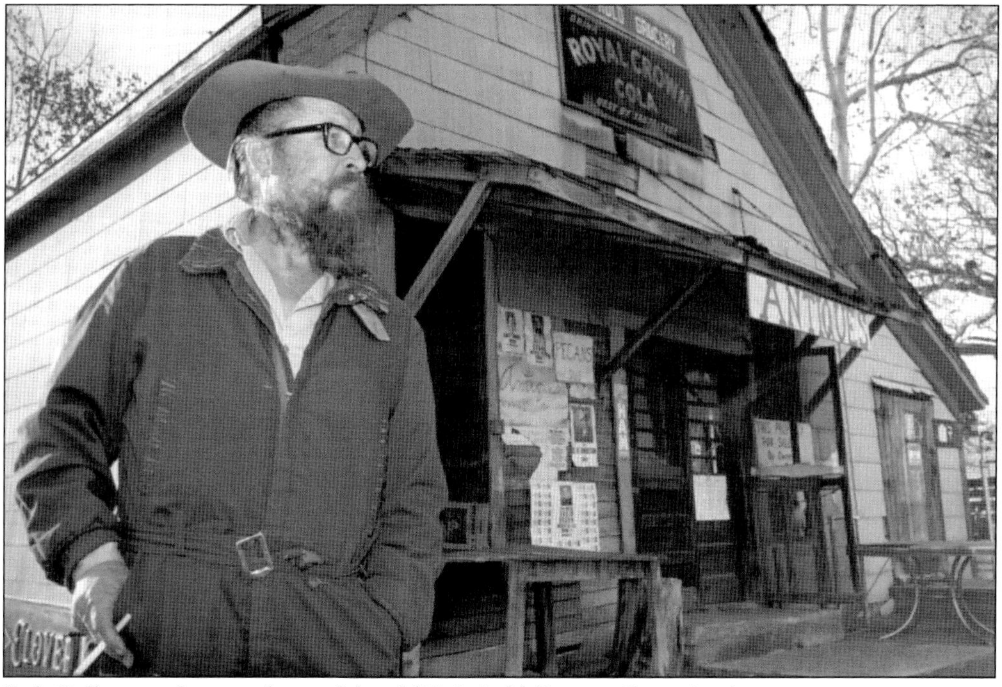

Dub Galloway relaxes in front of the old T. J. Auld Grocery Store. In the past, a country grocery store was more than just a place to buy groceries; it was one of the social centers of the community. People came to buy groceries and supplies, then stayed to visit with friends and neighbors and catch up on community news. Later the building housed an antique store. It burned in 2010. (Courtesy of CA.)

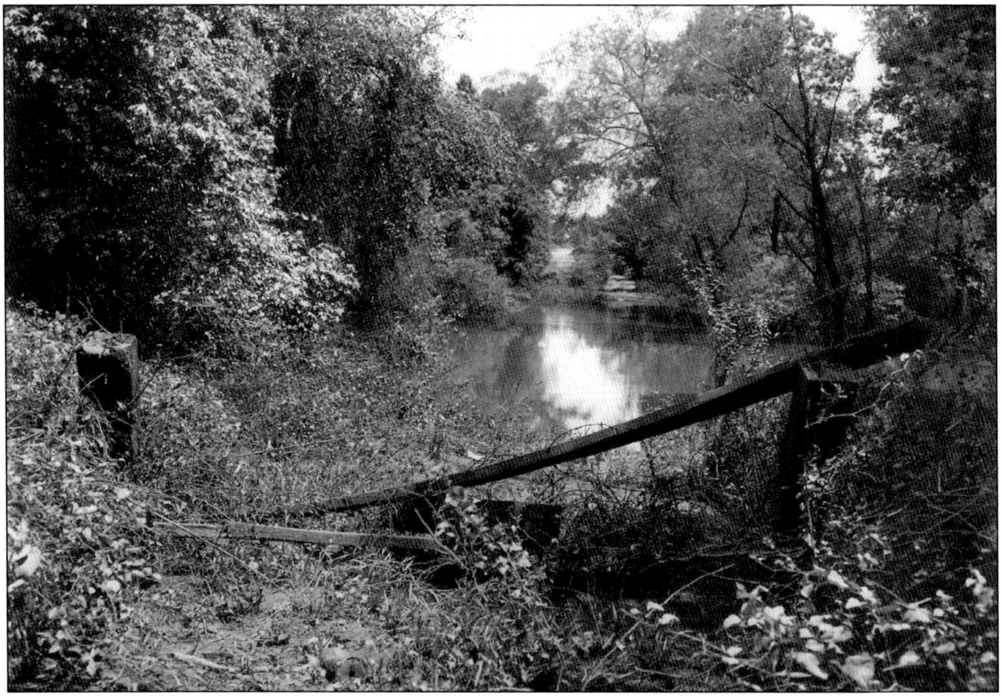

The photograph above shows a placid and remote Blackburn Crossing on the Neches River before Lake Palestine was built. This is the site where the dam was later built. (Courtesy of CA.)

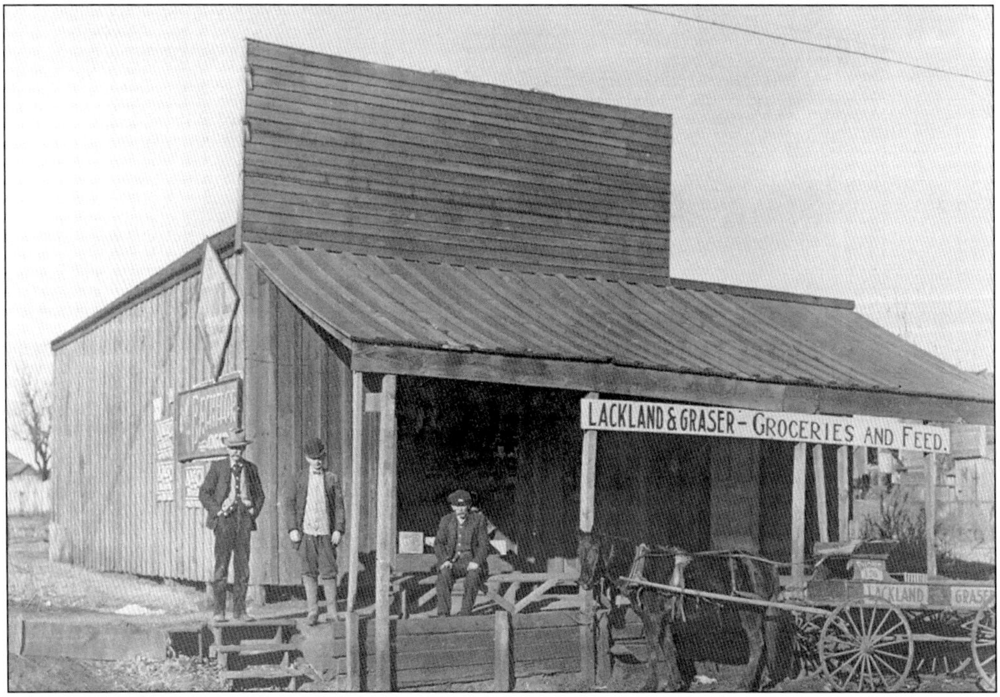

Lackland and Graser grocery and feed store was located in old town on the north side of the courthouse square. J. A. Lackland, on the left, is the only one identified. This photograph was taken between 1908 and 1910. Jackson Hanks law office is now located on this site.

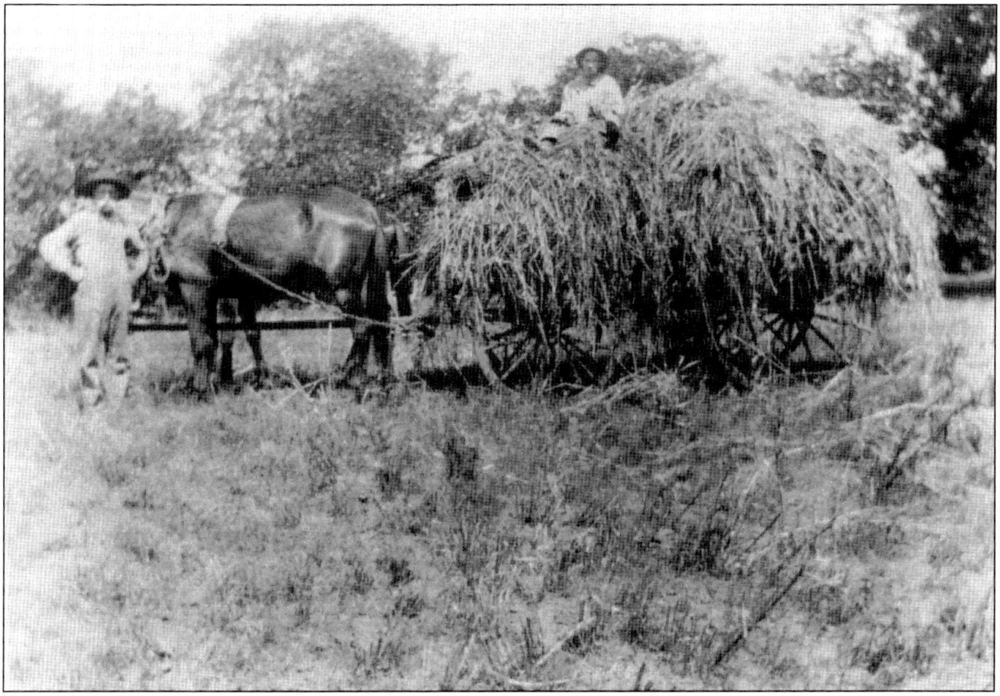

These two photographs are typical of farm life in Anderson County during the horse-and-buggy days. Above, the Elrod family is bringing in the hay in the Brushy Creek area. The photograph below was taken in the fall of 1898 in the front yard of Henry Ferdinand and Sarah Louise Winteroth Barthel. From left to right are Henry holding son Ernest John, six-year-old Mabel Priscilla, Sarah, and eight-year-old Gideon Henry. Their farm was located 4.5 miles southeast of Palestine. (Both, courtesy of PPL.)

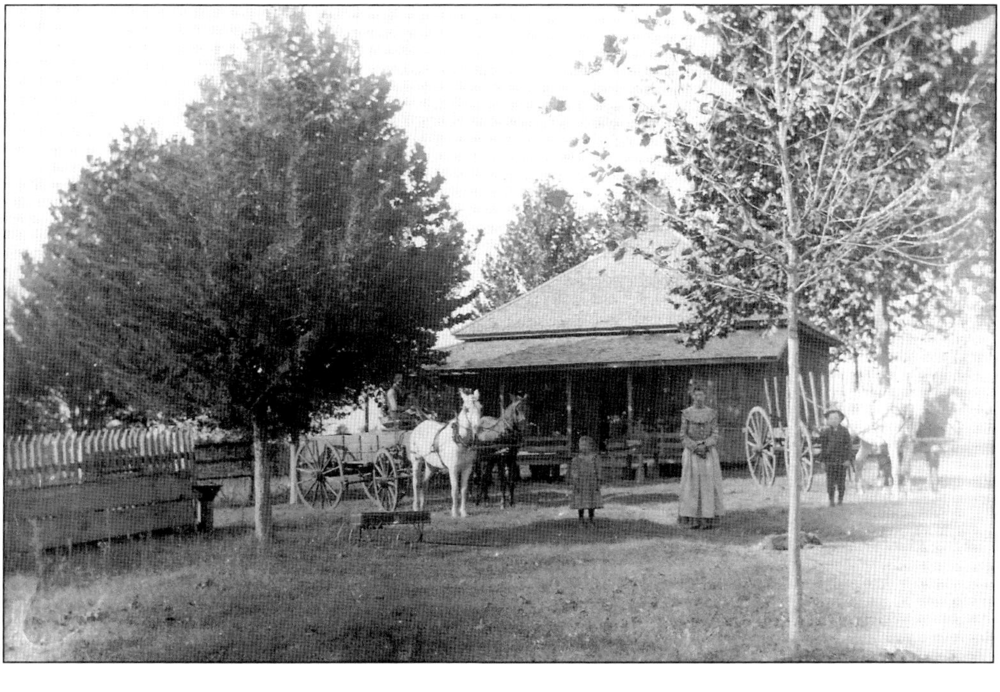

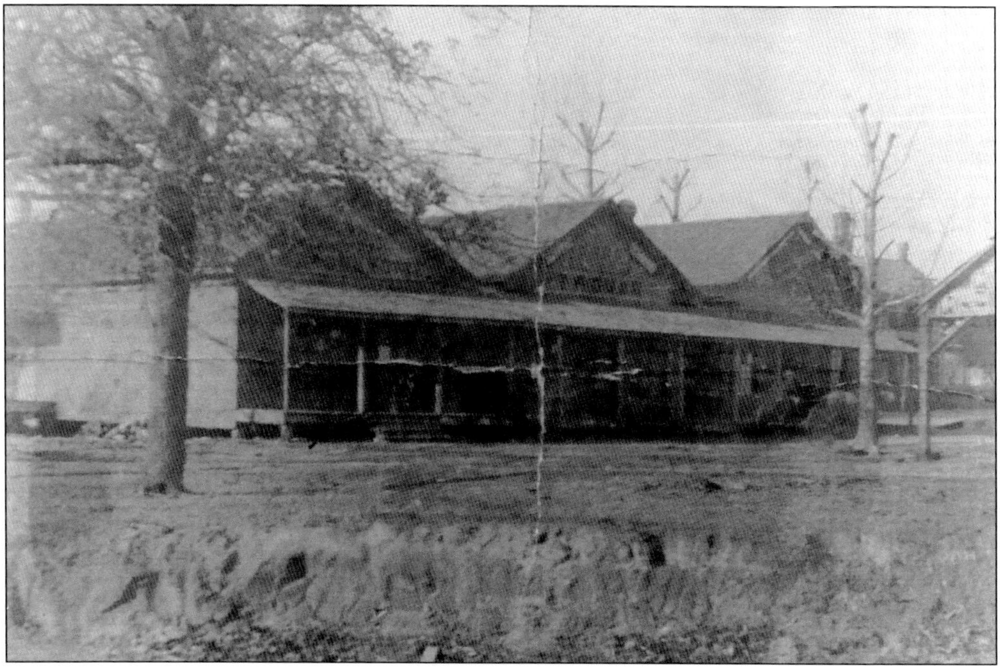

The town of Neches was established in 1872, the year that I&GN railroad was built through this section. The original name of Nechesville was later shortened to Neches.

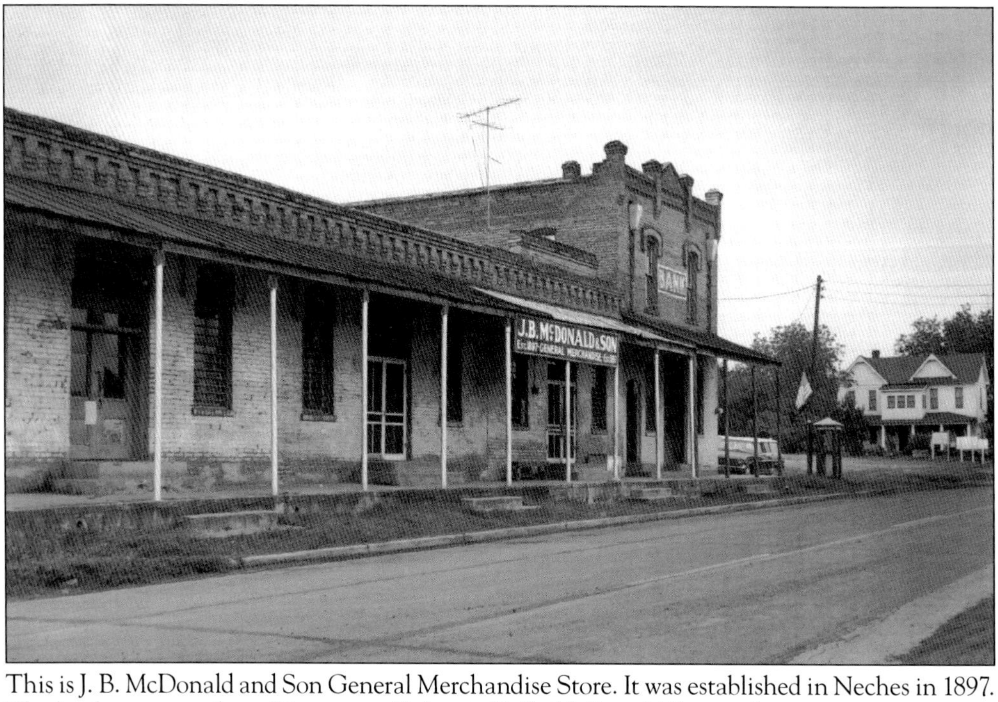

This is J. B. McDonald and Son General Merchandise Store. It was established in Neches in 1897. The bank was next door. (Courtesy of Johnnie Belle McDonald Faucett.)

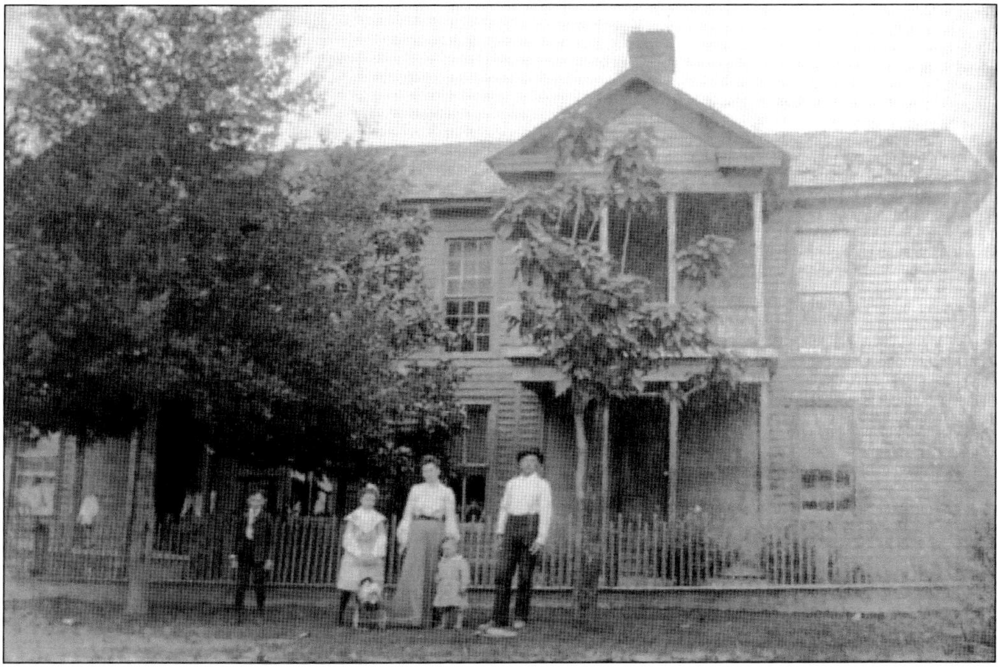

The first hotel in Neches was built by Murdock McDonald, a Scotsman who came from Moore County, North Carolina, in 1832. His descendants still maintain a residence on the property where the hotel stood. The hotel was torn down in 1908 and the Ballard home built from its lumber. (Courtesy of Johnnie Belle McDonald Faucett.)

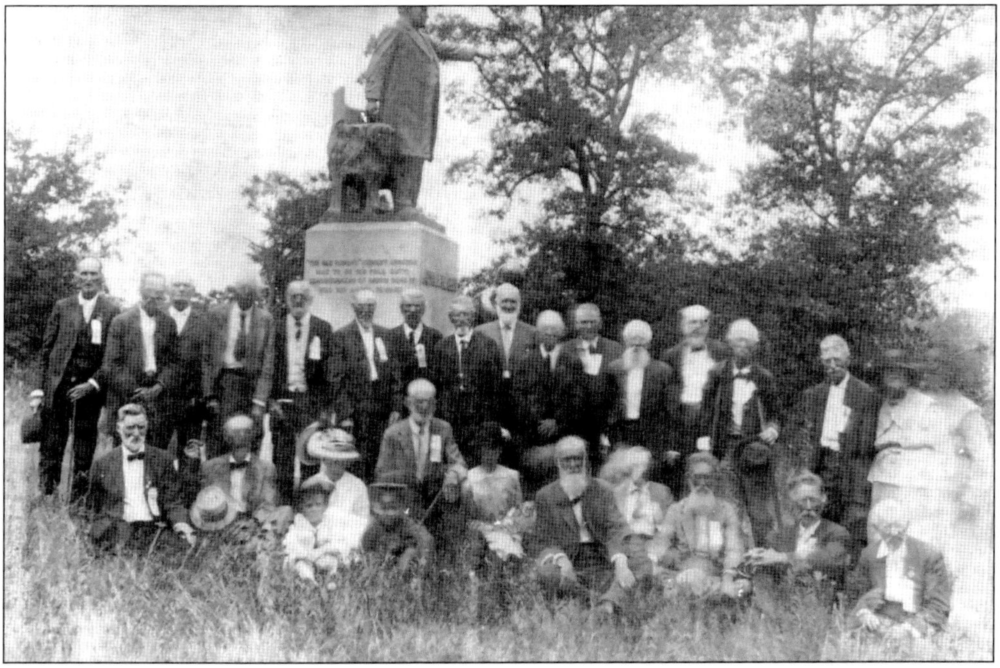

The Reagan monument pays tribute to the life of John H. Reagan. A group of Confederates gather around the statue in Reagan Park on Crockett Road. This photograph was taken around 1914.

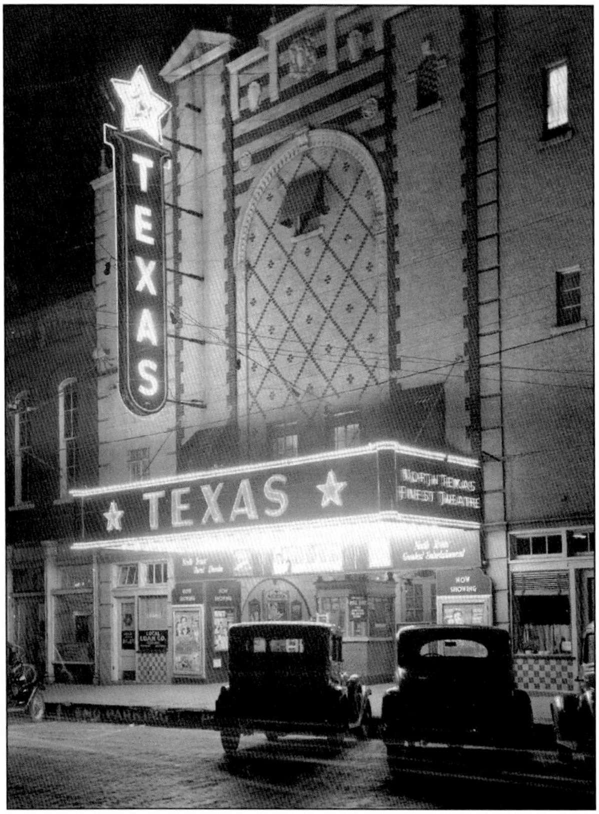

The Texas Theater at 213 West Crawford Street in Palestine opened in 1928. W. Scott Dunne designed the beautiful Spanish colonial structure. For those that grew up in the area, this is the site of some of their fondest memories. They spent hours mesmerized with their eyes glued to the images on the silver screen while munching their popcorn. It is now the home of the Palestine Community Theater, where live productions are regularly performed.

This is the Palestine Skeet Club. From left to right are (first row) Paul Dublin of Jacksonville, Luckett Kolstad Jr., and Frank Dublin of Jacksonville; (second row) Herman Eiler (ammunition salesman from Dallas), "Squat-Low" Aller (Winchester gun salesman of Dallas), Dr. Harry Haverlah, Fred Alford, unidentified, Alfred Moore, and Benny Liles. (Courtesy of Kathy Moore Odom.)

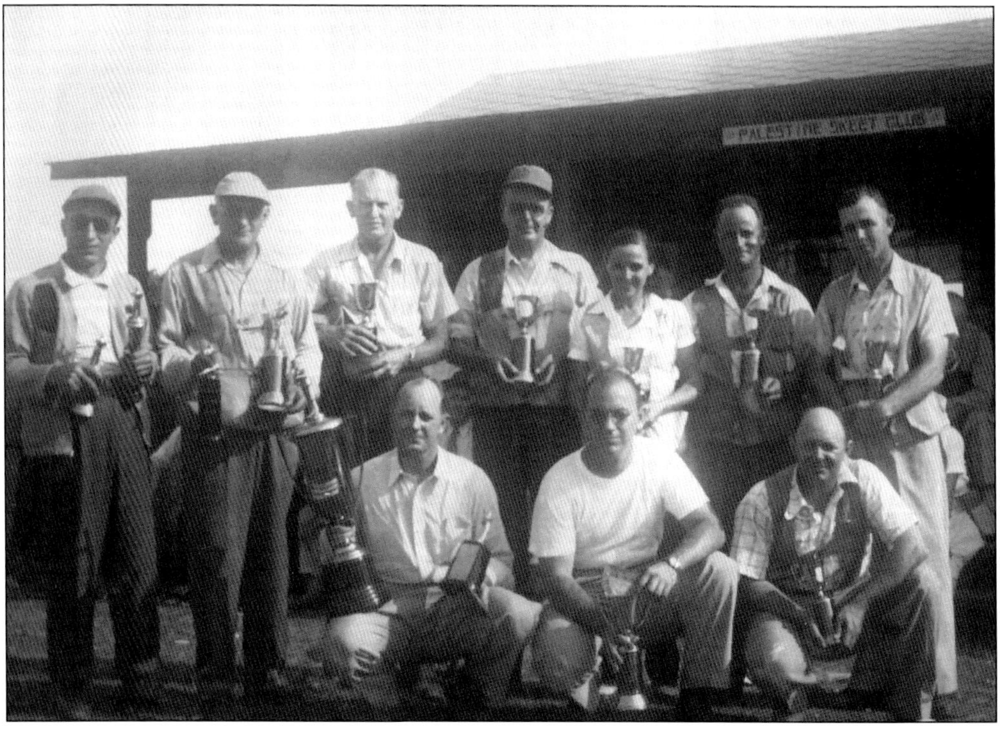

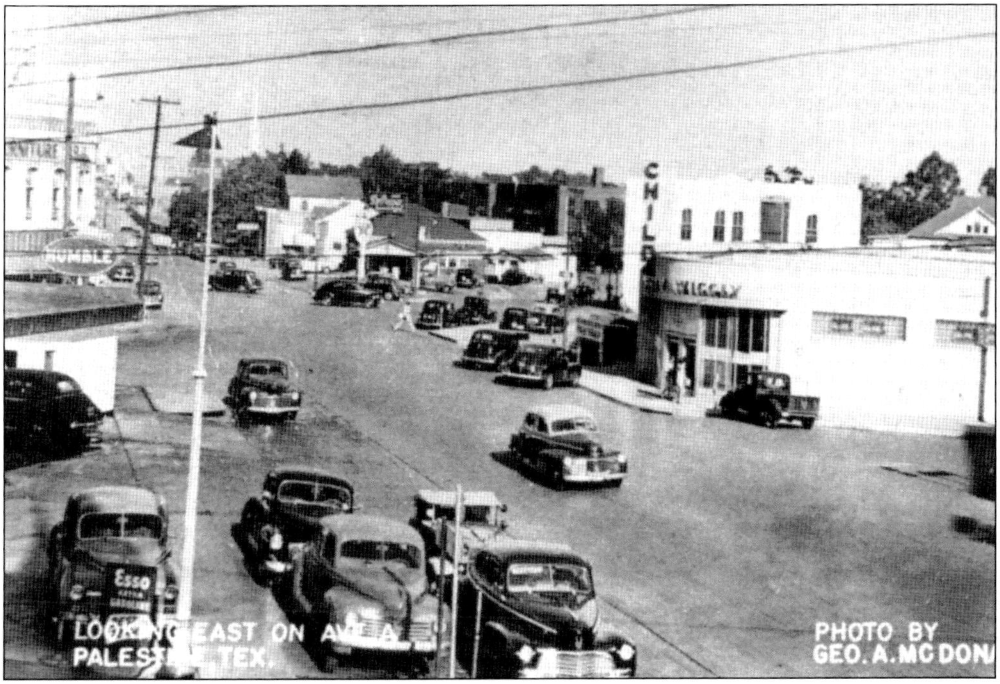

Palestine consists of two towns joined by Avenue A. The original town that grew around the courthouse square is known as Old Town. When the railroad arrived in 1872, the new part of town, or downtown, developed around the railroad depot on Front Street (now Spring Street). A new street, Avenue A, was built and became a vital corridor connecting the two towns. In 1874, a street car ran along the avenue. For many people, Avenue A brings back memories of watching countless parades march from the courthouse to downtown. The picture above shows the view looking east to the courthouse. It was probably taken from the Temple Opera House building. The picture below is taken from the courthouse looking west. Notice the county jail on the left and the First Presbyterian Church's steeple in the center.

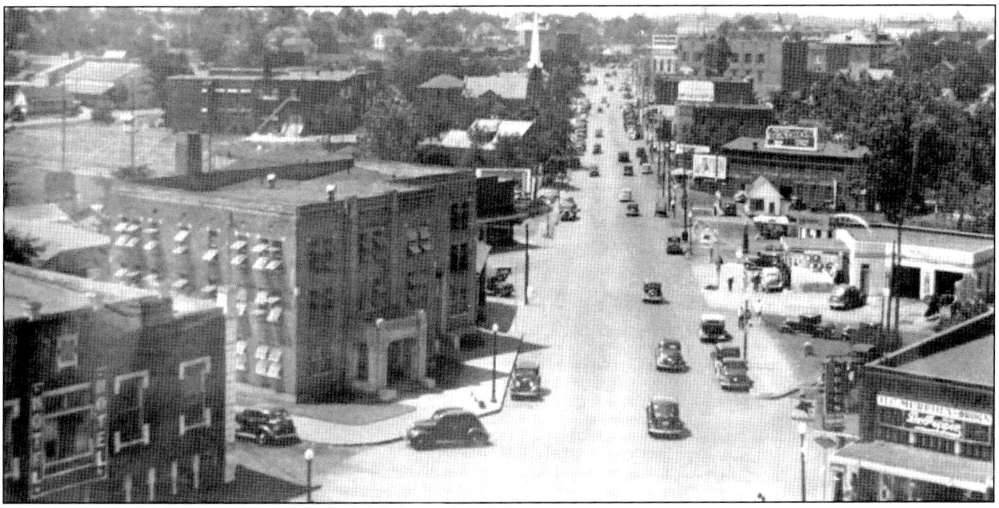

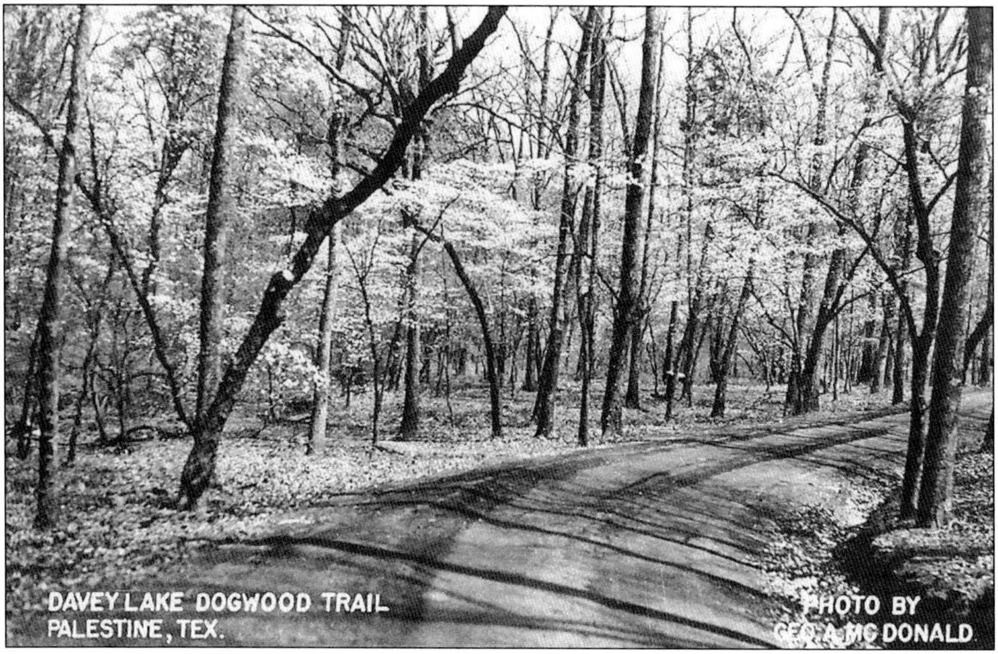

One of the major tourist attractions in Anderson County began one morning in 1938 from a conversation over coffee between Eugene Fish and Charles W. Wooldridge. They discussed how beautiful the dogwood trees were that year. Later Mr. Wooldridge went to the newspaper and suggested that out of town people be invited to come to Palestine to see the dogwoods. As a result, over 20,000 people drove to Palestine to see the beautiful blossoms. The Texas Dogwood Trails were incorporated in 1939. In 1941, the trails were routed through part of the Link family land. In 1944, M. A. Davey purchased the land through which the trails wound and donated it to Anderson County. The name was changed to Martin A. Davey Dogwood Park.

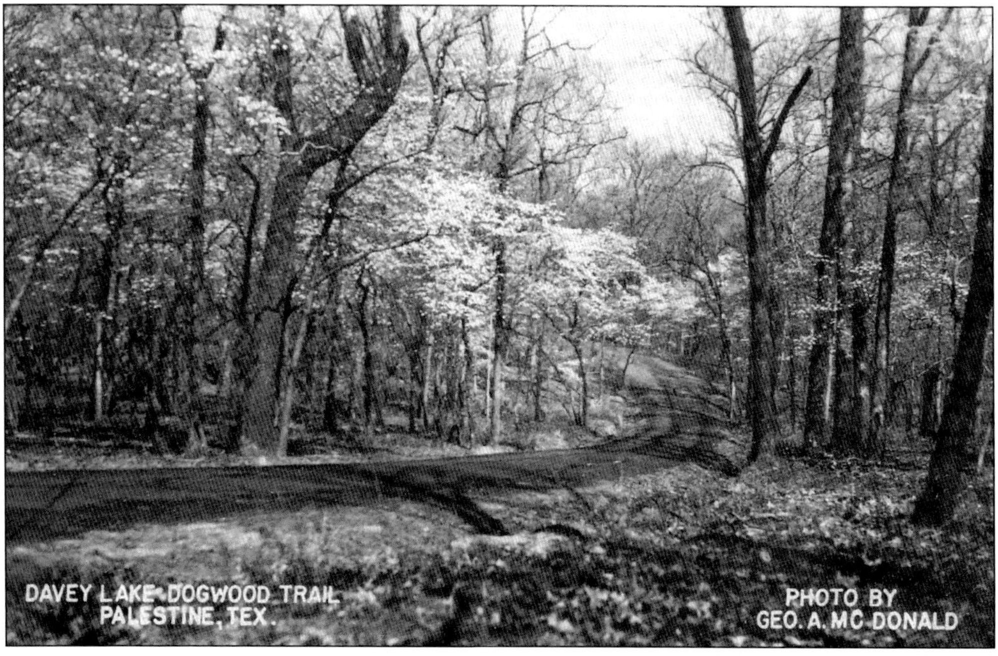

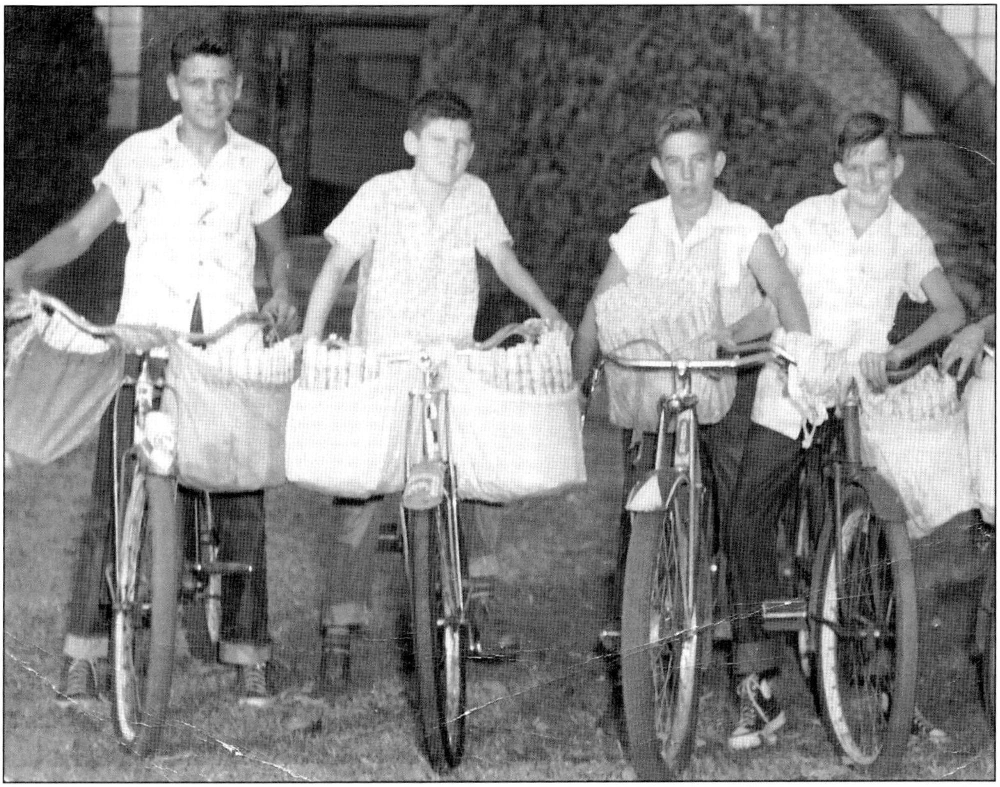

In 1950, it was a common sight across Palestine to see boys with a bag of newspapers strapped to their bikes riding down the street throwing the papers in customers' yards. Here are four of those enterprising paperboys, with Palestine High School in the background. They are, from left to right, Jimmy Odom, Terry Oxford, Bill Blount, and Kenneth Beard. (Courtesy of Jimmy Odom.)

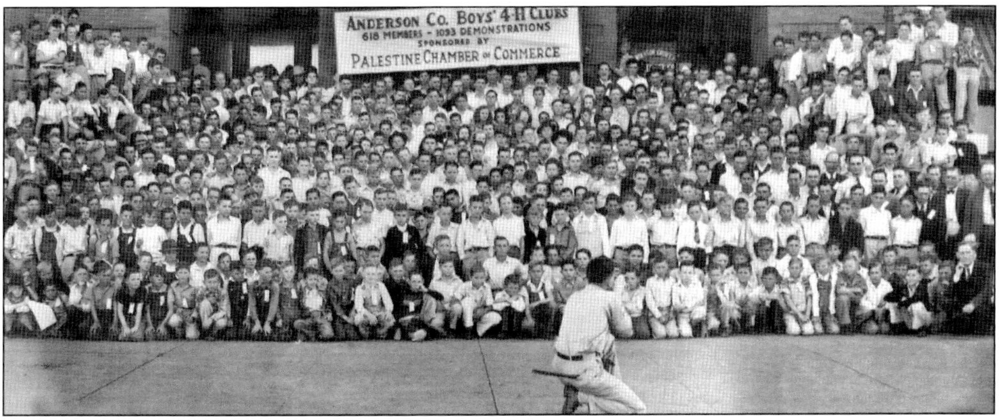

In 1906, the first 4-H Club organization was established in Texas. It is not known when the club first came to Anderson County. The original clubs were called corn clubs. Later they had pig clubs, beef calf clubs, and girls' tomato clubs. The Extension Agents chose to educate the youth because they were easier to teach than adults.

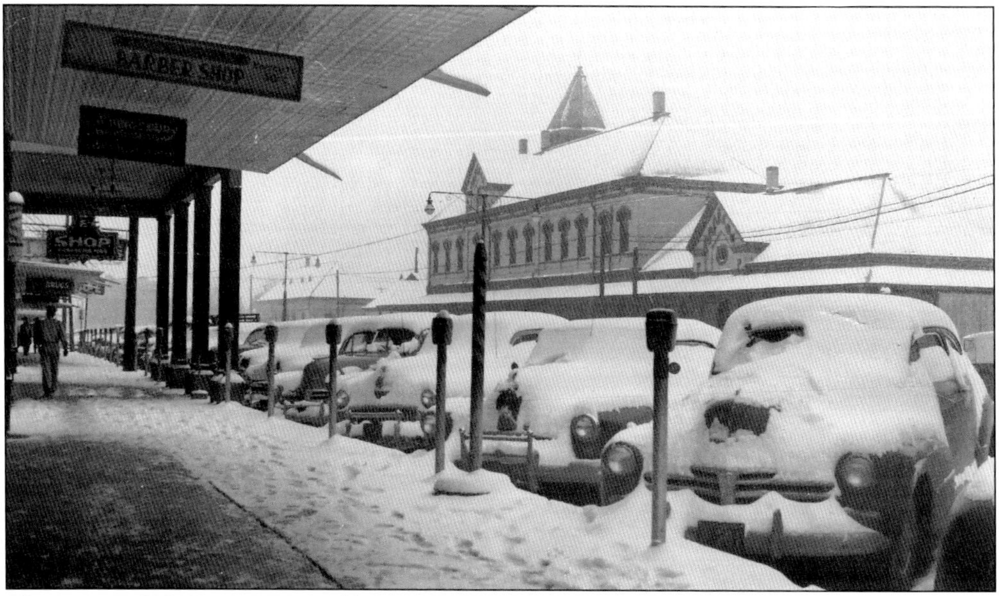

The winter of 1949 was a very cold, icy winter in Anderson County. It caused many hardships to both businesses and citizens. Electricity was lost when ice broke the lines, and driving was hazardous because the streets were treacherous. But in the midst of the chaos, the ice caused the beauty of a snowy wonderland. Pictured above, the cars along Spring Street are covered with snow.

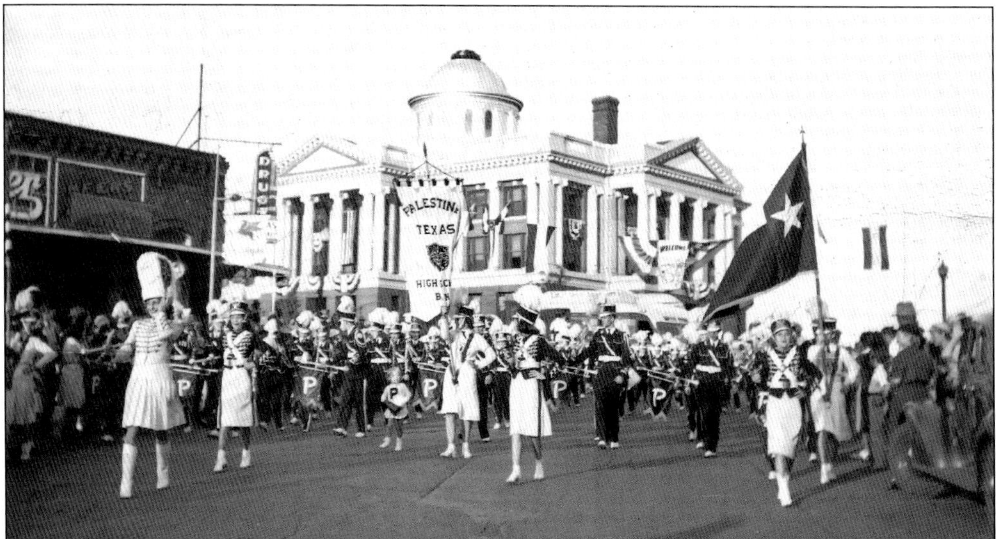

Each fall when the fair came to town, it was kicked off with a parade that left the courthouse, marched down Avenue A, and wound through the streets of downtown. This is the Palestine High School band in the fair parade on Monday, October 10, 1938.

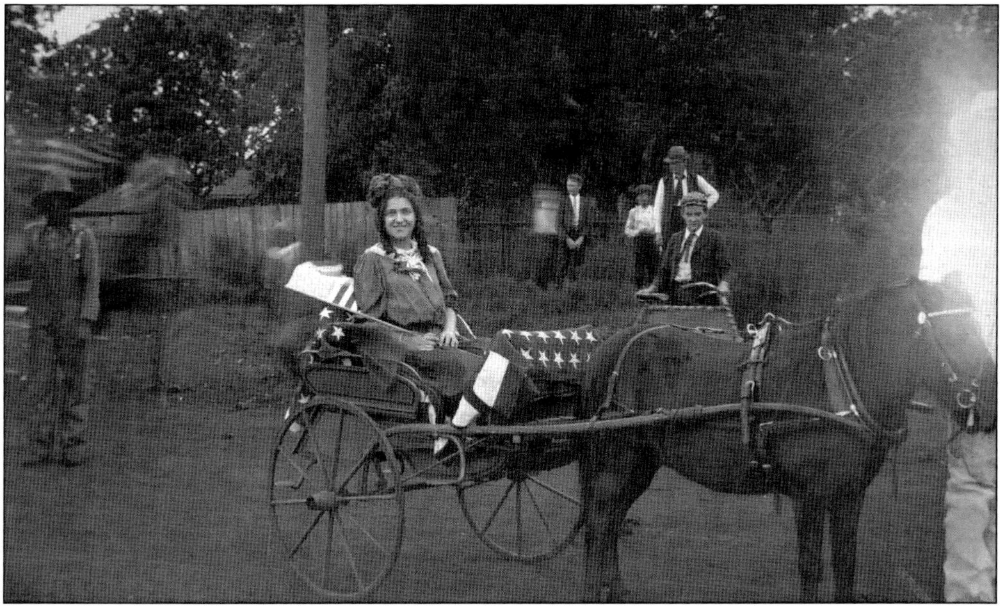

An unidentified lady is pictured at the East Texas Industrial Carnival and Fruit Show. (Courtesy of PPL.)

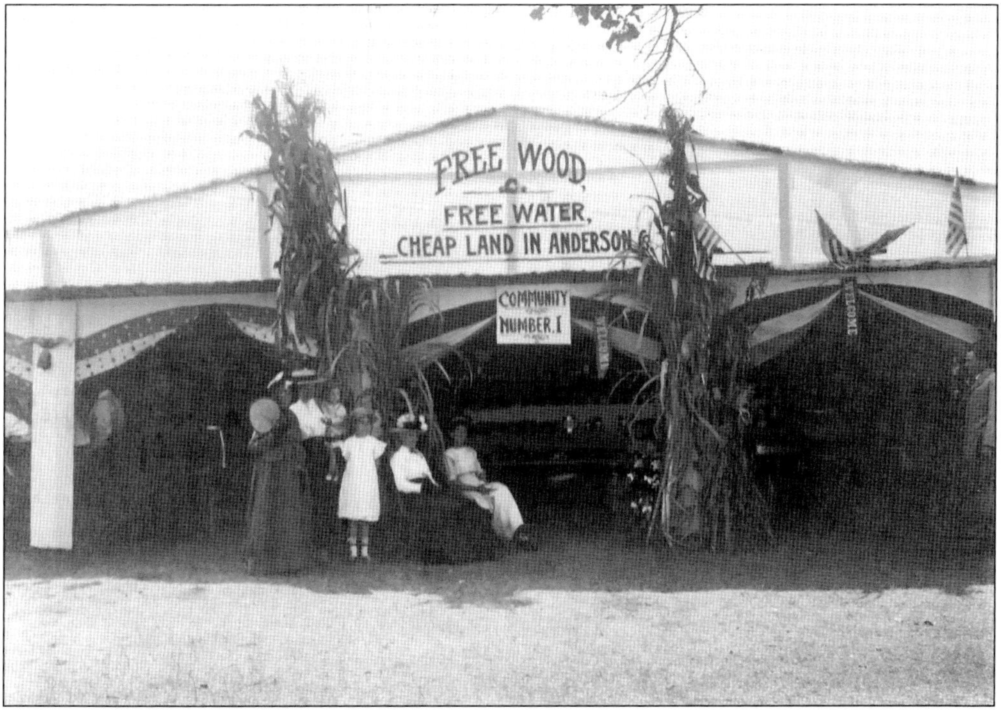

This photograph advertising free wood, free water, and cheap land in Anderson County may have been at the Great Fruit Palace that was held in Palestine on October 3–7, 1922. It featured horticulture, agriculture, and livestock. (Courtesy of PPL.)

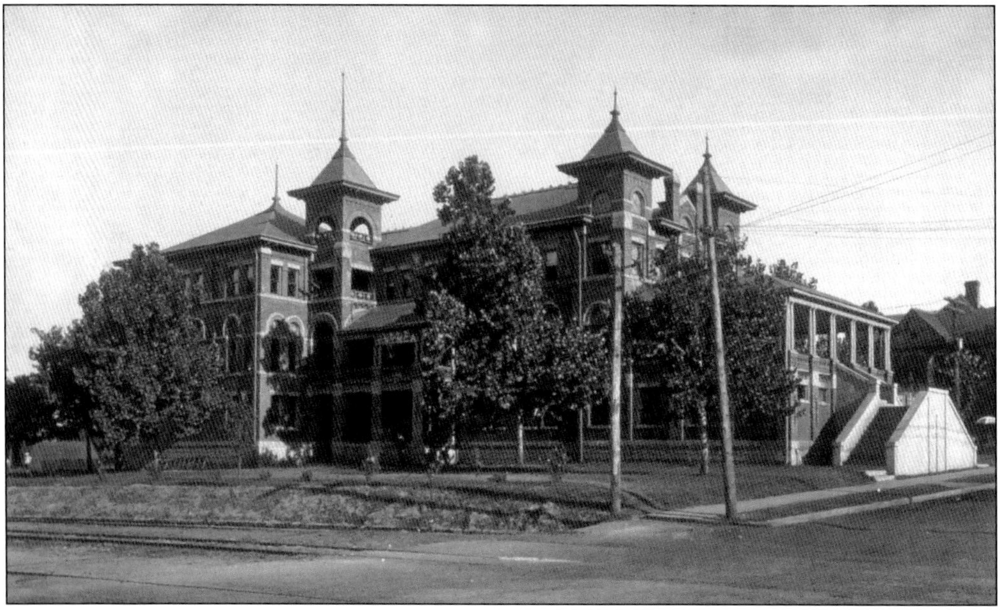

The new Railroad YMCA was opened on April 22, 1903, on South Magnolia Street near the railroad tracks. In addition to a dormitory, the building contained a gymnasium, swimming pool, bowling alleys, and other rooms for various activities. This photograph was taken in 1917. The "Y," as it was known, burned in the 1950s, and a new YMCA was built on Kickapoo Street. The site of the burned building was leveled and became a parking lot for the Missouri-Pacific Railroad General Offices.

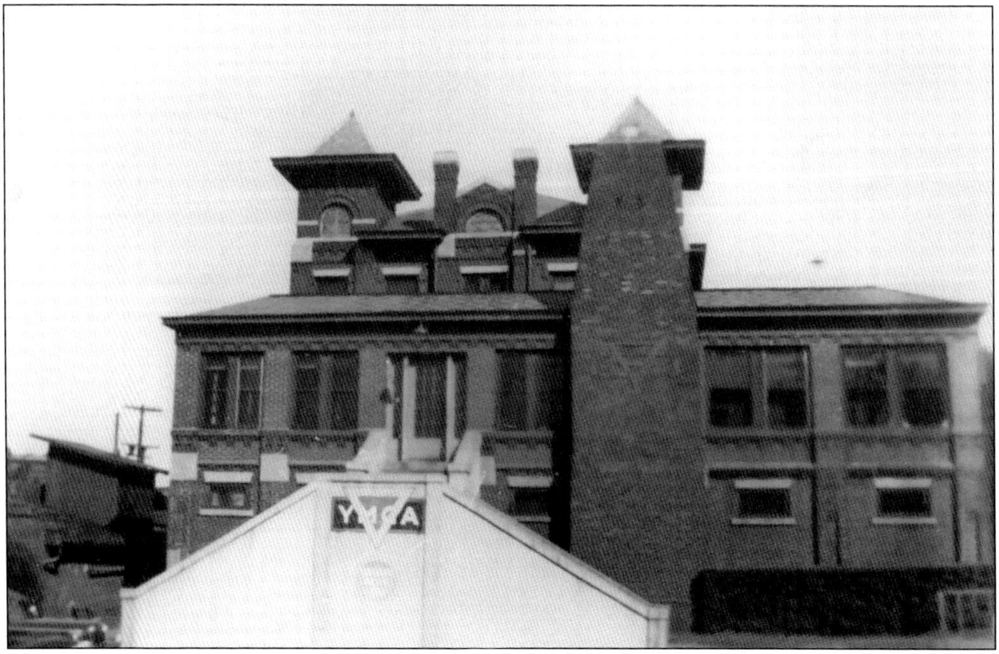

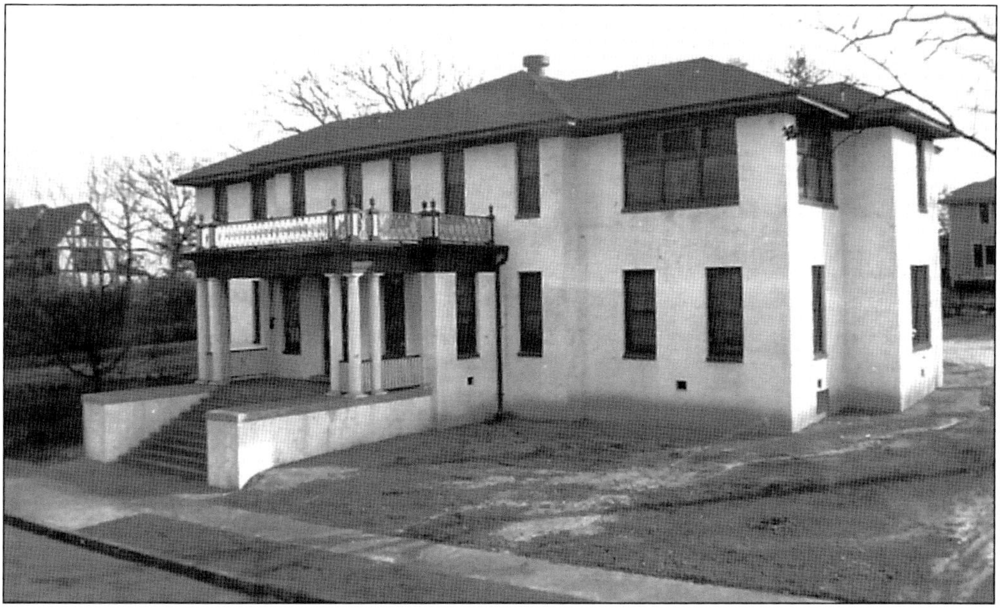

The Palestine Sanitarium at 318 East Neches Street and Sylvan Avenue was built in 1915. It was owned by Dr. A. L. Hathcock, and Dr. R. H. McLeon helped to establish it. In 1929, when a devastating tornado destroyed Slocum, the injured victims were brought to the sanitarium. From 1932 to 1952, Dr. Fred Felder practiced at the sanitarium.

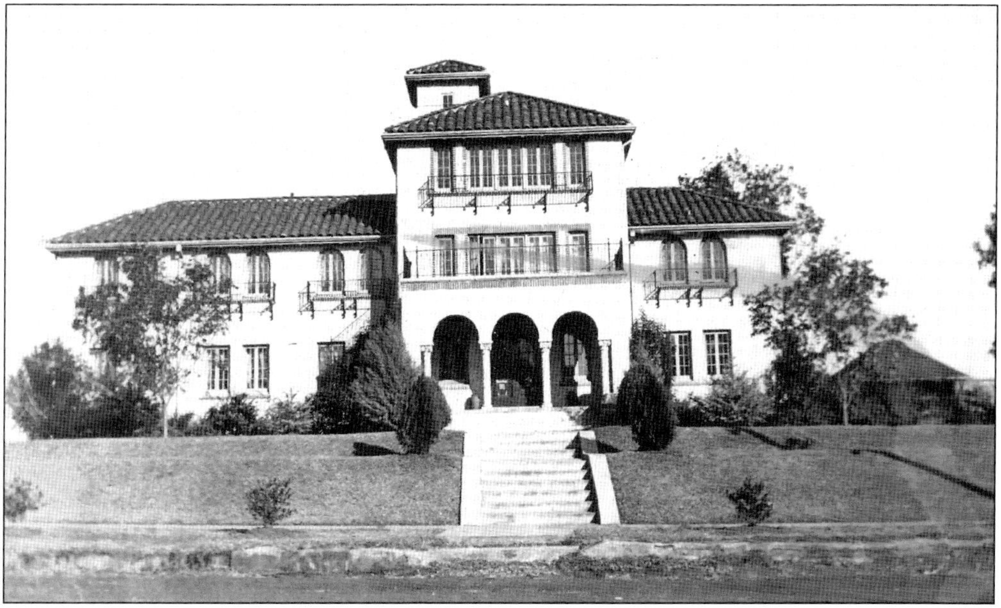

The Speegle Sanitarium was started in a small way in the home of Dr. A. Arthur Speegle, physician and surgeon, at the corner of North John and Greene Streets in 1916. One year later, he realized he needed larger quarters. As a result, he purchased an 11-room building located at 201 Palestine Avenue. Speegle Sanituarium was one of a very few institutions in Texas using gas as an anesthetic. In 1931, this was a modern hospital serving a 50-mile radius of Palestine. Dr. Arthur Speegle was born in Cullman, Alabama. His family moved to Palestine when Arthur was 11 years of age.

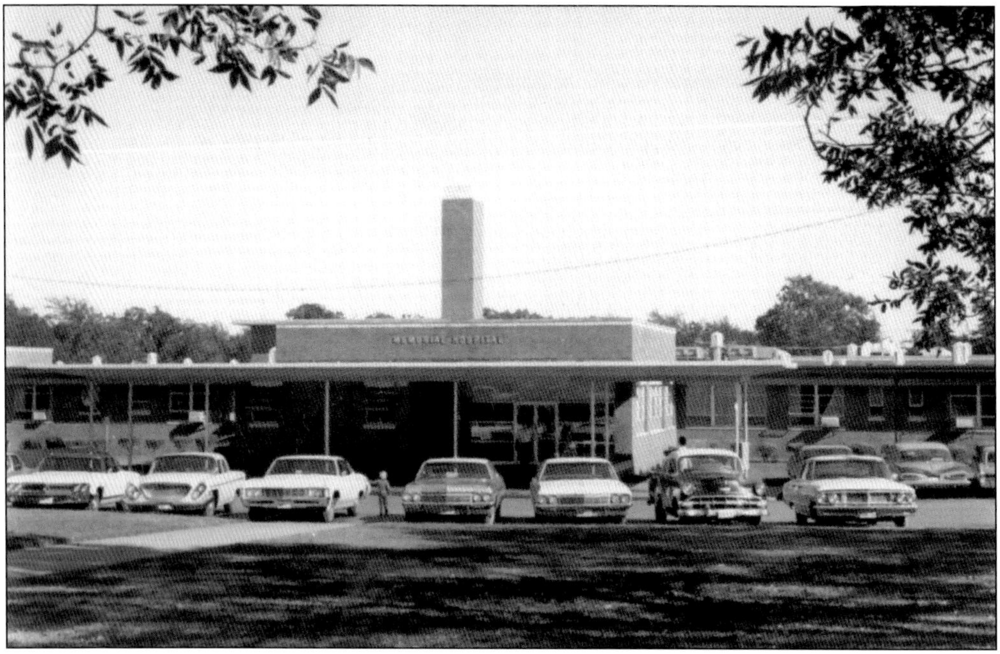

Memorial Hospital was officially dedicated on May 31, 1952. Originally the facility was owned and operated by the county, but it was later converted to a private foundation and not-for-profit community hospital. It was an 84-bed building and was constructed diagonally across an entire block on Palestine's south side. The room rates at the time would vary between $6 and $13, with most falling in the $8, $10, and $11.50 category.

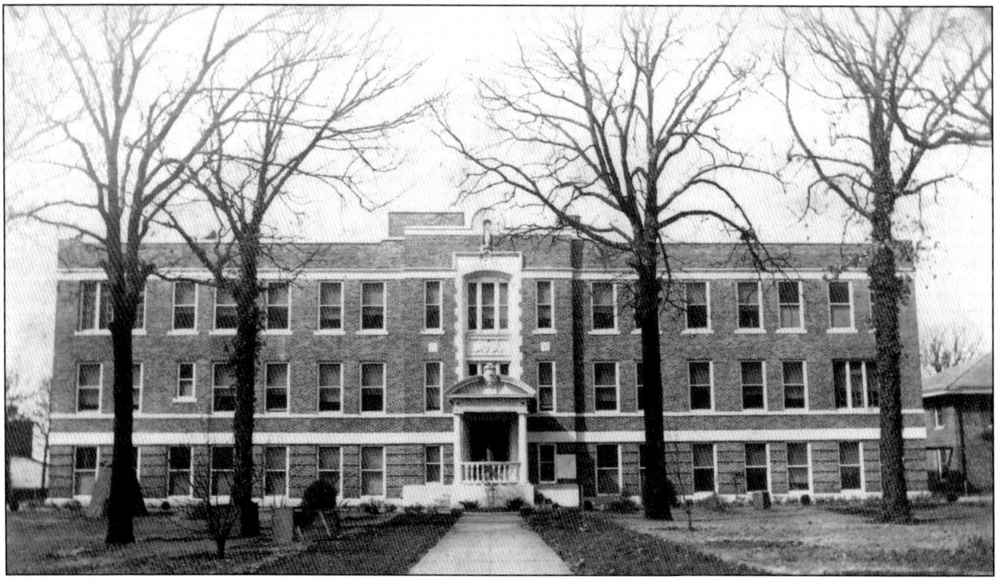

Missouri-Pacific Hospital was formally opened on April 1, 1922, for the care of railroad employees. It was a modern 75-bed, 2-story building in the 900 block of South Magnolia Street between Magnolia Street and the railroad tracks. In 1925, an additional brick structure was built to house the nursing students attending the school that had been established there. The hospital closed its doors on September 15, 1970, due mainly to reduced work force.

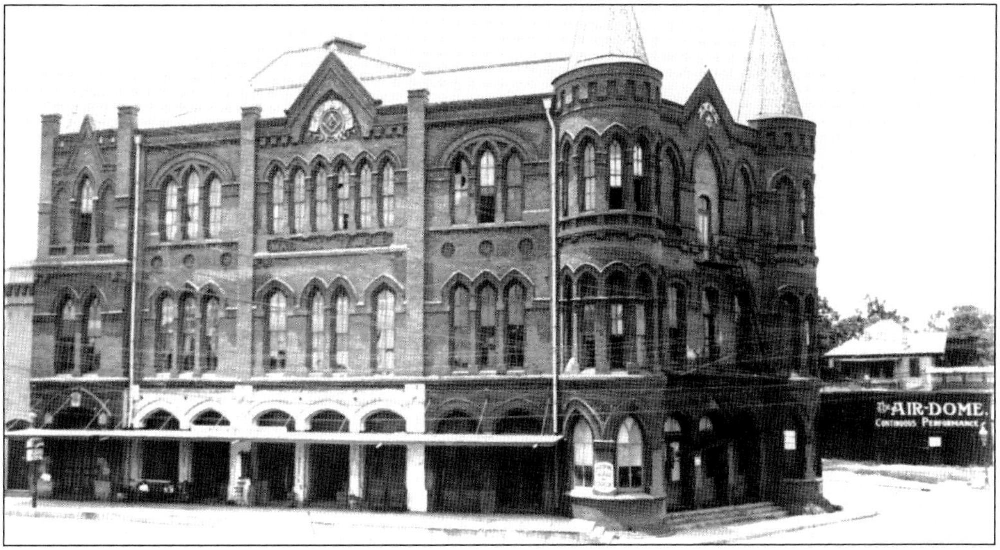

In 1879, a new Temple Opera House was opened at the intersections of Avenue A, Oak, and Main Streets. The ground floor was for mercantile businesses; the second floor was devoted to the opera house, which seated 700 people; and the third floor was for the Masonic Lodge. By 1882, there was only one surviving charter member of the Palestine Lodge. The beautiful building was of Gothic style with spires topping the two round towers. During the 1890s, many well-known performers came to Palestine to perform at the opera house. It was a place for beautiful weddings and elaborate dress balls. It was demolished in 1962. (Both, courtesy of CA.)

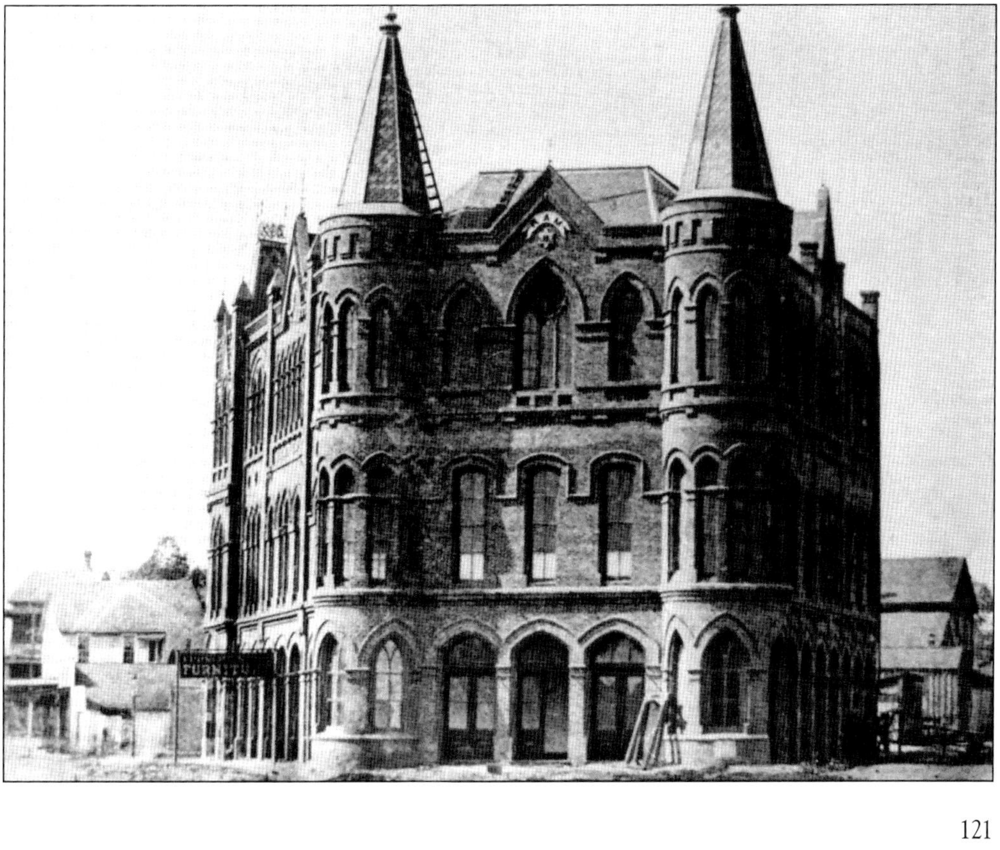

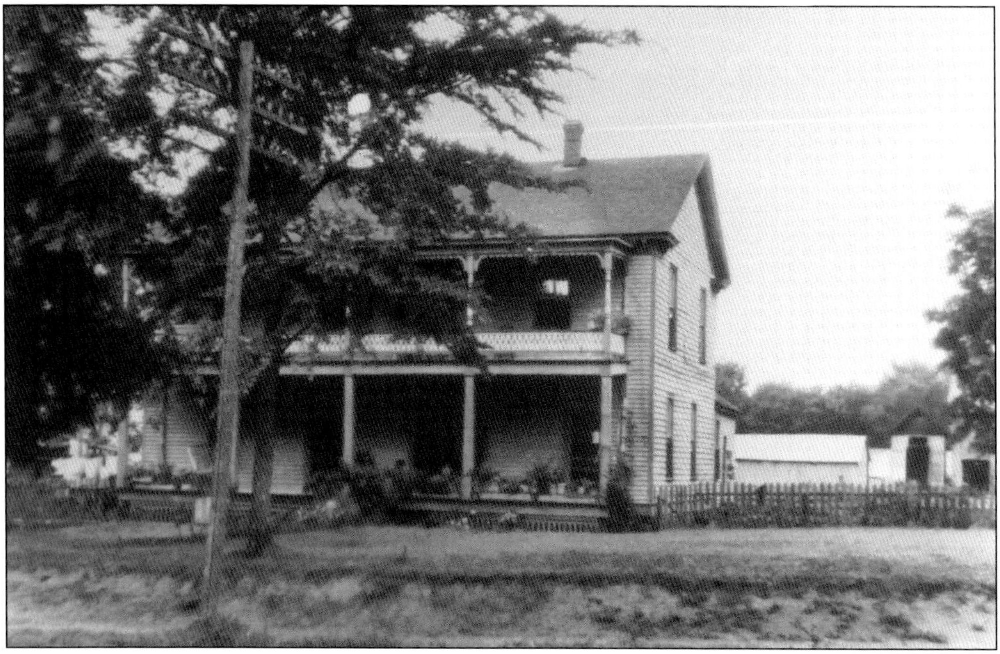

The second Masonic Hall was located on old Rusk Road at the present site of 914 East Lacy Street. The deed was conveyed for $2 on October 2, 1850, from George W. Dutton to A. E. McClure, worshipful master; Reuben A. Reeves, senior warden; and Robert W. Willett Jr., warden and brethren of Palestine Lodge of Full and Accepted Masons.

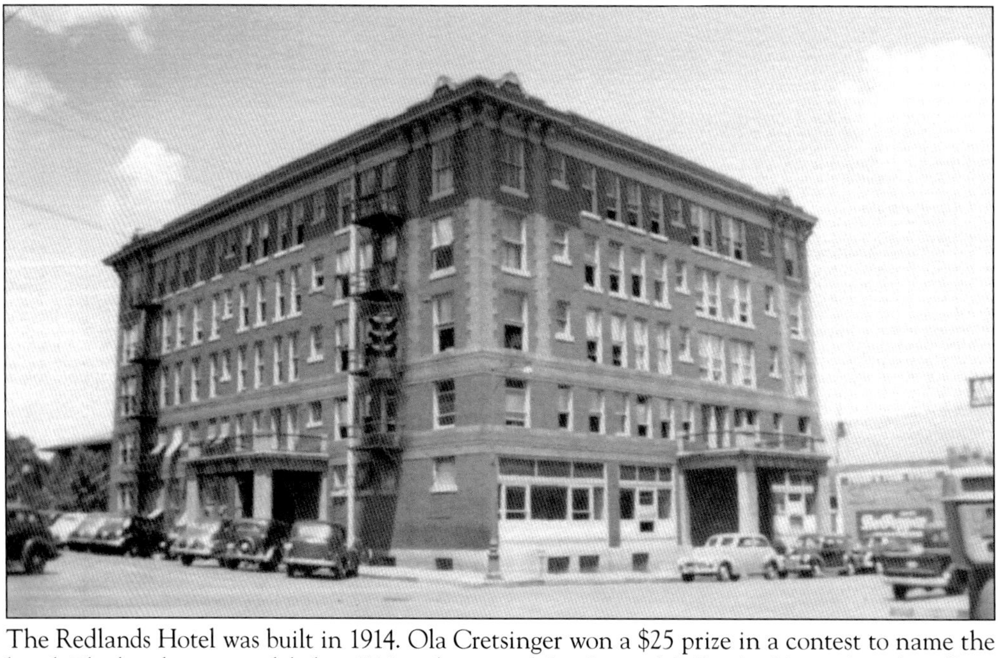

The Redlands Hotel was built in 1914. Ola Cretsinger won a $25 prize in a contest to name the hotel. The hotel was remodeled in 1919 and renamed the General Office building when the offices of the International and Great Northern Railroad moved their offices there.

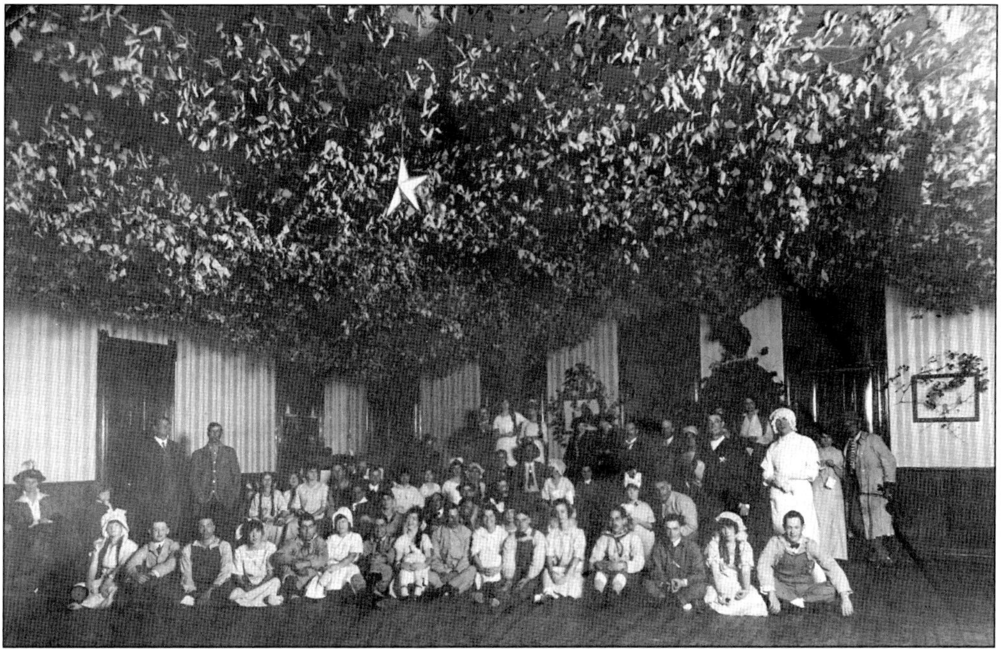

In the early 1900s, dances held in parks, pavilions, and dance halls were a very popular pastime. Many famous people appeared at the Murphy-Link Building at 319 West Main Street in Palestine. Pictured above is a group at the Elks' Thanksgiving dance held there on November 14, 1914.

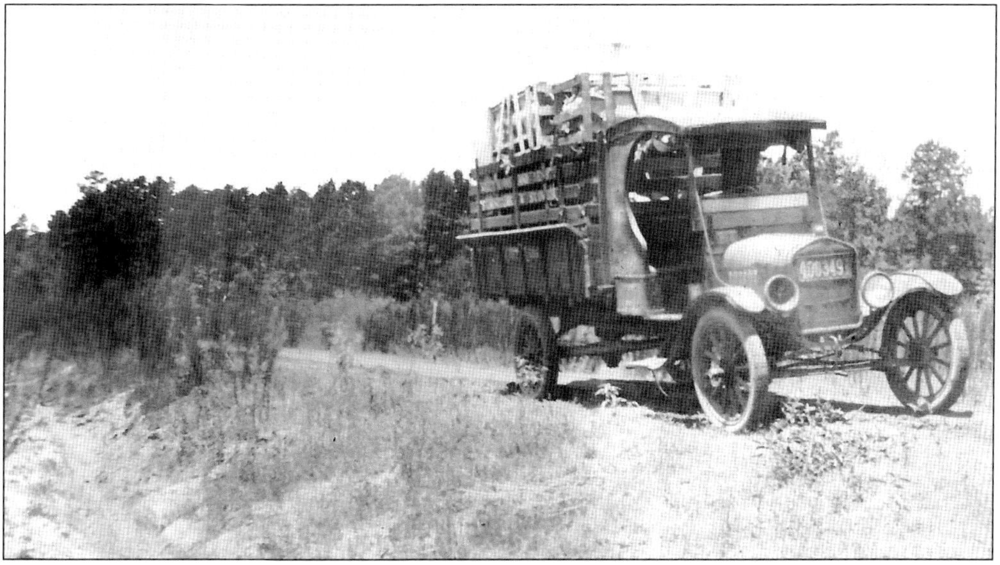

Stopping to cool off "Old Henry," this photograph shows John William "Will" Cockerham's farm truck en route to a Jacksonville store. John William was an Anderson County dairy and truck farmer. In 1882, he came from Louisiana to the Pleasant Springs community of Anderson County. He was the son of Jackson Elmore Cockerham, a Confederate veteran and farmer. Will married Maggie Smith in 1884 in Anderson County. (Courtesy of Connie Lenore Glenn.)

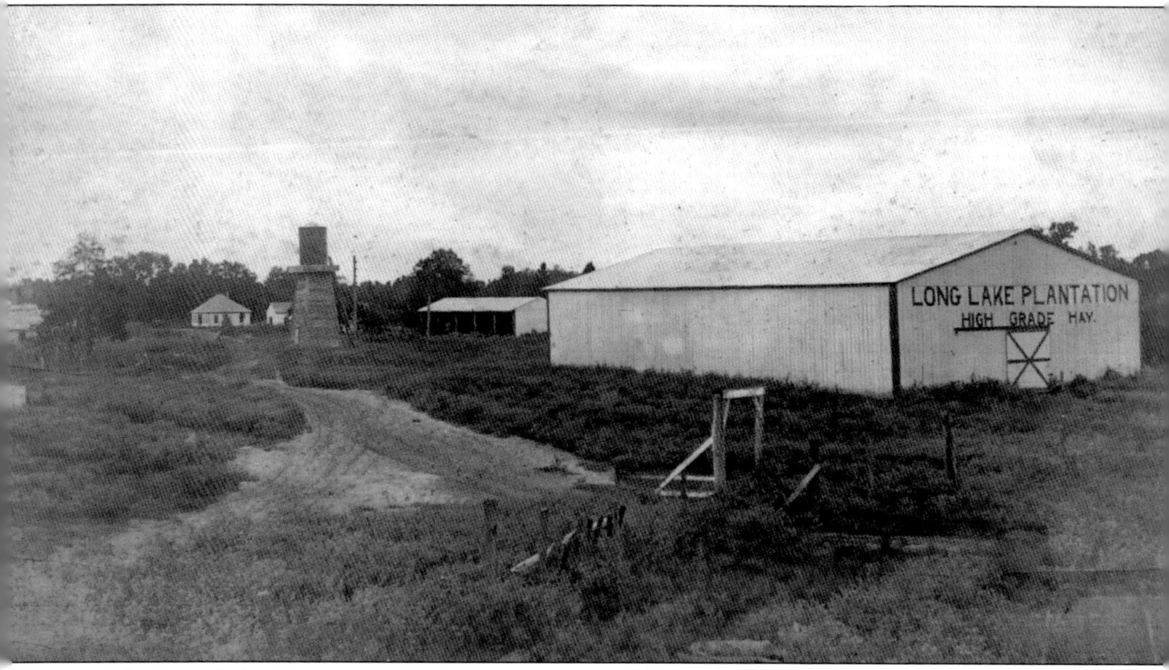

The Long Lake Plantation was the name given to the 4,200 acres of rich river bottom farm land purchased by Hugh Monnig in 1911. He placed the land under the management of his son, J. O. Monnig, who developed it for cotton production. The site was in an ideal location because it was on the International and Great Northern Railroad as well as a state highway. The Trinity River was also nearby. Soon the plantation became a trading and shipping center. As early as 1913, several unsuccessful oil wells were drilled in the area. In 1932, Tidewater and Seaboard Oil Companies drilled the first successful well on the plantation. It came in as a huge oil and gas well. (Courtesy of PPL.)

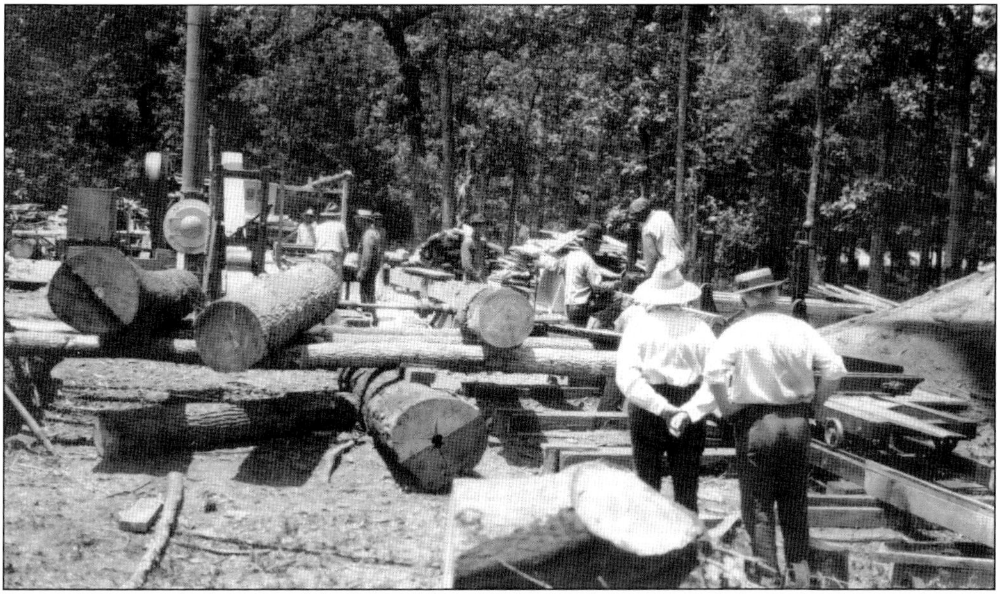

These photographs are of the sawmill on the Long Lake Plantation. The lush dense forests of East Texas made the lumber industry a major source of income in the days before the discovery of oil. The photographs on this page show the sawmill on the Long Lake Plantation. As with the cotton crops, the plantation's close proximity to the Trinity river, the railroad, and a major highway facilitated the transporting of the lumber to market. (Both, courtesy of PPL.)

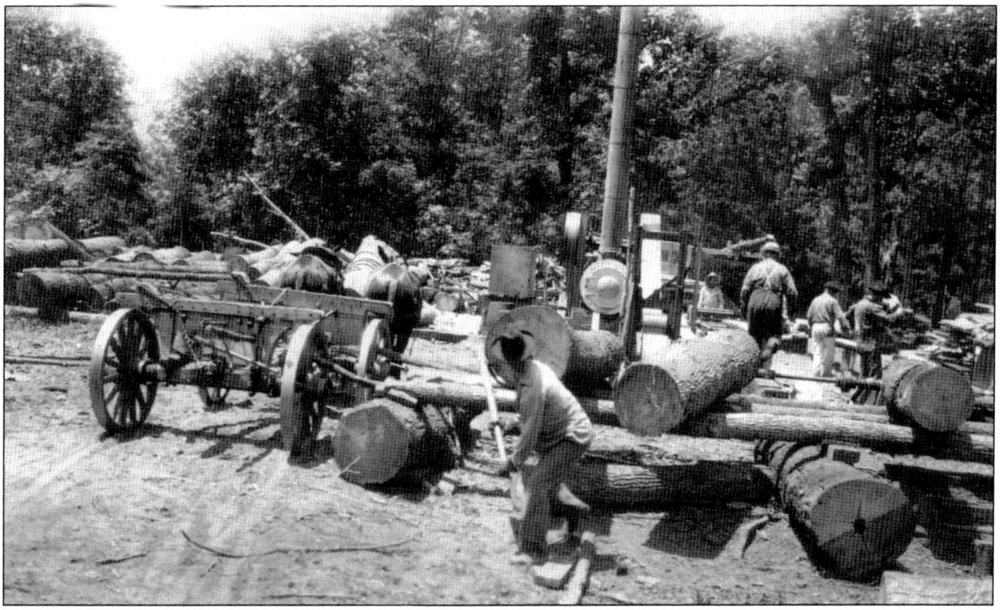

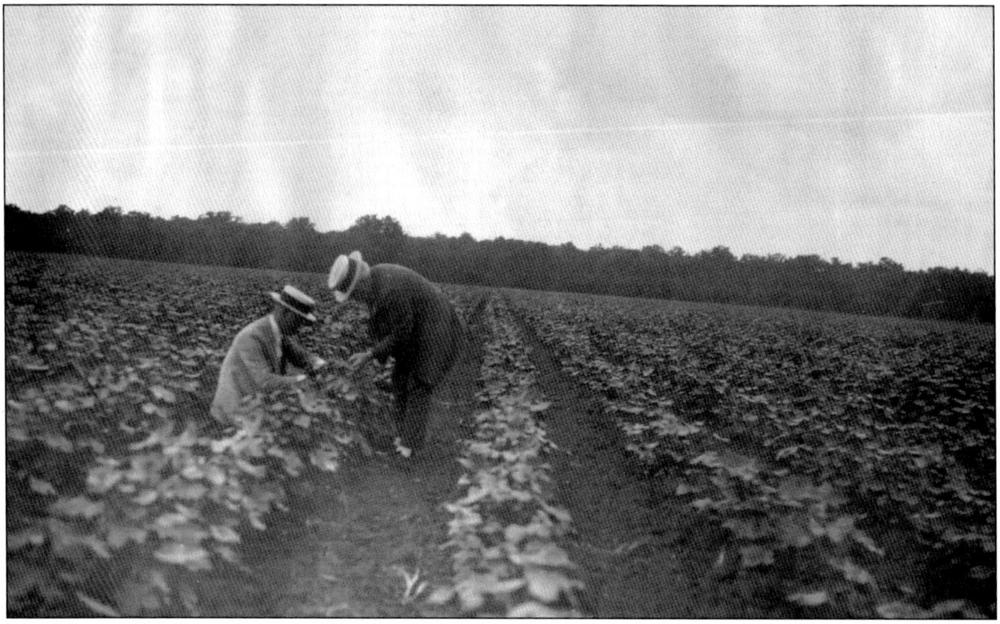

The Long Lake Plantation was developed for the production of cotton. It was very successful. The plantation grew into one of the largest cotton producers in the county. (Courtesy of PPL.)

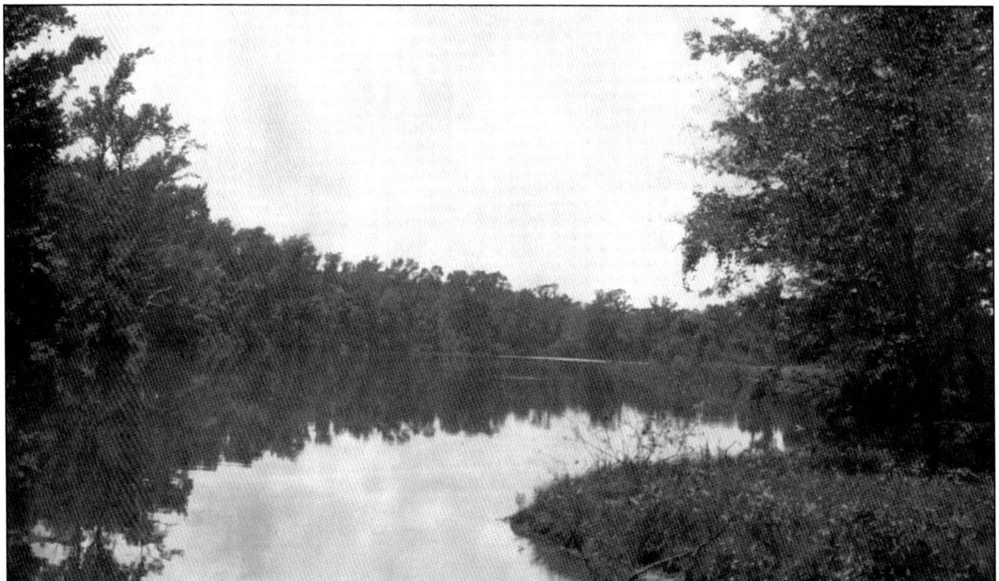

This is Long Lake, for which the Long Lake Plantation is named. The lake is .75 miles long and 150 yards wide. The bass and crappie fishing is excellent. (Courtesy of PPL.)

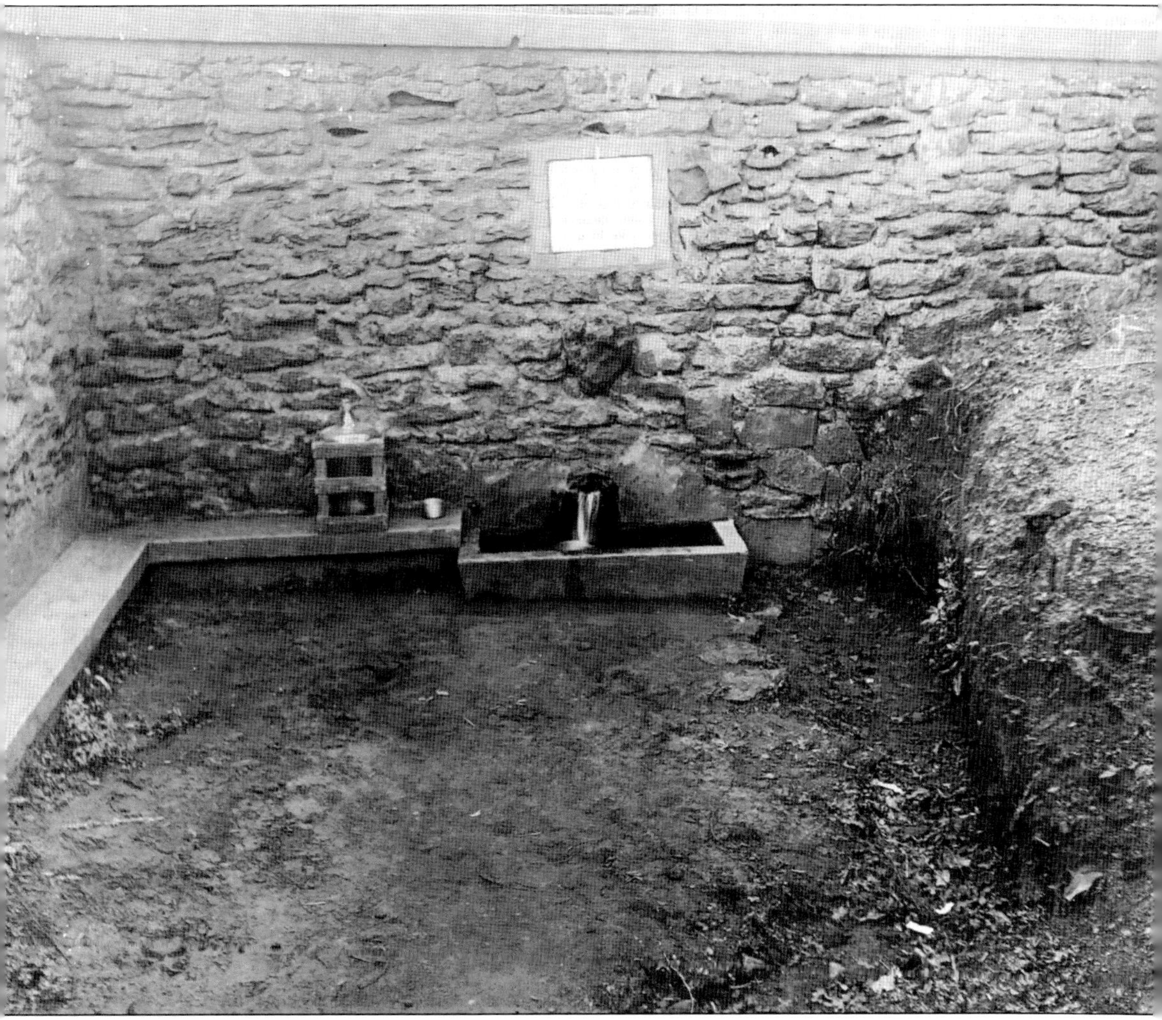

Just before North Jackson Street intersects U.S. Highway 287, a dirt road turns to the right. That road leads to a stone wall with a marble plaque inscribed with the following words: "Welcome to those who will be cleanly around this spring." Herbert and Jettie Bowden bought the "mountain" and its pure, flowing spring after they married in 1903. They built a general store and, a few years later, began selling the good spring water to the town folk, who thought it was better and healthier than the Palestine water. Bowden hauled five-gallon bottles of water to town in a horse-drawn wagon and later used two trucks. Some people brought their bottles to the spring to be filled. When Herbert Bowden died in 1952, Jettie Bowden moved into town. The spring no longer flows, and the area known as Bowden's Mountain is overgrown and mostly forgotten. (Courtesy of PPL.)